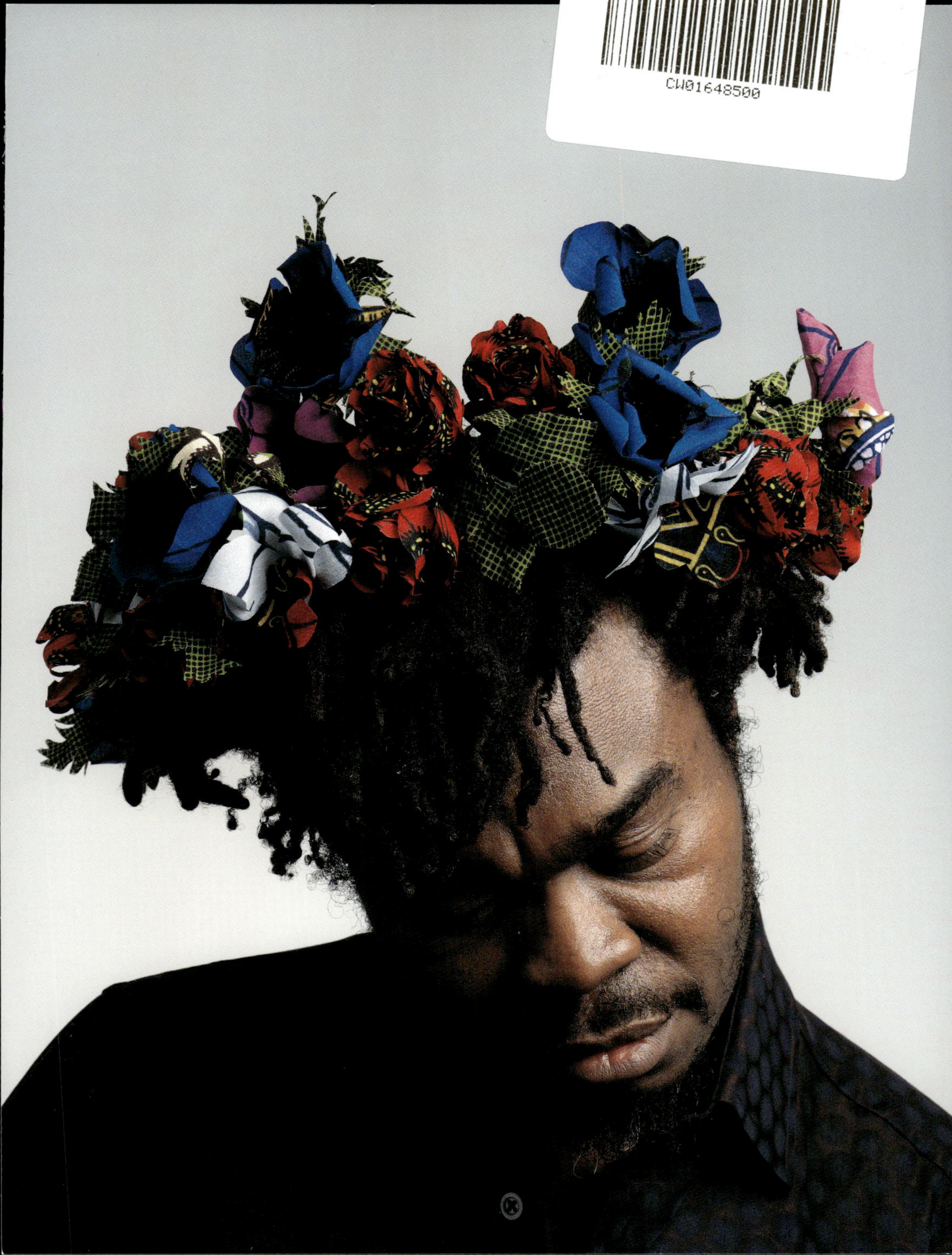

Flower Head, 2006
is a limited edition print for contemporary
created by Yinka Shonibare
Photo: Stephen White

992/3000

Contemporary Art and Memory

For Karen Trusselle, artist and rare friend who died just before the publication of this book.

Contemporary Art and Memory

Images of Recollection and Remembrance

Joan Gibbons

I.B. TAURIS
LONDON · NEW YORK

Reprinted in 2009 by I.B.Tauris & Co. Ltd
6 Salem Road, London W2 4BU
175 Fifth Avenue, New York NY 10010
www.ibtauris.com

In the United States and Canada distributed by Palgrave Macmillan, a division of St. Martin's Press, 175 Fifth Avenue, New York NY 10010

First published in 2007 by I.B.Tauris & Co. Ltd

ISBN: 978 1 84511 619 4 (Pb)

A full CIP record for this book is available from the British Library
A full CIP record for this book is available from the Library of Congress
Library of Congress catalog card: available

Typeset in Goudy by Dexter Haven Associates Ltd, London
Printed and bound in India by Rakesh Press

CONTENTS

List of Illustrations ix
Foreword xiii

Introduction 1

1. Autobiography: The Externalisation of Personal Memory 9

2. Traces: Memory and Indexicality 29

3. Revisions: The Reassembling of 'History' 52

4. Postmemory: 'The Ones Born Afterwards' 73

5. Enactments, Re-enactments and Episodic Memory 96

6. The Ordering of Knowledge: Museums and Archives 118

Epilogue – Oblivion: The Limits of Memory 141

Notes 149
Bibliography 173
Index 183

LIST OF ILLUSTRATIONS

1. Louise Bourgeois, *CELL (EYES AND MIRRORS)* in progress 1989–1993. Marble, mirrors, steel and glass, 93 x 83 x 86 inches; 236.2 x 210.8 x 218.4 cm.Collection Tate Modern, London. Photograph: Peter Bellamy. 11
2. Tracey Emin, *My Bed*. Mixed media installation Turner Prize Exhibition, Tate Gallery, London, 20 October 1999–23 January 2000. Photograph by Stephen White. Courtesy: White Cube/ Jay Jopling. 23
3. Felix Gonzalez Torres. *'Untitled' (Perfect Lovers)* 1991. New York Museum of Modern Art (MOMA). Clocks, paint on wall, overall 14 x 28 x 23/4 inches (35.6 x 71.2 x 7cm) Gift of the Dannheisser Foundation, Accc. no.: 177.1996. a-b © 2007. Digital Image, The Museum of Modern Art, New York/Scala Florence. Copyright © Felix Gonzalez Torres Foundation, Andrea Rosen Gallery, New York. 27
4. Rachael Whiteread, *House*, 1993 cast concrete. Commissioned and Produced by Artangel. Photograph courtesy of Artangel. 33
5. Miyako Ishiuchi, *Mother's 25 Mar 1916 # 31*, 2000, gelatin silver print 107.5 x 74.0 cm. Courtesy: Miyako Ishiuchi. 35
6. Miyako Ishiuchi, *Mother's # 49*, 2002, gelatin silver print 150.0 x 100.0 cm. Courtesy: Miyako Ishiuchi. 36
7. Nan Goldin, *Trixie on the Cot*, NYC, 1979. Cibachrome print, mounted on Sintra 27 3/8 x 40 inches (69 x 101.6 cm). Soloman Guggenheim Museum, New York. Purchased with funds contributed by the Photographic 45

Committee and with funds contributed by the International Director's Council and Executive Committee Members, 2002.

8. Bill Fontana, *Distant Trains*, 1984. Sound Installation with buried speakers, Anhalter Bahnhof, Berlin. Courtesy of the artist. 50
9. Judy Chicago, *The Dinner Party*, 1979 mixed media installation. Courtesy: Through the Flower. Copyright © DACS 2007. 56
10. Doris Salcedo, *La Casa Viuda VI*, 1995, wood, bone, metal 3 parts. Installation Distemper: Dissonent Themes in the Art of the 1990s, Hirschorn Museum and Distemper Garden, 20 June–September, 1996. Courtesy: Alexander and Bonin, New York. Collection Israel Museum. 61
11. Keith Piper, *A Ship Called Jesus*, 1991. Mixed Media, Installation view, Ikon Gallery, Birmingham, 1991. Courtesy: Ikon Gallery. Photography: Keith Piper and Spring Heel Jack. 66
12. Keith Piper, *A Ship Called Jesus*, 1991. Video projection with TV monitors, Installation view, Ikon Galler, Birmingham. Courtesy: Ikon Gallery. Photography: Keith Piper and Spring Heel Jack. 67
13. Yinka Shonibare MBE, *Mr and Mrs Andrews without their Heads*, 1998. Wax-print cotton costumes on armatures, dog mannequin, painted metal bench, rifle, 165 x 635 x 154 cm with plinth. Photo © National Gallery, Canada. Collection National Gallery of Canada, Ottowa. Copyright © Yinka Shonibare MBE, courtesy the artist and Stephen Friedman Gallery (London). 69
14. Christian Boltanski, *Autel De Lycée Chases (Altar to Chases High School)*, 1988. Six black and white photographs, 31 biscuit tins and six lamps 81.5 x 86.5 inches. The Museum of Contemporary Art, Los Angeles. Gift of Peter and Eileen Norton, Santa Monica, California. 81

15. Anselm Kiefer, *Your Golden Hair, Margarete*, 1981. Oil, emulsion, straw on canvas 51 3/16 x 67 inches (130 x 170 cm). Private collection. Courtesy: Anselm Kiefer. 84
16. Anselm Kiefer, *Sulamith*, 1983. Oil, acrylic and straw on canvas, with woodcut 114 3/16 x 145 11/16 inches (290 x 370 cm). Private Collection. Courtesy: Anselm Kiefer. 86
17. Art Spiegelman, from *MAUS I: A SURVIVOR'S TALE/MY FATHER BLEEDS HISTORY*, copyright © 1973, 1980, 1981, 1982, 1984, 1985, 1986 by Art Spiegelman. Used by permission of Pantheon Books, a division of Random House Inc. 91
18. Art Spiegelman, from *MAUS II: A SURVIVOR'S TALE/AND HERE MY TROUBLE BEGAN*, copyright © 1986, 1989, 1990, 1991 by Art Spiegelman Used by permission of Pantheon Books, a division of Random House Inc. 93
19. *[murmur]* Edinburgh, produced by New Media Scotland, 2007–2008. Map illustration © Jenny Proudfoot for Fifty Nine Ltd. 101
20. Janet Cardiff, *The Missing Voice (Case Study B)*, 1999, sound walk with personal CD player. Commissioned and Produced by Artangel. Images by Stephen White. 107
21. Pierre Huyghe, *The Third Memory*, 1999. Two-channel video and sound installation, 00:09:32. Dimensions variable. Solomon Guggenheim Museum, New York. Gift, the Bohen Foundation, 2001. Photograph by Ellen Labenski © The Solomon Guggenheim Foundation. 109
22. Jeremy Deller, *The Battle of Orgreave*, 2001. historical re-enactment. Commissioned and Produced by Artangel. Photograph by Martin Jenkinson. 115
23. Marcel Broodthaers, *Citron-Citroën*, 1974. Lithograph and screenprint on paper image: 1048 x 664 mm, Collection: Tate Modern, purchased 1977. Copyright © DACS 2007. 122

24. Mark Dion, *Tate Thames Dig*, 1999. Mixed media installation unconfirmed: 2660 x 3700 x 1260 mm. Collection Tate Modern, purchased with assistance from private benefactors 2000. Copyright © Mark Dion. 126
25. Susan Hiller, *From the Freud Museum*, 1991–1996. Mixed media installation, displayed: 2200 x 10000 x 600 mm. Collection Tate Modern. Purchased 1998. Copyright © Susan Hiller. 132
26. Susan Hiller, *From the Freud Museum*, 1991–1996. Detail, 'Sophia' mixed media. Collection Tate Modern. Purchased 1998. Copyright © Susan Hiller. 133
27. George Legrady, Composite image of various screens from the *An Anecdoted Archive from the Cold War*, 1993. An Autobiographical Archive according to the Floor Plans of the former Hungarian Worker's Movement (propaganda) Museum Palace of Buda Castle Building 'A' Budapest Clockwise: Floorplan; Stocks Brochure Page; Hungarian Posters, 1944–1948; Kissing Scene 1948 (1992); The Border Train Station in Hegyshalom (painting by Miklo Legrady, artist's brother); Mom in Canada (First summer in Canada, Ridgewood Ave) 1957; Old Flower Patterned Pottery and Breakfast, 1936; Father's Sports ID Card, 1953. Copyright © George Legrady. 137
28. Michael Landy, *Breakdown*, 2001, mixed media performance. Commissioned and Produced by Artangel. Photograph copyright © Michael Landy. 142
29. Becky Shaw (in collaboration with Michael Gill) *Twelve Museums*, 2002, transparent acrylic, scaled down photographs and miniaturised objects, Sackler Centre for Arts Education, Serpentine Gallery, exhibition view. Courtesy: Becky Shaw. 143

FOREWORD

The material covered in this book sits within some broad parameters, and I think it helpful to make these clear from the start. In the first instance, I feel it important to note what I mean by contemporary art, which encompasses a wide range of practices and now extends over a substantial period in history. Following critic Arthur C. Danto, I have treated contemporary art as a development that began in the 1960s with the diversification of avant-garde art after the post-war dominance of High Modernist abstraction. As Danto observes, this diversification saw the end of any a priori criterion concerning what art must be and left the museum without an overarching narrative into which its contents must fit.[1] While it might be argued that the word 'contemporary' carries connotations of that which is new or current, in terms of art it now covers a period of forty years or more and involves two generations of artists. Nonetheless, the term 'contemporary' obviously does not apply to all art produced in this still growing time span, and neither does it apply only to art that attempts a radical break with the past, which was perhaps the case with modern art. As critic Hal Foster, notes, there has been a twofold trajectory in the development of contemporary art. On the one hand, art has moved away from ideas of intrinsic value that dominated the High Modernism between the mid-1940s and mid-1960s and replaced the criterion of 'quality' with that of 'interest', from 'intrinsic forms to discursive problems', further characterising the paradigmatic shift observed by Danto. On the other hand, artists of the neo-avant-garde have not jettisoned the art of the past or situated themselves at its pinnacle, as was the case with High Modernism, but have engaged critically with its outstanding issues.[2] The artists that I discuss are contemporary because their art fits this notion of discursive practice. Their discursivity, of course, lies in the 'memory-work' they perform or in their critical response to ways in which that past has been previously construed and represented.

The second set of parameters concern the choices that I have made with regard to the scope of the book and which artists to include and which to leave out. This, I feel, has been a bit of a no-win situation. To include every artist who has addressed memory in his or her work would have made the survey so wide as to preclude the sort of analysis and comment that would render it a critical account, but to exclude artists that could have sat easily within the remit of the book opens it up to sins of omission. In the end, I have tried to achieve a balance between substance and scope, mindful that a single book can only cover so much ground and that it is the making of a contribution that counts. But, having made my choices, the danger became one of pigeonholing artists under the thematic headings of the chapters. To counteract this, I have been at pains to make connections and identify cross-currents between the content of individual chapters, pulling the discussion together from chapter to chapter into what I hope is an elastic or flexible whole. Nevertheless, in the end, although I have covered a considerable amount of ground, the field is still open to further excavation or cultivation as the case may be – and rightfully so.

Thirdly, while I have examined a wide range of memory-work in contemporary art, I have consciously avoided rehearsing theories of memory per se, drawing from them as and where relevant. I have put the artworks first and sought to explain approaches and attitudes mainly through ways in which memory has been conceptualised elsewhere in the arts and social sciences. Memory theory is wide and diverse, and not all of it is applicable to the ground that I have covered, but for those keen to gain an overview of the complexity of memory and its theory I would recommend The Stanford Encyclopedia of Philosophy (available online), which gives a comprehensive entry under 'memory' accompanied by a substantial bibliography. Bottom line, this book is an exploration of the many ways in which memory has been addressed in contemporary art. I have not allowed its content to be prescribed by theory but have sought to use theory in the interest of exegesis and extrapolation.

INTRODUCTION

The nightmare of having little or no memory is told in Christopher Nolan's film *Memento*, released in 2000. The severely amnesic main character has messages tattooed into his own flesh in order to conserve basic clues about himself and his history and he has to record even the most recent events by Polaroid if he is to retain them. Apart from providing the pretext for an effective thriller, the extremes of amnesia represented in the film underscore the fact that memory is one of the most vital of our faculties, the apparatus that allows for recognition (re-cognition) without which the powers of cognition itself remain transient and unframed. However, memory is never just a straightforward process of recording lest we forget and, even in the best equipped of minds, it can be a slippery mechanism. It can be both elusive and intrusive and we can rarely be completely sure of its fidelity to the events or facts that it recalls. Given such mutability, it is not so much the reliability or fallibility of memory that is at stake today but the way that memory is harnessed and deployed in the negotiations of life, from the 'little' moments and events of the private and the everyday to those 'grander' moments and events of formalised and public occasions. The claims that are made and the stories that are told in the name of memory can alter people's understanding of the world and, of course, alter the ways in which they act in or upon that world. With all of this in mind, I want to address the ways in which memory is valued and used today by examining it as it is deployed and represented in the context of contemporary art. What is also worth bearing in mind is that contemporary art has harnessed memory in such a wide variety of ways that it can readily be taken as representative of the range of attitudes towards and uses of memory in the culture as a whole. My claim is that such an exploration will contribute to a far more general understanding of both contemporary art and contemporary memory.

A good and accurate memory that can store and retrieve knowledge and experience used to be one of the most desirable attributes of learning and the acquisition of knowledge. The valuing of memory in this way has a long history. The ancient Greeks, for instance, depending largely on whether Plato or Aristotle was being followed, saw memory as a means of recovering divine knowledge of the ideal world or of recording experiential knowledge.[1] In both cases, what was required of memory was the ability to develop an effective means of retaining and recovering what were often vast quantities of knowledge and, in both cases, similar techniques were recommended for these processes. As the historian Frances Yates has shown, these mnemotechnics or memory skills were regarded as one of the liberal arts (alongside the sister art of painting in the Middle Ages and Renaissance). In its most spectacular instances, the art of memory often resulted in amazing displays of recollected data, from the recall of long complicated word sequences to the recital of epic poems such as *The Odyssey*, which the speaker could just as easily repeat backwards as forwards.[2] The apparatuses of memory that developed were referred to as 'the artificial memory', distinct from its opposite, the untutored and less regulated 'natural memory'. As will become evident, these categories are akin to Marcel Proust's notions of voluntary and involuntary memory, with the difference that Proust found authenticity in 'the natural' or involuntary memory rather than in the more organised recall of the automatic or voluntary memory.

The development of 'the artificial memory' was highly dependent on techniques of visualisation, such as the location of a piece of knowledge in an imagined, clearly defined locus (often a building) or the attachment of data or ideas to striking (and therefore more memorable) images.[3] In other words, the art of memory was essentially a visual art and remained so for centuries to follow, its skills of visualisation persisting even today in the sort of popular memory improvement courses found in the small ads. However, while memory is still writ large in the visual arts, the understanding of memory as a highly skilled art form that is essential to the production, retention and transmission of knowledge no longer carries quite the same value. A change in attitude towards memory and its importance began to take hold in the seventeenth century, when, for instance, British Empiricist philosophers laid stress not so much on memory as a vehicle of knowledge but as a type or form of knowledge rooted in experience.[4] Even so, memory was still often characterised in visual terms, with philosophers such as John Locke claiming that the knowledge that is recalled is frequently reproduced through images or sense impressions. Because of this emphasis on imaging or the formation of impressions, memory became closely related to the imagination. Two things emerge from this shift in thinking about memory that are significant for the understanding of memory today. The first is that the veracity of memory began to be questioned by some of Locke's contemporaries on the grounds that images and sense impressions are exactly that, never the real thing, making it difficult to distinguish memory images from those produced by the imagination. The second is that memory began to be actively co-opted as an agent for the imagination – the opposite of its traditional function as a means of accurate recall.[5] This use of memory for more fanciful purposes is evident, as Mary Warnock has amply demonstrated, in late eighteenth early nineteenth-century Romantic poets such as Samuel Taylor Coleridge and William Wordsworth, who frequently invoked memory as a means of access to the innocence of childhood and a means of access to the child's more authentic view of and participation in the world (Nature).[6]

The legacy of this understanding of memory as both a form of knowledge and an agent of the imagination is to be found early in the twentieth century in the work of Proust, who has become famously associated with memory through his extensive seven-volume novel *In Search of Lost Time* (*A la Recherche du Temps Perdu*, 1908–1922). In his quest for authentic personal knowledge, Proust, like Wordsworth and Coleridge before him, treated memory as something that has an emotional rather than an intellectually organised base – as an important constituent of a person's inner self.[7] Moreover, Proust was to recognise and comment on the important role that memory has as a creative power in bridging the gap between past and present in a way that connects personal truths to a wider audience or readership.[8] In developing this relationship between private understanding and its public expression, Proust's deployment of memory in literature is well in advance of and perhaps fundamental to many of the practices of contemporary artists of our time, as is the case with many of the artists discussed in chapter 1. In searching for 'lost time', Proust ponders on two types of memory: the voluntary and the involuntary. As Warnock has noted, Proust tends to characterise voluntary memory in terms of the production of images which convey the outer appearance of things, events or experiences.[9] Far more meaningful, on the other hand, is the sort of unsolicited recall sprung by the involuntary memory, as produced, for example, by the randomly encountered taste of a *petite madeleine*, which, uninvited, calls up an assemblage of sensation and emotion that is beyond the reach of the intellect and voluntary memory.[10]

Scepticism towards images is expressed in favour of a knowledge of the past that is more deeply embedded in the psyche and which can be evoked in its complexity, not simply by 'snapshots' of the event but by an everyday experience that manages to key into the whole host of sensations and emotions experienced in the moment or event. In making this contrast, Proust reflects some of the changes that were taking place in the avant-garde art of his own time between traditional forms of representation that are based on mimesis and new forms initiated by Symbolism that privilege subjectivity and the inner life and recognise the inadequacy of traditional forms of realism to express such states. This rejection of traditional mimetic forms by Symbolists such as Paul Gauguin or proto-Expressionists such as Vincent Van Gogh in the late nineteenth century opened up the floodgates to the plurality of approaches developed by the early twentieth-century avant-gardes, and most certainly paved the way for the plurality of practices that characterise contemporary art and that make much of it conducive to the evocation of involuntary memory. As will be seen, most of the works discussed in this book are not literal renderings of memory but are often allusive and suggestive of the past, tapping into our reservoir of emotions as much as into our store of cognitive knowledge.

The way that memory is valued, then, has shifted enormously from the idea of it being a storehouse of data which, given the right techniques, is recoverable in an ordered manner to the notion that it is a key to our emotional understanding of ourselves and the world. The present superfluousness of the old techniques of the art of memory is due in part to the existence of some vastly sophisticated systems that are literally artificial and exist outside the mind itself. These range from traditional catalogued and perhaps more limited material archives to the potentially ever elastic and ever-expanding virtual storage space offered by digital technology. Such archives, from libraries and museums to the internet, including those computerised databases that make libraries and museums accessible online, make the need for the memory skills associated with 'the artificial memory' largely redundant and have further affected people's attitudes towards memory. However, it is only the techniques of the traditional art of memory that have become redundant; storehouses of knowledge are still integral to the functioning of society, and have in fact been given a significant amount of attention in contemporary art. The critiques that have emerged of this sort of organisation and control of knowledge are discussed in the final chapter of this book alongside a discussion of archival practices as a methodology in the work of several contemporary artists.

In addition to these developments in archiving there has also been a recent discrediting of the accuracy and impartiality of memory with the emergence of 'false memory syndrome'. This issue gained particular notoriety in the 1980s, when techniques used for memory recovery in psychotherapy were found to be unsound. The querying of the accuracy of personal memories also relates to a mistrust of the memories that are constructed and represented as history. The viability of the traditional narratives of patriarchy, imperialism and colonialism were vigorously challenged in the second half of the twentieth century and disproved by the sort of reassessment of history called for and developed by marginalised groups and societies. This sort of undermining of the truth and authority of history is exemplified by Edward Said's landmark book *Orientalism*, published in 1978, which issued a clear challenge to the ways in which colonial history was constructed and biased.[11] It was further consolidated in the influential ideas of French theorist Michel Foucault, whose work is also underpinned by a desire to expose the ideological biases of history.[12] The result of the reappraisals of history that took hold in the latter half of the twentieth century has been a widespread recognition of the relativity of history, which has led to a favouring of memory as something which can maintain 'vital links with the surrounding culture'.[13] This move from history to memory is clearly manifest in the many recent attempts to reclaim lost and marginalised histories which have taken place within the remit of contemporary art, and which provide the focus for chapter 3.

In a nutshell, the subjective, or even the fictionalised, aspects of memory now seem to take precedence over trained and disciplined memory and its equivalent in history in the negotiations of the world. This is not to say that memory is no longer a vital agent of knowledge, without which our experience of the world would be ever transient and ever instantaneous; it is simply to say that the contingency of the knowledge that is held by memory is now widely understood, and that this has occasioned changes in its status and in the roles that it is given as a tool for understanding and navigating the world. The fact that memory is as vital as ever for knowledge of the self and for knowledge of the world is fundamental to the assertions I want to make concerning art and memory, in particular that art has become one of the most important agencies for the sort of 'memory-work' that is required by contemporary life and culture.[14] This returns to the key question of the ways in which memory is both necessary to and deployed in contemporary culture. Here, it is opportune to note that an increased preoccupation with memory in Western culture has already been signalled by a number of contemporary theorists, resulting in a growing body of scholarly works that have addressed the shifting significance of memory. In a move that recalls the shift towards subjective memory in the seventeenth and eighteenth centuries described above, this newer theoretical perspective has tended to explain the current understanding of and preoccupation with memory as a consequence of the shift from the more objectifying and universalising impulse of modernism to the more subjective, relativist ethos of postmodernism.[15]

Arguing along these lines, Andreas Huyssen, for example, clearly points to a relationship between the reordering of the notion of memory and the breakdown in the coherency of modernism's utopian narratives (the idea of the redemptive powers of technology, for example was severely tested by the carnage of the two world wars of the last century). Further to this, Huyssen argues that our current obsession with memory derives from a crisis in the belief in a rational structure of temporality, signalled in the early twentieth century in the works of Henri Bergson, Marcel Proust, Sigmund Freud and Walter Benjamin (who represent an underside to the universalising tendencies of modernism, prefiguring postmodernism).[16] For Huyssen, this crisis in the way that time is perceived and experienced has become even more evident in the way that both time and history have been collapsed by an information revolution that threatens to make categories such as 'past and future, experience and expectation and memory and anticipation' obsolete. Hence, the current preoccupation with memory can be seen as an attempt

> to recover a mode of contemplation outside the universe of simulation and fast-speed information and cable networks, to claim some anchoring space in a world of puzzling and often threatening heterogeneity, non synchronicity and information overload.[17]

In other words, Huyssen sees the current preoccupation with memory as a way to 'find a new mooring' in an age of uncertainty. It does not matter if memory is now deployed more subjectively or that 'the old dichotomy between history and fiction no longer exists'.[18] In our postmodern condition of contingency and relativism, it seems that there is no way in which the fictional or confabulatory aspects of memory can be denied. This aspect of memory surfaces in chapter 5 in which I discuss enactments and re-enactments in art as memory practices. The fictional aspects of memory bring the discussion back to the dilemma of what is important, or even radical, about memory in contemporary Western culture. For Susannah Radstone, the crux of this issue is not just the ways in which memory is harnessed or deployed but, rather, the tensions and equivocations that are produced by the ambivalences of memory.[19] In characterising the significance of memory as a matter of tension and equivocation, Radstone notes the way that memory tends to occupy a number of threshold or liminal positions: not only those borderlines which exist between subjectivity and objectivity, the outer and the inner world, the self and society, but also the boundary that exists between forgetting and remembering, the tensions of which have enormous implications given the potential for a purposeful use of memory to transform the present into a better future.[20] As will become evident from much of the material covered in this book, the borderlines identified by Radstone resemble the sort of ambiguous and marginal territories that are frequently haunted by contemporary artists, who often seem to thrive on the tensions and equivocations that go with such territories.

The understanding of memory as a set of liminal practices invokes one of the best-known early twentieth-century writers on memory, the French philosopher Henri Bergson, who defined memory as the intersection of mind and matter.[21] It is a short step from this to see art as constituting a similar intersection, but, in this case, acting as a 'memory-object' or a memory-work that intervenes and forms a connection, as Proust knew, between the work and a number of minds – or, better, a number of persons.[22] In performing this function, art provides a locus in which the re-cognitions and reconfigurations of memory can be communicated and shared. The idea of 'places' in which memory is harboured is central to the work of contemporary French theorist Pierre Nora. Nora expresses the notion as *lieux de mémoire*, which does not necessarily refer literally to places but to sites that may just as easily be objects or events as actual places.[23] Like other contemporary theorists, Nora sees memory as overtaking history in the significance it holds for the culture, which, in line with Huyssen, he puts down to an acceleration of history due, in part, to the media and the 'ephemeral film of current events'.[24] In effect, the privileging of memory over history represents a freedom of knowledge which, when accessed in *lieux de mémoire*, can become less prescriptive and, like Proust's *madeleine*, allows a transformation 'from the historical to the psychological, from the sociological to the individual, from the objective message to its subjective reception, from repetition to rememoration'.[25] Again, this notion of *lieux de mémoire* is easily transferred to many of the products of contemporary art, especially those that carry actual traces of events or experiences, but this notion of *lieux de mémoire* figures in chapters 3 and 6 in particular, in which traditional historicising practices and the traditional location of 'historical' knowledge are questioned.

Each of the thematic approaches that I have identified in the representation of memory in contemporary art occupies a chapter in the book. Of course, the distinctions I make between different approaches are never so clear-cut in reality, and I pay attention to overlaps and correspondences as I go along in the interest of producing a more cohesive account At the same time, I make no claims to a definitive account, and I am aware that there are a number of relevant artists who I have missed out from my discussion. To have made a broader survey would have resulted in a far more superficial account and a skating over the surface. Nevertheless, it seems timely to conduct an overview of the approaches and attitudes that are taken towards memory in contemporary art practices, despite the obvious limitations of surveys (which, after all, have the virtue of leaving room for further study). Indeed, given the amount and variety of attention paid to memory in contemporary art, it is rather surprising that it has been written about only sporadically in relation to particular artists or particular exhibitions. One of my aims in writing this book, therefore, is to bring existing studies together and build on them to form a larger and more comprehensive picture of the varied and numerous forms or roles that memory is given in this arena of cultural practice.

In doing this, I intend not just to produce a critical survey but to explore the preoccupation with memory in contemporary art with a view to understanding of the ways in which memory has assisted in the construction of knowledge, values, fantasies, desires and beliefs in the late twentieth and early twenty-first centuries. Contemporary art is an ideal vehicle for this sort of enquiry because it is characterised by a vast spread of heterogeneous practices that allows for almost any number of approaches to be taken in relation to any one of its major thematics, and consequently allows the complexities and contradictions of that thematic to be widely aired. Conversely, a study of the way that a major thematic such as memory has figured in contemporary art has the advantage of providing a thread by which some of the often overwhelming diversity of contemporary art can be harnessed, contextualised and understood.

With these sorts of consideration in mind, I have divided my account of contemporary art and memory into a number of themed chapters that address key ways in which memory has been dealt with by contemporary artists. The first chapter addresses autobiographical works of art and is an exploration the ways in which memory is presented as a personal narrative and of the implications of making the private public. The next discusses works that constitute memory traces and involve the use of objects, photographs and sounds that were part of or link to the original memory, leaning on now well-rehearsed notions of indexicality in photographic theory. The third, on revisionist memories, maps a number of recovered social and political histories and puts them into the context of the current tendency to privilege memory over history. In this chapter I also begin a discussion of museums and galleries as *lieux de mémoire* that I pick up in my final chapter. This leads on to chapter 4, which is dedicated to issues concerning and strategies of remembrance of the Nazi Holocaust, in which I examine the debates over the speaking of the unspeakable and make use of Marianne Hirsch's notion of 'postmemory'. Shifting key somewhat in chapter 5, I then move into a discussion of enactment and re-enactment as relational or participatory forms of memory-work that are more emotionally and, in some cases, somatically connective. In my last chapter, I turn my attention to the ways in which artists have represented and critiqued methods through which knowledge and data, as aspects of memory, are ordered and stored by specialised and authoritative institutions such as the museum and archive. Finally, I end with an epilogue which also serves as a conclusion, and which introduces the (already lurking) theme of oblivion and the issue of forgetting as not just the converse of memory but as essential to the successes of memory.

1

Autobiography: The Externalisation of Personal Memory

Autobiography assumes a variety of forms and involves a range of practices. In literature alone, it encompasses 'the memoir, the confession, the apology, the diary and the "*journal intime*"', as well as less testimonial forms such as novels, drama and poetry.[1] On another front, the revealing of personal histories has become a popularised practice through mass media such as tabloid newspapers or television – the chat show serving as an obvious example. Equally, autobiographical information has become a key part of the everyday administration or institutionalisation of our lives – in the filling out of insurance forms, applications for finance or social benefit, the recording of medical histories and so on.[2] Operating on so many levels and in so many forms, autobiography plays a key role in Western culture and has come to represent a key issue of our time: the relationship of the private to the public. With this in mind, this chapter addresses the ways in which a number of artists have represented their histories and walked the often delicate path between the public and private spheres. I begin with a look at the prehistory of autobiographical art in self-portraiture, but for the main part this chapter is concerned with the work of artists who have made personal experience rather than the mirror-likeness of portraiture the lynchpin of their self-representations. What will become evident is that the current openness of expression in contemporary art has allowed for the terms in which autobiography is figured to be stretched and tested in new and significant ways.

The first artist to make self-portraiture a trademark of his work was, of course, Rembrandt van Rijn (1606–1669). In a series of self-portraits that lasted his adult lifetime, Rembrandt brought a psychological depth to his self-imaging that went further than a simple chronicling of his changing appearance. Indeed, the amount of self-scrutiny that Rembrandt applied to himself in the seventeenth century was without precedent in the art of any culture and coincides with the emergence of the individualist self in the West. As literary historian Michael Mascuch has shown, this new tendency was expressed in part by the spread of new, more popular, practices such as personal almanacs and diaries. Until this point in history the model for autobiographical writing had been set by St Augustine in his *Confessions* and sat within a clear framework of religious and moral piety. By the seventeenth century, 'the spiritual notebook was losing its status as instrument, and acquiring a new status as an object created by a subject; that is, an autonomous text, deliberately wrought by an individual intending it to represent some aspect of his personality'.[3] This corresponds with the view expressed by Rembrandt's contemporary Constantijn Huygens, that portraiture is 'the wondrous compendium of the whole man – not only of man's outward appearance but in my opinion, his mind as well'.[4]

The nature of Rembrandt's gaze is crucial in relation to this access to the inner man. As art historian Gen Doy has pointed out, seventeenth-century portraitists were well aware of the way that the painted eye creates an illusion of captivating the gaze of the viewer wherever he/she may be positioned in relation to the painting, and even of following him/her around the room.[5] But this alone is not enough to make the gaze compelling; in conjunction with this simple illusion, Rembrandt's eye contact obtains because, while unflinching, there is something indefinable in it and it is almost constantly troubled. Again following Doy's commentary on seventeenth-century portraiture in relation to notions of the self, it could be said that the nature of Rembrandt's gaze bears the hallmarks of the sort of individual self-scrutiny that is associated with the philosopher René Descartes (1596–1650) – the notion of a self-conscious, self-defining subject which, despite challenges from postmodern theorists, remains deeply embedded in the culture.[6] Aligned with the compelling yet vulnerable nature of Rembrandt's gaze, it is also a notion that privileges or encourages a romanticised interpretation of Rembrandt's personality by those who read his self-portraits as autobiography.

However, the 'story' of Rembrandt's life that emerges as the self-portraits follow on from one another is not an autobiography that looks back on the past to give it narrative shape. The majority of his images are not retrospective, and only a few serve to mark a life event such as his marriage to Saskia Uylenburgh in 1634. Instead, they are indicative of how Rembrandt wanted to present himself at a given time, in some cases to aid his pursuit of fortune and, in later life, to support his fame. The autobiography offered by the self-portraits has been constructed from without by critics and historians, who, as Gary Schwartz points out, insist on seeing Rembrandt as 'a sensitive human being with great spiritual depths' despite historical evidence to say that this was not typical of his conduct and character as experienced by his contemporaries.[7] The self-images that Rembrandt offers seem, rather, to represent the selective nature of memory, both on the part of the artist, who presents a preferred view in order to memorialise himself, and on the part of the viewer, who, in the vein of Romanticism, wants to believe in the depths of humanity that Rembrandt shows us. In crude Freudian terms, Rembrandt may be said to present us with mementos of his ego-ideal (or, rather, a long series of ego-ideals) which act both as a conscience and as a counterpoint to the baser realities of his life.[8] By extension, the 'thinking' self that Rembrandt

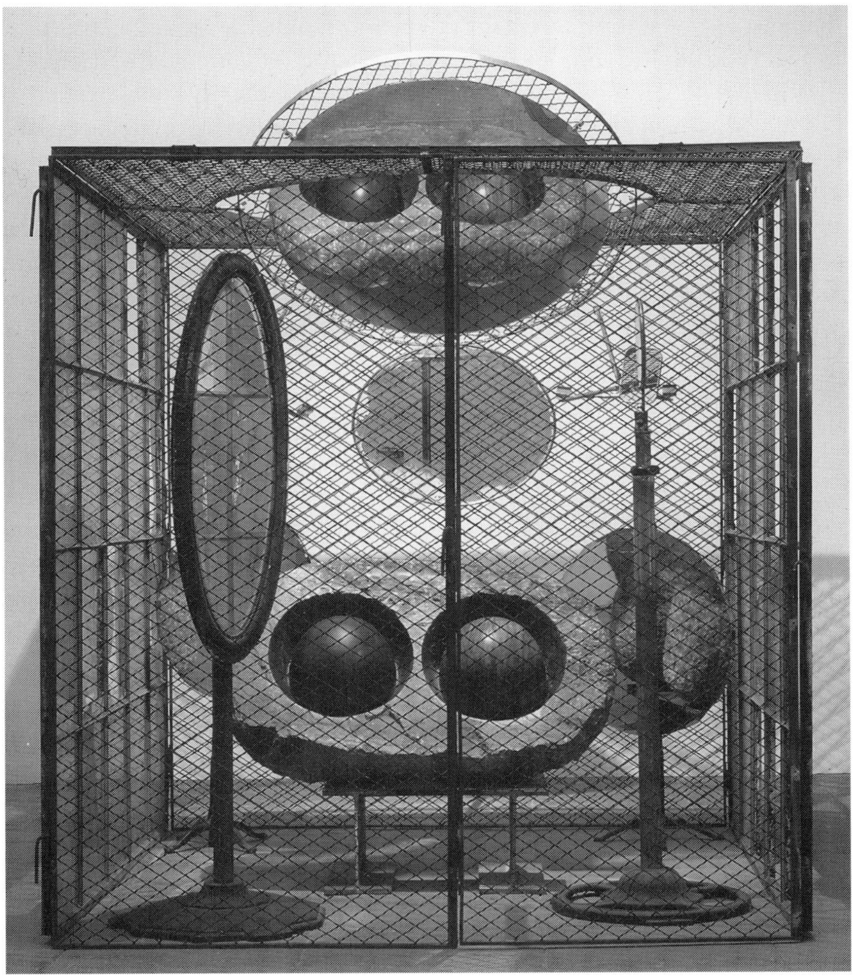

Figure 1: Louise Bourgeois, *CELL (EYES AND MIRRORS)* in progress 1989–1993. Marble, mirrors, steel and glass, 93 x 83 x 86 inches; 236.2 x 210.8 x 218.4 cm. Collection Tate Modern, London. Photograph: Peter Bellamy.

portrays can serve as a kind of collective ego-ideal, and, as such, may be a key factor in his undeniable popularity.

But the ego-ideal that Rembrandt presents is far from one of perfection, and the reason why Rembrandt's self-portraits consistently find a widespread relevance is perhaps that they are not idealised, but touched by what art historian, Simon Schama, has called 'the poetry of imperfection'. Even as Rembrandt seeks to impress with accessories and costume, his face is subject to 'the pranks and indignities suffered by all mortal flesh'.[9] In contrast to the human frailty expressed in his facial features, Rembrandt's tendency to put on a show of material status in nearly all his self-portraits is also noted by Schama, and seen to be especially poignant in the self-portrait of 1658 held in the Frick Collection, New York. Here, despite being in the depths of misfortune, the artist presents himself not only with dignity but also in a rich costume that defies his circumstance (alongside a face that is, nevertheless, a continuing testimony to the vagaries of time and experience).[10] Memory, of course, is inherently selective and there is a proven tendency to rework the original facts of an event or experience in a way that coheres around the wishes and values of the person remembering.[11] So, while the actual truth value of Rembrandt's self-portraits may be in doubt, what is important for his viewers are the human truths that they appear to embody.

In terms of memory or memorialisation, Rembrandt provides documents of himself that in chronicling physiognomic changes are literally autobiographical (the tracing of a life), but these traces, as already noted, are constructed in the present tense and most often bear a distant relationship to his actual circumstances and life events, and work more at the level of commemoration. This was echoed to some degree two hundred and fifty years or so later in the work of Rembrandt's compatriot, Vincent Van Gogh (1853–1890). Yet, while Van Gogh's recordings of his own likeness are also numerous and run a wide gamut of changing circumstances, they are more a poignantly truncated record in relation to a short lifespan and show a more rapidly changing self-image. In addition, while Rembrandt's troubled gaze is often reiterated, Van Gogh's self-portraits are more overtly diaristic than Rembrandt's. His self-images reflect the actualities of his life far more directly and, in that respect, construct an autobiography based more closely on his life circumstances.

Van Gogh's self-portraits shift from the conventional realism of the earlier self-images to an attempt to reinvent himself as a progressive and urbane artist when he arrives in Paris in 1886, as in *Self-portrait with Light Felt Hat and Bow Tie*, in which his dress is that of the fashionable townsman and his palette is lightened to match that of the avant-garde. But this is soon followed by self-portraits that document his changing mental state and re-identification with workers and peasants. This is strikingly shown in the portraits he made of himself showing his bandaged ear in January 1889, in the aftermath of his first major mental health crisis in Arles, and in the bleakness of his penultimate self-portrait painted in St Remy in September of the same year (Nasjonalgalleriet, Oslo). In contrast to Rembrandt's tendency to hide the particular circumstances of his life, Van Gogh's often painful baring of both life and soul makes the private public and paves the way for the confessional practices associated with the autobiographical art of the late twentieth and early twenty-first centuries. In this respect, his self-portraiture not only signals a paradigmatic shift in the genre of self-portraiture but expands the nature of the 'memory-work' that it performs.

Nevertheless, changeable as the self-portraits are in relation to Van Gogh's health and circumstances, they almost all fit within the conventions of the mirrored likeness, usually head and shoulders, although sometimes with an arm and hand holding a palette. Exceptions to this format are found in two extraordinary self-images in which Van Gogh has substituted his face, firstly for that of Christ (*Pièta*, 1889, after Delacroix), and secondly for that of Lazarus (*The Raising of Lazarus*, 1890, after Rembrandt). In appropriating familiar compositions and religious iconography that are already ingrained in cultural memory, Van Gogh finds a vehicle for themes of death and resurrection pertinent to his situation both as an invalid and an artist. In this, he asks to be remembered as a victim and martyr to the larger forces and conditions that worked against him, both in his struggle to develop successful interpersonal relationships and in his struggle to become a successful artist in his own time.

A similar strategy is frequently replayed in the work of the last self-portraitist that I want to discuss, the Mexican artist Frida Kahlo (1907–1954), who conflates autobiographical symbolism with cultural symbolism in a way that again sets particular terms for the 'memory-work' that her art involves. For the most part, Kahlo's self-imaging divides into two dominant approaches: one which abides by the conventional format of the mirrored image (either head and shoulders or full-length), with personal attributes that often allude to the larger socio-political context that she inhabits; and one in which she illustrates or stages key moments in her life in a mise en scène of some sort. Representative of the first approach is a work such as *The Two Fridas*, 1939. In this large piece, Kahlo positions two seated full-length images of herself as if mirror images of each other – except that one wears what appears to be a colonial-style wedding dress while the other wears the traditional Tehuana costume of a south-west Mexican woman. A divided self is immediately suggested, but simultaneously denied by the entwining of the two figures with major blood vessels that grow from the exposed heart of each Frida. Painted at the time of her (temporary) divorce from leading Mexican muralist Diego Rivera, the 'colonial Frida' is the Frida that Rivera espoused while her 'twin' represents the Frida that Rivera had in fact encouraged and helped mould – the representative of an independent postcolonial Mexico.[12] Significantly, the heart of the 'colonial Frida' is broken and sprouts an artery that divides, ending on one side in a severed state, staining the wedding dress, and on the other the heart of the 'Tehuana Frida', which is whole and which sprouts a further independent artery leading to a miniature portrait of Rivera's head.

As others have observed, the personal can be seen to blend with the political in much of Kahlo's work. In this case, the micro-politics of her relationship with Rivera are mapped onto the macro-politics of postcolonial identity, the tenuously linked hearts symbolising the pulls and stresses that the duality of identity exerted on Kahlo, born of a German father and Mexican mother and divorced from a man who she felt had refused to love her European side. While the bleeding heart can be seen as a symbol of Kahlo's personal anguish, it is also central to both the iconography of Christ's martyrdom and that of Aztec ritual sacrifice, functioning equally in both traditions as an emblem of suffering and surrender.[13] In the almost diagrammatic fusion of the personal with larger cultural meanings, the separations and entanglements inscribed in the painting allude to rather than replay or restage the events or circumstances of Kahlo's life. While the iconography is deeply encoded, the stylised technique and symmetrical composition also play a large part in the way that Kahlo chose to memorialise the dualities and inner conflicts of her identity.

In contrast, the self-images that depart from traditional portrait formats are different not only in the introduction of narrative but also because they introduce an element of retrospection and historicisation. However, works such as *The Henry Ford Hospital* (1932) and *My Birth* (1932) are more than simple recordings of past events; they are also, both literally and metaphorically, a reframing of these events. As art historian Gannit Ankori notes, *The Henry Ford Hospital* not only replays the trauma of miscarriage but overtly addresses a much broader trauma of identity. Kahlo herself referred to the piece as an 'anti-nativity' and represented herself as La Llorona, the weeping woman from Mexican folklore, who in various versions stands for evil, extreme violence, bad motherhood and sexual deviance.[14] Similarly, *My Birth* draws a complex relationship between personal and collective history and mythology, compounded by an atemporal combination of Kahlo's own birth and the death of her premature foetus in a single image, in which she is 'born but gives birth to herself'.[15] Thus, while more historically specific than *The Two Fridas*, *My Birth* and *The Henry Ford Hospital* also make similarly broad cultural references, connecting the personal to culturally shared mythologies and histories. This interweaving of personal memory with religion and myth not only allows for hindsight but also generates insight into the interweaving of personal memory within larger cultural schemes.

As Ankori suggests, the painting can be seen as an image of rebirth, a response to recent events that must have caused Kahlo to dwell on the idea and experiences of motherhood (a failed abortion, the adjustment to oncoming motherhood and a quickly ensuing readjustment to the miscarriage and the death of her own mother). On the other hand, Kahlo rejects any conventional image of mother and child, exposing the carnal reality of the female body, allowing Kahlo to rethink her identity as a woman.[16] However, despite this flouting of iconographic convention, the work takes a conventional form – that of a domestic retablo, a votive image that is used to give thanks for escape from disaster, usually accompanied by an inscription.[17] In this case, however, the inscription is conspicuously missing from the scroll at the bottom of the painting – a telling absence, given Kahlo's habit of inscribing the scrolls in her more conventional self-portraits. The reason for the absence of the inscription becomes obvious when it is remembered that the painting refers back to the miscarriage depicted in *The Henry Ford Hospital*, in which personal disaster had been neither avoided nor overcome. Moreover, the missing inscription can also be read as a sign of the unspeakability of trauma – the inability, as Cathy Caruth notes (after Freud), of being able to fully assimilate trauma as it occurs and the need to find belated and symptomatic or allusive ways of reviving the crisis in order to remember it.[18]

In works such as *My Birth*, the practice of self-portraiture shifts in a way that is to prefigure later approaches to autobiography in contemporary art and the ways in which it functions as memory. Given that Kahlo's self-portraits have begun a process in which the past is reworked as a means of understanding the self in its larger context, it is useful to introduce the notion of *Nachträglichkeit* (loosely translated here as 'retroactivity' or 'hindsight'). *Nachträglichkeit* is a psychical process mentioned many times by Sigmund Freud, whereby an original experience is reconstituted, retranscribed or rearranged in relation to ongoing circumstances – not only to replay the experience but to gather new meaning and endow it with a psychical effectiveness that has been lost by the repression of the experience.[19] As literary theorist Nicola King has recently shown, *Nachträglichkeit* forms an important counterfoil to the notion of memory as the simple excavation of the forgotten or repressed, as is clearly the case with *My Birth*.[20] As King has noted, the metaphor of excavation quickly calls to mind Walter Benjamin's thoughts on memory and history and the methods he used to chronicle his native city of Berlin. Here, memory is not an instrument for exploring the past but the medium through which that which has been known or experienced has to be processed – the soil that has to be dug and turned over. But, importantly, this act of digging not only reveals deeper hidden strata but also necessitates a re-seeing (review) of the strata which had to be excavated.[21] Again, memory is complexified by a conflation of past and present, in which that which is retrieved is contingent on what is felt or experienced in the present and becomes as much a feature of the present as of the past.

After Kahlo, this synthesis of past and present plays an important role in the mapping of autobiography in the work of the US-based French artist Louise Bourgeois (born 1911), in which the function of memory is not only to recall, reconstitute or reconcile the past but also to construct and represent the present. While Bourgeois is now widely known for the autobiographical basis of her work and its attention to memory, this aspect of her work did not begin to make a widespread impact until the 1980s with her major retrospective at the Museum of Modern Art (MoMA) in New York (1982), followed by one in Frankfurt in 1989 and another at the Serpentine Gallery in London (1995). Until the first retrospective Bourgeois had been seen, and saw herself, largely in terms of her competencies as a Modernist/Late Modernist artist, positioned in relation to dominant strands of modern art such as Formalism (Brancusi in particular) and biomorphic Surrealism, contrasting influences which suggest early on, as Frances Morris has put it, that Bourgeois is a case apart, whose 'career refuses to answer to narrative unfolding and does not mesh with an avant-garde notion of modernism'.[22]

In terms of the foregrounding of autobiographical content, a watershed occurred as early as 1974, when Bourgeois produced the first work to make reference to a particular memory from childhood entitled *The Destruction of the Father,* in which she rendered the family dinner table as a large cavity, grotesquely and significantly reminiscent of the interior of the mouth. *The Destruction of the Father* was the first of many cathartic works in which Bourgeois has exorcised childhood memories and fears. In this case, it was the fear that was regularly produced at the dinner table by the overbearing behaviour of her father that was invoked, and turned into a private fantasy that involved the dismemberment and cannibalisation of the father by Bourgeois and her brother and sister.[23] In line with the notion of *Nachträglichkeit*, that which had been repressed resurfaced at an appropriate moment – at a time when revision and reconstitution of the experience could be safely and expediently revived as part of a process of healing in order to strengthen Bourgeois' sense of self in the present. In the artist's own words, *The Destruction of the Father* 'deals with fear – ordinary, garden-variety fear, the actual physical fear that I still feel today. What interests me is the conquering of the fear; the hiding, the running away from it, facing it, being ashamed of it, and finally, being afraid of being afraid.'[24] It is also worth noting in this context that *The Destruction of the Father* was worked on during the year following the death of Bourgeois' husband, the art historian Robert Goldwater – undoubtedly a period of intense psychological adjustment and reassessment.

In the late 1970s, Bourgeois was also beginning to analyse earlier works in terms of her life history. This is evidenced in an interview with Susi Bloch in 1979 in which she speaks of abstracted figure sculptures, such as *The Blind Leading the Blind* (1947–1949) and *One and Others* (1955), in terms of 'a reconstruction of the past'.[25] However, the most explicit announcement of her developing preoccupation with the past is witnessed in 'Child Abuse', an insert in *Artforum* in 1982 at the time of her retrospective at the Museum of Modern Art.[26] It is here that Bourgeois claims that 'everything I do was inspired by my early life' and speaks openly of the effect that she felt her governess, Sadie, had had on her family relationships (that Sadie became her father's mistress, that her mother could tolerate the situation and that Bourgeois felt betrayed both by her father and by Sadie). However, this is more than an outing of family intrigue in that Bourgeois gives further insight into the way that she sees memory in relation to her art: 'It is the attitude of the poet who never finds the lost heaven and it is really the situation of artists who work for a reason that nobody can quite grasp.' Art is the medium through which she comes to terms with and transcends a painful and imperfect past, and memory is the thematic basis of her sculptures and installations:

> They are my documents. I keep watch over them… To reminisce and woolgather is negative. You have to differentiate between memories. Are you going to them or are they coming to you. If you are going to them, you are wasting time. Nostalgia is not productive. If they come to you, they are seed for sculpture.[27]

From the mid-1970s onwards, then, Bourgeois' work is continually built upon personal experience, whether in a more abstracted form such as in *Twosome* (1991), a huge phallic mechanical installation piece which stands for the relations of the family and house as well as bodily functions such as birth, sex and excretion, or in the Cells installations that incorporate far more specific iconography from her past.[28] The Cells occupy the bulk of Bourgeois' production during the 1990s and, after *The Destruction of the Father*, may be seen as her most specifically autobiographical works. Assuming the form of rooms that the viewer looks into rather than enters, the Cells invoke a memory technique first recorded by ancient scholars in which memories are linked to imaginary objects and images and arranged in the rooms of an imaginary building, ordered visually for the easy retrieval of information or experience.[29] The only thing is that, for Bourgeois, the exercise is not to systematise or to objectify memory, as is the case with the ancient art of memory, but to find a physical expression not only for that which has occurred but also for the complex of emotions that accompanied the experience. Objects and spaces are not organised programmatically in a way that resembles the conscious mind. Instead, Bourgeois compresses the space and objects of her cells so that the effect is not that of a room that can be easily 'read' or inhabited. A suggestive play of meaning is created through juxtapositions of objects and accessories that resemble the comparatively unregulated realm of the unconscious mind rather than the well-ordered house.

Sometimes these spaces are constructed with salvaged wooden doors and panels, as in *Cell 1* (1991), and sometimes they are sealed off with industrial wire mesh, as in *Cell (Eyes and Mirrors)*, 1989–1993 (fig. 1). While the memories are domestic in origin, the 'rooms' show little sign of homeliness or housekeeping (indeed, some are evocative of workshops rather than domestic living spaces or combinations of the two). Instead they are made of found materials and evoke gaol-like enclosures that, for Bourgeois, 'give meaning and shape to frustration and suffering'.[30] Furnishings and accessories gathered within the cells are orchestrated to evoke the past and the pain that is embedded in it, ranging from found or period objects that refer to Bourgeois' childhood in her mother's tapestry workshop, such as the industrial band saw in *Cell (Arc of Hysteria)*, 1992, or the pivoting mirrors in the aforementioned *Cell (Eyes and Mirrors)* or the spindles and skeins of thread in *Red Room (Child)*, 1994, to actual objects from Bourgeois' own life, such as the clothes in *Cell (Clothes)*, 1996, or the perfume bottles in *Cell 2* (1991).

Alongside the management of the present through the past and vice versa that is central to *Nachträglichkeit*, the decontextualisation and recontextualisation of materials and objects in these works clearly harks back to Dada and Surrealist strategies whereby additional and unplanned associations are generated by new juxtapositions. In this, the objects and the spaces Bourgeois creates for them are more than illustrations of a life history and more than a making public of the private; they also allow for broader subliminal responses. As Robert Storr has put it,

> [T]he content of her art is not primarily autobiographical but archetypal, an astonishingly rich, nuanced, sometimes alarming, sometimes funny and almost always startling fusion of classical personifications of human passions and terrors, Symbolist variations on them, Freudian reinterpretations of both, and direct or indirect transcription of her own unblinking glimpses into the murkiest waters of the psyche.[31]

While rendering Bourgeois' private life public, the personal history in the Cells is theatrically and obliquely staged through a mixture of props in a way that produces an ambiguous and complex edginess – an uncanniness, 'a sense of unfamiliarity that appears at the heart of the familiar', which I would argue obtains even without knowledge of Bourgeois' life history.[32] This more suggestive approach is not the case with the work of the next artist who I want to discuss, Tracey Emin (born 1963), whose autobiographically based works tend to cut to the quick and are largely characterised by their directness.

This is not to say that Emin's work lacks complexity, nor that is without ambiguities; far from it, as the several authors contributing to *The Art of Tracey Emin* (2001) have amply demonstrated.[33] It is to say, rather, that the forms that Emin employs are seemingly more explicit and that the references to life events are more blatantly put. Bourgeois may have found an iconography that dealt with her own past, but, as Storr has suggested, she employed it in a way that enabled it to connect with the sort of sublimated or generic pain and suffering that lies buried deep in the human psyche. Emin, on the other hand, constantly foregrounds specific events, experiences or emotions from her past, which she frames within familiar forms and materials of mass or popular culture. In doing this, she makes both her sufferings and pleasures directly accessible, although not so much calling upon us to share them as to witness them, so that, in contrast to the shared psychical engagement demanded by Bourgeois' installations, the control and ownership of the memories and feelings that Emin makes public lies clearly with the artist, not the viewer.

This brings me to the much-repeated notion that Emin's art is essentially confessional, which I would suggest, at most, is only partly true. The gestures Emin makes are declarative displays of a private life in which the soul is bared. As noted at the start of this chapter, autobiography is historically rooted in confession, and confession, stemming from earlier religious and more recent psychoanalytic practices, now survives widely in the broadcasts of mass media, which frequently act as moral purveyors of the behaviour of their subject – the chat show again furnishing a familiar example.[34] Emin's art, however, does not sit comfortably in a shared moral framework, as is traditionally the case with confessional practices. This is as evident in Emin's written work, in which her accounts of psychological and sexual abuse and rape are remarkably lacking in recrimination (although the men involved are shown to be ultimately weak and ignoble).[35] Similarly, episodes from her life in which her own behaviour might bring strong moral censure are guiltlessly and guilelessly told, causing Jeannette Winterson to suggest that some of the rather crass and insensitive revelations in *Strangeland* (2005) 'should have been edited out by someone that loves her'.[36]

Rather than meeting a need to confess, the self-absorption of Emin's work can be seen as a means by which she copes post-traumatically with the cruelties and abuses of her life – something that is shared with Kahlo and Bourgeois. As will be seen, Emin has developed a wide range of approaches and strategies through which she stages past events and experiences. At times, these traumas are dealt with almost in terms of archival documentation, as in her appliquéd tent *Everyone I Have Ever Slept With, 1963–1995* (1995). This provocatively titled piece was included in the well-publicised *Sensation* exhibition at the Royal Academy (1997) that brought the generation of artists known as YBAS (Young British Artists) firmly into the Establishment. While in common parlance 'to sleep with someone' is a euphemism for having sex with them, Emin is literal in the title of this work and commemorates family members and platonic friends as well as sexual partners and aborted foetuses. In effect, Emin provides reminders of the many intimacies that her bed has been host to but does not attempt to differentiate between them nor to disclose the relationships involved, so that if we want to know more about who is named we have to go to whatever is available in other sources. Nevertheless, the sewn-in names represent memories, which the viewer reads under quite intimate conditions – in order to see the names in full, he/she has to get inside and lie on his/her back (almost as if lying in bed). Details of the memories represented are not up for sharing in the viewing of this piece and nothing is actually confessed. Alongside the naming of her dormitory companions, it is the idea of the intimacies and associations of the bed that Emin opens up for scrutiny. And, as Renée Vara has suggested, the tent adds substantially to the meaning of the work, its iconography (for Emin in particular) going back to the Tibetan tent as a site of that which is ritualistic and contemplative. Significantly, given such nomadic origins, Emin's tent was to 'roam different galleries' and provide more widely placed opportunities for contemplation, in this case the contemplation not only of who has been slept with but what this might mean in terms of human intimacies.[37]

At other times Emin's works make more explicit references to her past, as in the appliquéd wall hanging *Mad Tracey from Margate, Everyone's Been There* (1997). In this work, a mixture of aphorisms vie with one another in the manner of a graffitied wall, some of which clearly echo the sort of humiliations that Emin experienced while growing up in Margate. In other pieces, such as the video *Why I Never Became a Dancer* (1995), Emin's humiliating experience is put into narrative form. Here, Emin relates her teenage truanting and accompanying sexual encounters against compilation footage of Margate, the mise en scène of her adolescence. However, although it is more specific in its recollections, *Why I Never Became a Dancer* is, again, non-confessional. It provides key autobiographical details but the events are presented in a way that, firstly, gives a record of her experiences and, secondly, that squares the record in terms of the humiliations she endured. She does this towards the end by dedicating the video to the men who managed to publicly shame her out of a dance competition. The final sequence shows Emin, having long escaped from Margate, dancing with considerable style in a venue in central London, at the end of which she names the individuals who taunted her. This is memory as redress and retribution, and, as an example of *Nachträglichkeit*, it shows Emin now in control of a past that once threatened to destroy her emotionally.

Of course, Emin's work runs a far wider gamut than these few examples demonstrate, and the stuff of which memory is made varies from piece to piece. Many works mix pain and pleasure, as in most of the wall hangings, and much of the verbal content she employs across a range of media is couched in double entendre. Countering these conflations and ambiguities, Emin's choice of medium is an important factor in the way that the works are read. Appliqué has both the familiarity and reassurance of its folk or craft origins and, from this vantage point, the viewer can feel at home or comfortable with the medium (it is also one of the forms which underwent rehabilitation in second wave feminist art in the 1970s).[38] Another favoured medium, neon, as I have discussed elsewhere, brings associations of Emin's home town and is a familiar part of most urban landscapes in the West.[39] The video forms that Emin appropriates, as Lorna Healy has noted, are also familiar from popular culture, from the camera shake of the home video to the body language and camera angles of the pop music video, and, indeed, to the incorporation of pop music into some video works.[40] So, while the subject matter is not always fulsome, Emin by no means makes the terms of engagement with her works difficult or obscure. Moreover, in selecting forms from popular culture in this way, Emin uses a method of representation that parallels the way that memories themselves are frequently mediated and reshaped using images and forms that are familiar and readily available in the wider culture.

And so it is with *My Bed* (fig. 2), the focal point of Emin's 1998 entry for the Turner Prize, an unmade bed with soiled sheets, knickers, condoms, etc. For all the sordid aspects of the piece, *My Bed* again portrays Emin's life in forms that are actual and familiar and, in this case, quite domestic. Writing on the autobiographical status of *My Bed*, Sidonie Smith and Julia Watson see it as a radical artwork that pushes at the boundaries between life and art – not through unconventionality of form or the method of representation (the bed is, after all, in the Dada tradition of the ready-made), nor even that of the life represented, but through the 'convergence of anti-art and extreme artistic self-reference'.[41] As the two authors note, the implicit contract of trust between author (artist) and reader (viewer) that has been held as the crux of the literary genre of autobiography by seminal theorist Philippe Lejeune does not apply.[42] Just as Emin does not show any consistent obligation towards confessional practices, neither does she offer to negotiate any kind of pact with her viewers concerning what she represents and how she represents it.[43] For Smith and Watson, *My Bed* is a happy blend of avant-garde practices and personal content that crosses established paradigms of autobiographical practice.

On a more general level, Smith and Watson take advantage of the motif of the unmade bed as something that can stand for the state of autobiography as a genre in the late twentieth and early twenty-first centuries. Autobiography imagined as an unmade bed is 'inescapably a rumpled one – much slept in; still warm, if soiled; and haunted by conspicuously absent bodies'. Smith and Watson use *My Bed* as a vehicle to raise questions not only concerning the boundaries between art and life but also concerning the boundaries of autobiography, claiming that Emin takes autobiography to 'the outer limits of the practice of memoir' although, for me, as much could be claimed with regard to Kahlo and Bourgeois' autobiographical works. In short, artists such as these have brought autobiography to a point at which its parameters and practices have expanded and diversified in a way that provides a radical alternative to the narrative conventions that predominate in its literary forms.

In spite of this diversification of practice, however, there is an inescapable issue that applies to all manifestations of autobiography: the relationship of the private to the public, which brings with it the associated issue of the relationship of the personal to the political. As Leigh Gilmore has noted in her book *The Limits of Autobiography: Trauma and Testimony* (2001), self-representation is constantly burdened by 'its public charge to disclose a private truth'.[44] This again harks back to Lejeune's notion of a 'pact' or 'contract' between reader and author in literary autobiographies in which the expectations of both are tacitly agreed, although, as Lejeune more recently notes, the terms of the contract will vary from reader to reader.[45] In other words, the bond between reader/viewer and author/artist is always positioned at this interface between the public and the private, which is variable and elastic in the forms that it can assume. As Paul John Eakin similarly observes, autobiography is not contingent upon an autonomous self but a self that is relational.[46] This contingency extends to the relationality of the self to the public context in or for which the autobiography is produced and consumed. And, as Dipankar Gupta has also argued, the private and the public are all too often offered up in a simplistic binary opposition which ignores the historical specificity and the individual complexity of each of these categories – something which is characteristic of the range of practices already discussed in relation to Kahlo, Bourgeois and Emin.[47]

There is no doubt that the intrusions of the mass media into personal lives and the gratuitous use of electronic technologies of surveillance have turned the relationship of the private to the public into a highly contentious and sensitive issue in contemporary life. Nonetheless, because it is voluntarily given, autobiography is able to escape any accusation of intrusion into the private and carries the issue rather differently, especially when the limits and forms of autobiography are stretched or mutated in the various ways already described in the work of Kahlo, Bourgeois and Emin. However, despite their individually differing radicalisations of the genre, all three artists have a shared emphasis in the sort of experiences they reveal in public – the working through and coming to terms with personal trauma. This, in turn, can be seen as part of a more general cultural preoccupation with pain and damage, which Gilmore perceives almost as a characteristic of the zeitgeist (it is worth remembering here that the works of both Bourgeois and Kahlo have only recently achieved recognition and that it is largely for this content in their work). Gilmore further argues that it is trauma that is at the heart of the limit testing of self-representation and that it is at the negative limits of pain that radical forms of autobiography emerge.[48] In short, limit-testing

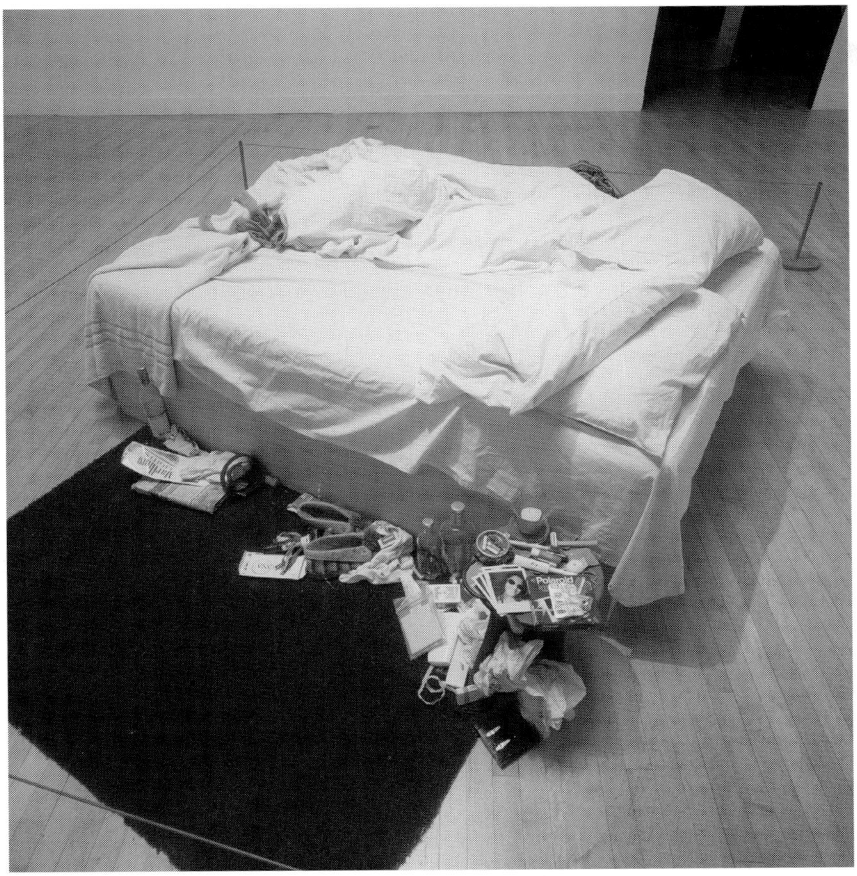

Figure 2: Tracey Emin, *My Bed*. Installation Turner Prize Exhibition, Tate Gallery, London, 20 October 1999–23 January 2000. Photograph by Stephen White. Courtesy: White Cube/ Jay Jopling.

autobiographical works not only juggle the relationship of the private to the public in a complex network of relational attitudes and circumstance, they do this specifically by opening their wounds to public probing. As has been seen, Kahlo, Bourgeois and Emin have all achieved this balancing act in their own ways – with Emin emerging as the most contentious of the three, due perhaps to the tabloid-friendly nature of her subject matter as well as to the exposure that her life itself has been given in the media in general.

The final artist I want to include in this chapter has similarly pushed the boundaries of autobiography but taken the issue of the private and the public further by consciously foregrounding it in much of his work. This is the late Cuban-born American artist Felix Gonzalez-Torres (1957–1996), who was chosen posthumously to represent the United States in the 2007 Venice Biennale. Gonzalez-Torres' work is emotionally low-key in comparison to that of Kahlo, Bourgeois and Emin, who wear their hearts openly on their sleeves. One reason may be that personal injury or trauma does not figure so conspicuously in the work of Gonzalez-Torres, which nevertheless was deeply affected and informed by his own experience of HIV and AIDS – the cause of his partner's death in 1991 and of his own in 1996. Another reason is the rather different terms in which he figured his memories, which draw from Minimalism both in the more formal placement of the work within the gallery and in the use of serial objects as components of the works. However, while Minimalism famously struck new spectator relations in the breaking down of the conventional barriers between viewer and work (the absence of frame or plinth, for instance), Gonzalez-Torres stretched these relations even further by building particular forms of interactivity into the works.

Typical of this approach are the untitled paper stacks that Gonzalez-Torres began to make in 1988, which in their allusive, mostly text-based content are as much neo-Conceptualist as they are neo-Minimalist. Many of these serve as a form of remembrance, at times autobiographical, as in *'Untitled' (Loverboy)* (1990) or *'Untitled' (Ross in LA)* (1991), and at times more broadly political, as in *'Untitled' (Memorial Day Weekend)* (1989), a now commercialised holiday in the United States, or *'Untitled' (Monument)* (1989), which carries the text 'Ten men came only three returned'.[49] However, while these pristinely cut floor pieces mimic abstract Minimalist works, their formal authority and integrity is compromised, as viewers are invited to take pieces of paper from the stacks, which are then constantly under replenishment. Not only does this continue the undermining of the autonomy of the work that was central to Minimalism, but it enables 'memory-work' to operate at the level of physical interaction with the work.

Yet, while the paper stacks represent new ways of representing and sharing memory, even they are not as radical or extraordinary as the pieces that are made up of stacks or piles of sweets or candies. Again, there is a clear obligation to Minimalism in the way that these pieces occupy floor space, usually in a corner of the room, as with *'Untitled' (Fortune Cookie Corner)* (1990), or sometimes, as with *'Untitled' LA* (1991), arranged to occupy the gallery floor.[50] And, again, many of these works make autobiographical reference. What is unique to them, however, is the proposition that the memory be eaten – physically ingested rather than kept as a souvenir or trophy (which is inevitably the fate of many of the giveaway items). This literal incorporation through the mouth brings a psychosomatic dimension to the work in which the body not only becomes a receptacle for memory but also the means of forming a communal bond between those who share the act of eating. Not only are the private lives symbolised in the works made public but the public is asked to absorb them into their own bodies and, in doing so, establish a symbolic bond with the person or persons represented, and perhaps with one another in the social context of the exhibition. In this, the social interaction required by the candy-based works may be likened to the many ritual practices of shared eating that act metaphorically for incorporation into the social body, from family meals to ceremonial feasts.[51]

In making his work participatory, Gonzalez-Torres has reconfigured the relationship of the private to the public. As already noted, this is a relationship that is of constant issue in Gonzalez-Torres' work, and perhaps nowhere more obviously than in billboard projects that are public by virtue of the spaces that they occupy. While a number of these works again addressed broader political concerns that have impinged on Gonzalez-Torres' life, such as gay history, AIDS and US military imperialism, there is one that stands out in particular for the fusion of the personal and the political, the private and the public. This is the billboard depicting an unmade double bed, produced in 1992, the year following the death of Gonzalez-Torres' partner, Ross, from AIDS. The poster shows a recently vacated bed with imprints left on the pillows. However, while depicting such intimate subject matter, the manner of representation is highly aestheticised, working through low-key harmonies of colour and tone and a flattened composition. To me, this reduction in or absence of colour and form amounts to a sublimation of grief that chimes with Gonzalez-Torres' acknowledged need to distance himself from his pain by placing this image in a public arena. And, as I have noted elsewhere, it is an image that in its aesthetic of absence brings to mind notions of the sublime invoked by Jean-François Lyotard in relation to modernist monochromatic painting.[52] Following Immanuel Kant's notion that the sublime exists in being able to comprehend incomprehensibility itself, Lyotard claims that what is at stake in modernist abstract painting is the representation of 'something which can be conceived which can neither be seen, nor made visible'. The answer to this dilemma of representation, according to Lyotard, lies in Kant's notion of 'formlessness, the absence of form, as a possible index to the unpresentable'.[53] Gonzalez-Torres' bed seems to both embody and resolve Lyotard's dilemma of unrepresentability, not only because of the absence of narrative specificity and the relative formlessness of the image but also because it provides an index to the unpresentable – to death itself, to that which is overwhelming and ultimately unknowable.

Nancy Spector also notes the lack of narrative detail in the image, which, she suggests, renders it ambiguous and more open to the subjectivities of the viewer.[54] But this lack of narrative specificity also allows for a connection to be made with an event in recent legal history which was concerned with the regulation of homosexual practices in the privacy of the home. The case of *Bowers v. Hardwick* had been brought before the Supreme Court in 1986, which ruled against sexual privacy for gay men and lesbians in their own homes, declaring them liable for prosecution for acts such as sodomy if against the law in the state in which they lived.[55] In effect, the bed, which is normally the most private of spaces, was subjected to public control; as Gonzalez-Torres puts it, 'It was ruled that the bed is the site where we are not only born, where we die, where we make love, but it is also a place where the state has a pressing interest, a public interest.'[56] The 'bed billboard' was, therefore, both a subtle and complex piece of autobiography that conflated a personal tragedy with a wider political issue, and in bringing them together in the public realm served both to commemorate a personal tragedy and extend the debate over sexual privacy.

Even more than Emin's bed with all its specificities, the blending of the private and public in this work provides a clear example of the breakdown of the conventions of autobiography in the late twentieth century. Even when his works are exclusively autobiographical, Gonzalez-Torres is enigmatic and allusive. Typical of the sort of oblique autobiographical references formed in his work is *'Untitled' (Loverboys)* (1991), a piece made up of 355 pounds of white and blue cellophane-wrapped sweets that in some versions is sited in the corner of the gallery and at other times laid out more centrally on the floor. The weight is specific, representing the combined weight of Gonzalez-Torres and Ross, and the combining of the weights in a single pile of sweets speaks to the intertwining of two lives – in Spector's words, 'a double portrait of two men in love'.[57] For Gonzalez Torres, it was also another way of letting go, of dispersing the pain of witnessing the drawn-out loss of his partner.[58] Another strategy was to represent the relationship by means of pairings or intertwinings that represented the notion of ideal lovers. In *'Untitled' (Perfect Lovers)* (1991) (fig. 3), two identical clocks are placed side by side, their hands moving in synchronicity. While anchoring it in his own relationship, Gonzalez-Torres universalises the ideal of two perfect lovers, and deliberately so, in order to eschew and even skew homophobic reactions;

in his own words, 'Two clocks side by side are much more threatening to the powers that be than an image of two guys sucking each others dicks, because they cannot use me as a rallying point in their battle to erase meaning.'[59]

A similar pairing is the set of two identical mirrors, *'Untitled' (March 5th) # 1* (1991), one of several works that feature the date of Ross' birthday as a subtitle. The second of them, *'Untitled' (March 5th) #2* (1991), was the first of his light bulb pieces in which the cords of two light bulbs run up from sockets near the floor to be knotted together at a height of around 10 feet, leaving a further 14 inches of cord to hang down with cords intertwining. As Andrea Rosen notes, the piece is particularly poignant, underpinned by the knowledge that one bulb can burn out before the other.[60] Other light bulb pieces became more elaborate and assumed varied configurations on floor or walls or strung as a curtain in the middle of a gallery, but, as Rosen also notes the light bulb pieces as a group of works were meant to refer to the twenty-four most important events and concepts that Gonzalez-Torres would like to memorialise. And, again, they are both tied to particular experiences and a testimony of the artist's need to maintain a dialogue between the

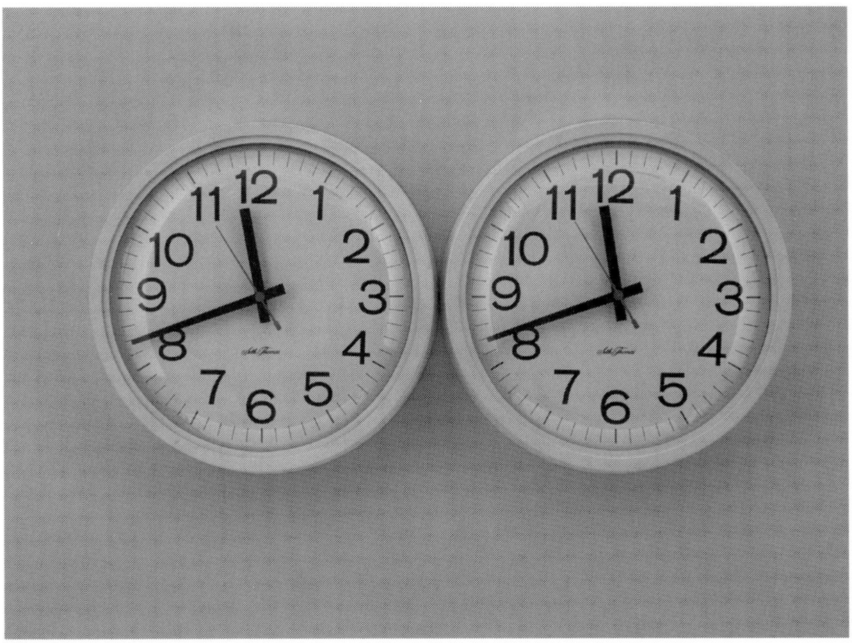

Figure 3: Felix Gonzalez Torres. *'Untitled' (Perfect Lovers)* 1991. New York Museum of Modern Art (MOMA). Clocks, paint on wall, overall 14 x 28 x 23/4 inches (35.6 x 71.2 x 7 cm). Gift of the Dannheisser Foundation. Acc. no.: 177.1996. a–b. © 2007. Digital Image, The Museum of Modern Art, New York/Scala Florence. Copyright © Felix Gonzalez Torres Foundation, Andrea Rosen Gallery, New York.

personal and the social. In Gonzalez-Torres' own words, 'I'm a person who lives in this society and I'm a product of this society and this culture. I'm not only a reflection, I'm that culture itself…'[61] While this obviously returns to the notion of incorporation into the social body that is implicit in the candy works, it further suggests that Gonzalez-Torres wanted his memories to be as collective as they are personal.

The embeddedness of autobiographical practices in a larger cultural context found in Kahlo's work is again made obvious in Gonzalez-Torres' statement. But his work operates allusively and subliminally, more akin in this respect to that of Bourgeois. Gonzalez-Torres addresses the political and social limitations of his life through forms and strategies of representation that test the limits of autobiographical practices, and, in introducing participatory strategies, he is to my mind the most innovatory of all the artists in this chapter in developing ways to represent and share personal memories. In my next chapter I continue to examine the work of artists who represent highly specific or personal memories but, while autobiographical content continues to figure, particularly in the work of Miyako Ishiuchi and Nan Goldin, the emphasis will also be on the way that the choice of an indexical medium affects the status and impact of the memory represented.

2

Traces: Memory and Indexicality

In this chapter I want to explore works that anchor memory through an indexical relationship with the subject represented, works that almost literally 'trace off' the actual world. To do this, I begin with a discussion of the work of Rachel Whiteread, whose sculptures are essentially direct casts taken from objects – or, better, the surfaces of objects that hold traces of the object's 'life' until being frozen in time by the casting process – and whose works, I argue, come as close as can be to a pure indexical relation. However, the most widely used medium in the visual arts that embodies an indexical relationship to its subject is photography, which until the advent of digital photography, with its ability to produce pure simulacrums, could always claim an existential relationship, no matter how tenuous, with what has actually existed.[1] In discussing representations made through the indexicality of the photograph, I have selected two photographers whose approaches allow me to cover key aspects of this way of anchoring memory. Here, an examination of Miyako Ishiuchi's close-up photographs of her mother's ageing body and the personal possessions left behind after her death (which, equally, show the traces of her life) will lead on to discussion of Nan Goldin's documentation of her close friends (her 'family'). A number of Goldin's friends and peer group have subsequently died, giving the posthumous status of memento mori to works that were initially conceived as memoirs. In addition to photography and video, Goldin uses sound, a medium with indexical properties that is rare in art but capable of highly evocative and immersive effect. The indexical immediacy of sound is central to the work of the last artist I want to discuss in this chapter, Bill Fontana, whose acoustic memory-works work on a less personal level, but capture and hold the particular ambience of places of special cultural or historical significance.

The traces that I identify in the works of all the above artists are, to one extent or another, connected to themes of death, loss and absence, although more distantly so in Whiteread and Fontana's work. Following on from chapter 1, the work of the two photographers also has a strong autobiographical lean, and as noted at the end of that chapter might have as easily fitted in that discussion. However, I have let the medium lead in the examination of memory in their work, which, broadly speaking, belongs as much to the context of family photography as it does to what I have shown to be the very elastic genre of autobiography. As is becoming evident, there is often a crossover between types and categories of memory or 'memory-practice'. This will be an ongoing feature of this book and is exemplified by the inclusion of the work of Doris Salcedo in the next chapter. As will be seen, Salcedo's work is also characterised in some cases by indexical relation to the subject as well as by themes of death and absence, but, at the same time, it moves into installation and foregrounds the central theme of that chapter, which is recovered histories and restitution.

That many representations are linked indexically to the thing they portray is famously discussed in the work of US philosopher Charles Sanders Peirce (1839–1914). Peirce spoke of three types of sign, the index, the symbol and the icon, signalling various relationships between the object and its representation – the signifier and the signified. In Peirce's scheme of things, the index is characterised by an existential relation to the object, as opposed to the symbol, which is a code that is entirely independent of the physical characteristics of the object (as in linguistic or geometric signs), and the icon, which refers to analogous and purely mimetic types of representation (as in figurative art or figurative language).[2] The indexical sign may involve abstraction or, indeed, may be heavily mimetic, but it is distinguished by the fact that the signifier retains at least something of the existential 'having been thereness' of that which is signified.[3] As direct casts from an object, the indexical status of Rachel Whiteread's (born 1963) sculptures is obvious and has played a substantial part in the interpretation of her work. But, as Peirce himself notes, the index is constantly vulnerable to 'degeneration' and seldom exists in a pure form. Examples of this pure or first order of indices are given by Rosalind Krauss in her 1977 essay 'Notes on the Index: Part 1', and include a footprint, a medical symptom or a cast shadow.[4] Here, the indexical relation is so close as to be almost integral, and, close as Whiteread's casts come to this status of direct attachment to the signified, they are essentially traces off the object and not part or an extension of it, and so are degenerate, or at least in the first stages of degeneracy. As Neville Wakefield has noted, the relationship between the representation and the represented in Whiteread's work is not one of a physical continuum but, rather, one in which the cast is separated, if only infinitesimally, by means of a release agent.[5] For Wakefield, the separation is 'synaptic', a charged gap between the object and its cast, 'a space of release' and a space that is 'heavily impregnated with memory', through which interiority and exteriority can form a two-way traffic and one which, due to the traces of lived experience captured in the casting, is as much redolent with somatic memories as with emotional associations.[6] The notion of an imperceptible but highly charged space between object and cast has also been taken up by Susan Lawson, who (following Derrida) refers back to Duchamp's notion of *infra mince*, a pellicle-like interface at which signification is mediated or deferred.[7] Memories are figured at this interface, but at the same time they are in deferral, present only in the form of traces – not icons, not symbols, but indices.[8] As importantly, however, this *infra mince* space, this space of release, is a liminal space at which both the fact of the object and its representation, imaginings and associations overlay one another. Moreover, as a space that is indexical, it is also dependent on the properties of the medium that, in turn, determine not only the nature of the representation but also the nature of the memories that are carried by it.

The importance of the medium and its indexicality for the formation of meaning becomes clear when Whiteread's early work is compared to examples of Emin's work, discussed in the previous chapter. As with Emin's work as a whole, Whiteread's early casts were rooted in her own formative experiences and were an attempt to capture the feel and actuality of those experiences – in effect, to memorialise them through objects that were representative of this period in her life and redolent in association with it. Like Emin, Whiteread also chose domestic and everyday objects or furnishings as her vehicles, with the mattress standing out as typical of the artist's forays into memory at the time. Yet, how different can works that share the same themes and motifs be? Emin's works are all too actual, present and detailed for the comfort of many, while Whiteread's are representations that mark the absence of the object and give only surface details, the material differences of which have been abstracted by the transformation into a single, usually monochrome material such as plaster. Emin recreates the 'lived-in-ness' of her bed, for instance, by presenting a real bed, real bedclothes, passingly real dirty underwear (which, if true, could give some indexical status to the work) and real condoms, blinding us with an overload of what might be seen as circumstantial evidence of her life. Whiteread, on the other hand, gives evidence that is almost forensic in status, due entirely to the indexical relations that govern the casting processes that she employs.

In *Untitled (Yellow Bed, Two Parts)* (1991), for example, Whiteread cast the base and mattress of a divan bed in dental plaster, a finely ground plaster that picks up on minute detail with accuracy. In this case the plaster not only reveals the creases in the mattress but absorbs some of the staining that had occurred on it, again revealing forensic-like traces of its past life. But, as with all of her casts from domestic objects, the objects selected are not actually personal to Whiteread, despite rumours to the contrary.[9] Another bed piece,

Shallow Breath (1988), has been said to be a cast of the bed that either Whiteread had been born in or her father had died in. It was, in fact, a found object, but, as Patrick Elliot notes, it nevertheless relates to Whiteread's personal memories and preoccupations. The deathbed was something that she became vividly aware of from a television documentary that she had seen as a child, and the title *Shallow Breath*, relates to her father's heart condition.[10] So, while sprung from and connected to Whiteread's own memories, they are generic objects which Whiteread saw as 'very much a part of London's detritus' and, as such, the memories they embody are also of a generic order, specific in their surface detail but both allusive and elusive with regard to the history behind these details. As casts of identifiable domestic environments, other works, such as *Ghost* (1990) and *House* (1993) (fig. 4), are obviously not so indeterminate in their history. But, again, Whiteread resisted being pulled into the specifics of their history, saying of *House*, for instance, that, although she had met the previous occupants of 193 Grove Road, she felt 'uncomfortable' in the knowledge that she'd cast their history, while not intending to 'intrude in that way'.[11] As Simon Watney has noted, *House*, in particular, embodies a whole complex of historical associations and memory, located as it is

> at a complex intersection between different and frequently conflicting sets of collective memories (and forgettings) – about the gulf between the ideal and the imaginary worlds of 'childhood' and 'home', and our actual remembered (and forgotten) childhoods and homes. And much more besides.[12]

Many of Whiteread's works are not replicas of the originals, as would be the case when the mould is used to recast the object. They present the inverted surfaces of the first stage of the casting process in three dimensions so that a negative of the object is rendered that corresponds to the original detail for detail and mirrors the size and scale of the original, but falls short of actually reproducing the original.[13] This shortfall alters the presence of the object from the here and now to one of absence or of 'the thing that has been there', to invoke Roland Barthes' characterisation of photographic indexicality.[14] *House*, like other objects cast in the same way, freezes time in a manner that has been attributed to photography, except that the photograph, as John Berger notes, cuts across the continuum of time, whereas works such as *House* or *Ghost* mark the end of a time span or the lifespan of the object.[15] Because of its public presence and the publicity that it gathered, the frozen moment encapsulated in *House* transcends the residual memories inscribed in the casts of the walls, windows and doors and, in doing so, brings together 'questions of house construction and of housing; our deep ambivalence about domesticity and "family values"; parenting; the relation of the "public" to the "private"; the effects of World War II in British popular

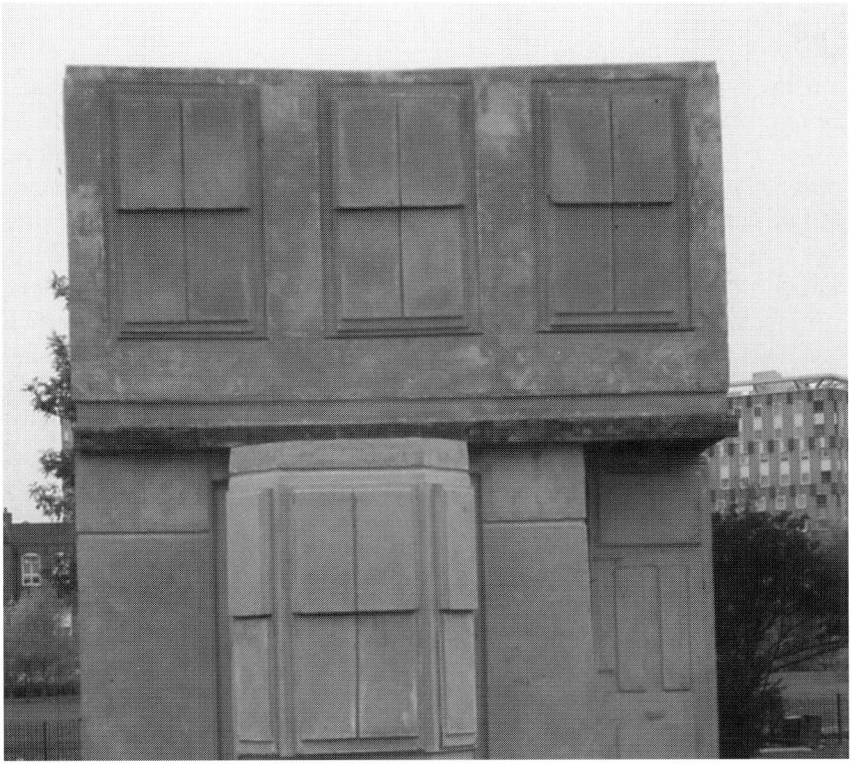

Figure 4: Rachael Whiteread, *House*, 1993. Commissioned and Produced by Artangel. Photograph courtesy of Artangel.

memory; the relationship between art criticism and commercial journalism; notions of "neighbourhood"; and so on'.[16] In its scale and isolation on razed land, it also served temporarily to monumentalise all these issues.

Although freezing time in the same way, *Ghost* lacks much of this broader contextual signification. A cast of a Victorian parlour, it is similar in iconography and similar in age to *House* but smaller in scale and scope, fitted to gallery representation rather than the public realm. Nevertheless, big enough to command a large room on its own when shown in a gallery, it also has the feel of a monument, some say a mausoleum. And, indeed, Whiteread went on to make commemorative monuments that place the relationship between casting and memory in another context, such as *The Holocaust Memorial* (1995–2000) at the Judenplatz in Vienna, or the more elusive *Monument* (2001), which occupied the empty plinth in Trafalgar Square in 2001. However, I want to end my discussion of Whiteread's work by noting the way in which the casting technique used in pieces such as *House* and *Ghost* not only preserves residual memories that are co-extensive with the life of the object but does so in a way that creates a 'space' for play of the imagination and free association, so that the work functions both to remind (re-mind) the viewer of the past and to liberate his/her thoughts and feelings in the present. While this seemingly returns us to the notion of *Nachträglichkeit* discussed in chapter 1, it is not the same process of working through specific memories as a means of psychotherapy, as in the work of Kahlo, Bourgeois and Emin. The details traced on the surfaces of Whiteread's casts were once a part of someone's life, but they reveal only pared-down traces of that life. They indicate that there is a story embodied in the work but everything is stripped down to surface details and effects, which are robbed of the expressivity and specificity of their original colour and original materiality. A process of reduction has taken place which, while physically subtractive, allows for a counter-process in which additive meanings can be built through the viewer's own memory, imagination and knowledge of social and cultural history. Not *Nachträglichkeit* as such, but a similar opportunity nevertheless for recall and revision.

The Japanese photographer Miyako Ishiuchi (born 1947) also adopts methods of representation that monumentalise her subjects and that deprive them of their original colour in a way that detaches them from their quotidian contexts and meanings. But her works differ from Whiteread's in three important ways. Firstly, the medium – that of photography – although again indexical, generates a trace of a different order from the imprint left by the cast. Secondly, Ishiuchi's subject matter is based directly on the representation of the human body and its accessories rather than alluding to it more obliquely, as Whiteread does, through casts of the objects and spaces that the body lives in and moves among and within. Thirdly, her subjects are often directly connected either to her personal history, as in the early documentary series such as *Yokosuka Story* (1977), which depicts the American military base that was also her home town, or to *Mother's* (2000–2005), which memorialises her mother through images of her body and personal belongings (figs 5 and 6).

That the photograph has a particular indexical relation to the real was recognised by Peirce himself, who in his typology of signs noted that photographs are characterised by a physical connection to the thing photographed. But, at the same time, Peirce recognised another important characteristic of the photograph, which is that it is 'in dynamical connection both with the individual object, on the one hand, and with the senses of memory of the person for whom it serves as a sign, on the other'.[17] As with Whiteread's casts, the photograph has the status of a 'degenerate' sign, and the gap that this degeneration produces between the object and its photographic signifier opens up a space in which new meanings and relationships can be produced. And, although indexicality is important for evidencing the

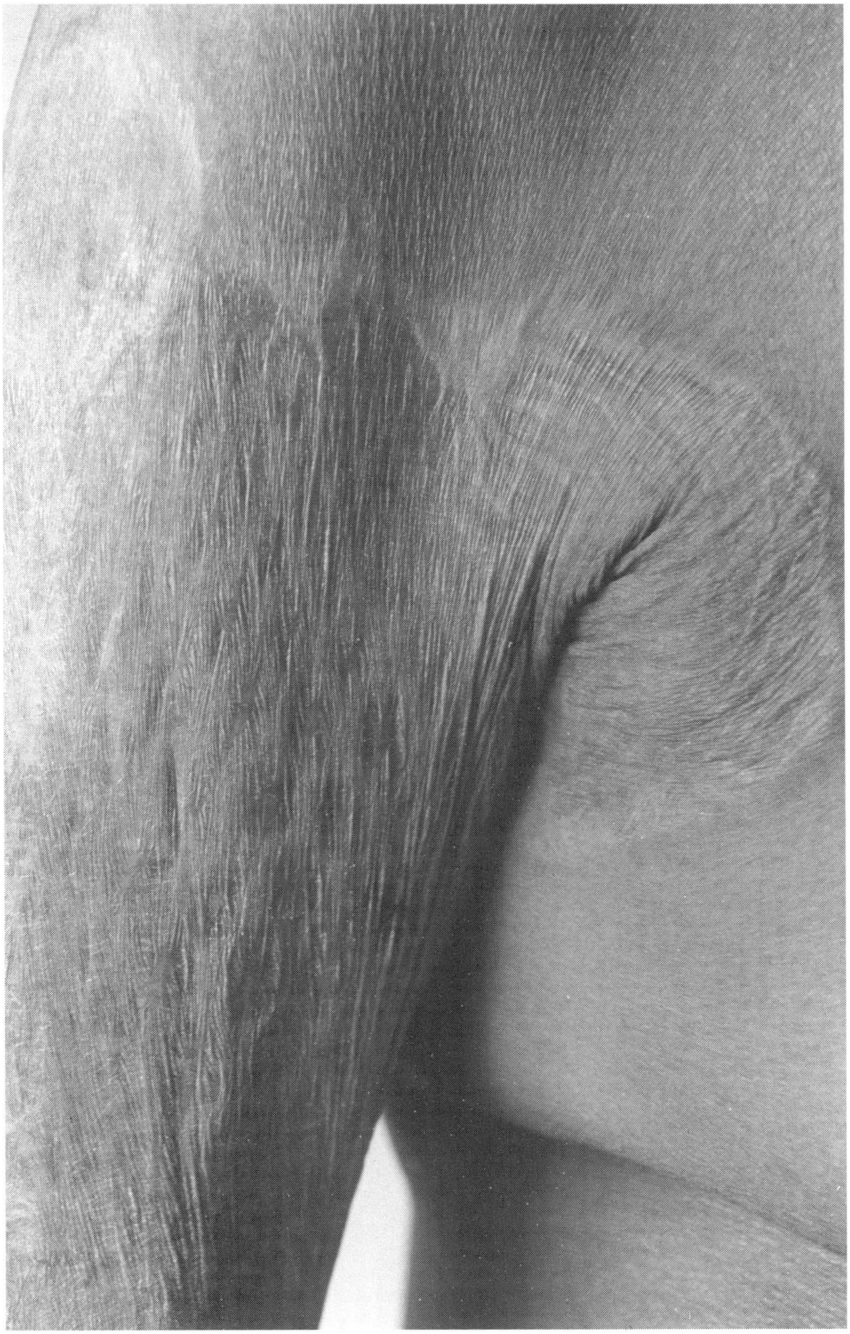

Figure 5: Miyako Ishiuchi, *Mother's 25 Mar 1916 # 31*, 2000, gelatin silver print 107.5 x 74.0 cm. Courtesy: Miyako Ishiuchi.

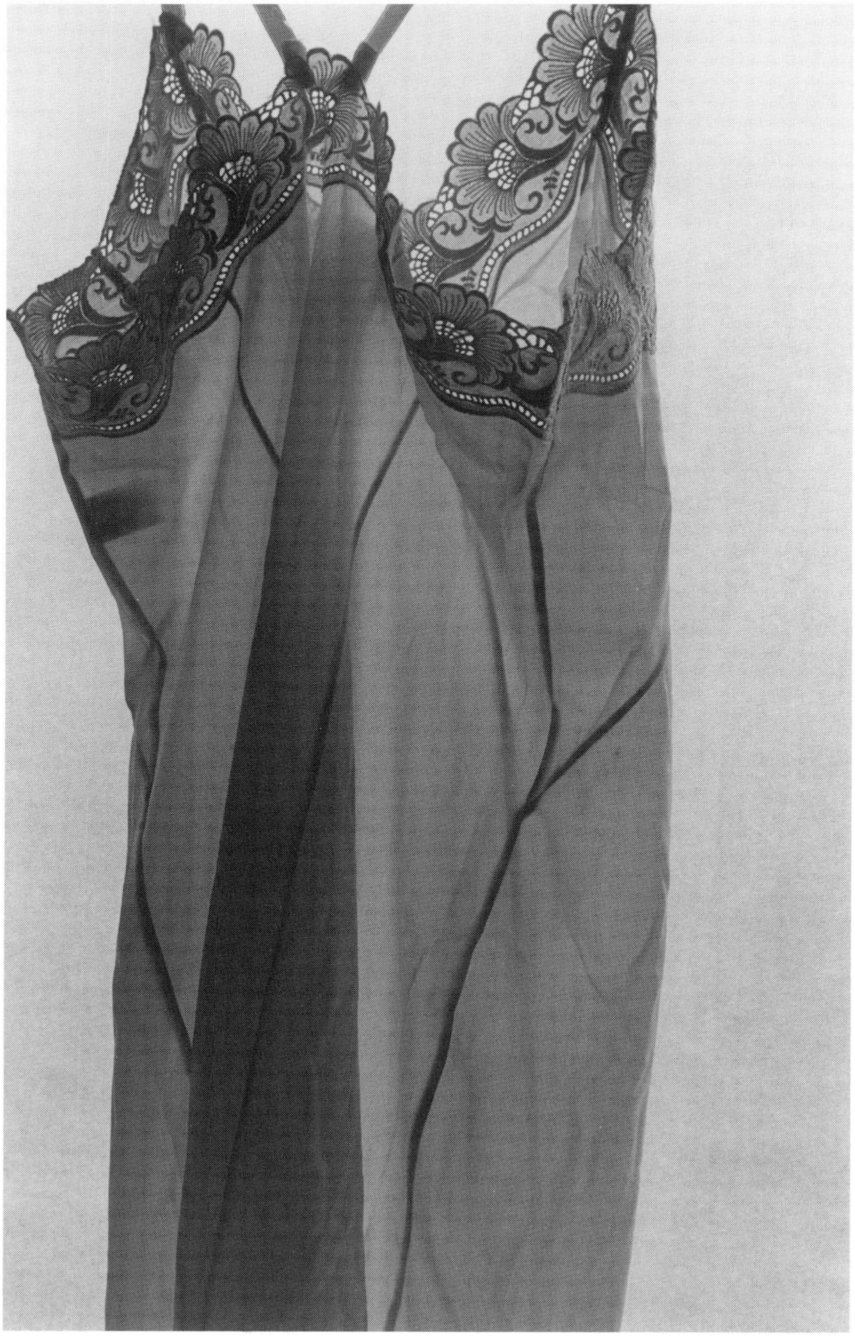

Figure 6: Miyako Ishiuchi, *Mother's # 49*, 2002, gelatin silver print 150.0 x 100.0 cm. Courtesy: Miyako Ishiuchi.

existential status of things represented in photographs, it does not provide the whole story as far as photographic representation is concerned by any means. As Victor Burgin has argued, the viewer comes to the photograph with pre-textual knowledge; for instance, conventions of representation can be and are borrowed from other arenas of visual practice, such as painting, in addition to which the viewer brings foreknowledge of the cultural meanings attached to the things represented.[18] For Burgin, this means that 'the naturalness of the photographic image is a deceit. Objects present to the camera are already in use in the production of meanings and photography has no choice but to operate on such meanings.'[19]

Moreover, photographs have as much transformative potential as they have evidential powers, and the two can most often be said to work hand in hand with one another. As Allan Sekula has pointed out, 'Photography is haunted by not one, but two "chattering ghosts", the spectre of bourgeois science and the spectre of bourgeois art.'[20] In distinguishing between the two main roles that photography played in the nineteenth century (scientific and artistic), Sekula writes both of the truth value and of the magical qualities attributed to the daguerreotype, which, on the one hand, had proved far more accurate in its representation of things than painting and, on the other hand, had functioned as a fetish object which could 'penetrate appearances to transcend the visible'.[21] But, whether photography is seen in terms of its artistic or scientific roles, indexicality is an important factor and it can signify not only an existential but a spiritual connection with the real, or both at once. The photographic process involves a ghostly transference of the real (the loss of corporeality) in which objects are dematerialised and transformed into images, so that the connection to the real is not just a transmutation assisted by certain mechanical and chemical processes, it is also alchemical, and, as Barthes would have it, astonishing and metaphysical.[22] Indeed, photography, from its early years, was associated with the 'marvellous', and seen as a form of natural magic. As the eminent Victorian photographer William Henry Fox Talbot put it in his presentation to the Royal Photographic Society in 1839,

> The phenomenon [photography] which I have now briefly mentioned appears to me to partake of the character of the marvellous, almost as much as any fact which physical investigation has brought to our knowledge. The most transitory of things, a shadow, the proverbial emblem of all that is fleeting and momentary, may be fettered by the spells of our 'natural magic', and may be fixed for ever in the position it seemed only for a single instant to occupy.[23]

As will be seen, Sekula's example of the daguerreotype both as an empirical likeness and a fetish object, as well as the notion that photography involves a form of ghostly transference and the finding of the 'marvellous' in the insignificant, is especially pertinent to the discussion of Ishiuchi's work that follows.

I first met with Ishiuchi's work at the 2005 Venice Biennale, where she was the sole exhibitor in the Japanese pavilion, showing images from her series *Mother's* (2000–2005). These works were monumental in effect, largely because of their size (the smallest being 32.5 x 22 cm, the largest 206 x 100 cm), the choice of frontal viewpoints, symmetrical compositions and the scaling up of the image into close-ups, whether body parts or body accessories. Many were also monochromatic, lending gravity through the absence of colour, although several were in colour, countering the more evocative monochromes with a fairly uncompromising realism. But another almost immediate effect was brought about by the subject matter, that of Ishiuchi's mother and her most personal accessories, which led me straight into the territory opened up by Barthes in *Camera Lucida* (1980). In addition to their monumental presentation, the images are all extremely poignant and, en masse, are resonant of Barthes' quest for a definitive image of his mother in part two of the book – not an image of his mother as she looked, but one which spoke of her in essence, found eventually in a single photograph of her as a child in a winter garden (which he declined to reproduce).[24]

In a similar vein, Ishiuchi epitomises her mother, although, in this case, it is through intimate reminders of her, which on their own do not reveal her mother in essence but cumulatively result in a sense of knowing her – through her skin, her clothes and signifiers of habitual body care, such as hairbrushes, cosmetics and even her false teeth. But, even though there is no single definitive image for Ishiuchi, the correspondences with Barthes' experience of looking through old photographs of his mother are strong. Barthes, for example, speaks of the effect of looking at a photograph of his mother as a young woman:

> Here, around 1913, is my mother dressed up – hat with a feather, gloves, delicate linen at wrists and throat, her 'chic' belied by the sweetness and simplicity of her expression. This is the only time I have seen her like this, caught in history (of tastes, fashions, fabrics): my attention is distracted from her by accessories which have perished; for clothing is perishable, it makes a second grave for the loved being. In order to 'find' my mother alas, and without ever being able to hold on to this resurrection for long, I must, much later, discover in several photographs the objects she kept on her dressing table, an ivory powder box (I loved the sound of its lid), a cut-crystal flagon, or else a low chair, which is now near my own bed, or again, the raffia panels she arranged above the divan, the large bags she loved (whose comfortable shapes belied the bourgeois notion of the 'handbag').[25]

I quote this extract from Barthes at length simply because it reads almost as a programme for Ishiuchi's *Mother's*, which also starts with a period photograph of her mother looking both chic and demure and culminates in a number of images of her mother's personal items, hairbrush, lipsticks, gloves, shoes, undergarments, etc. But this is not the only way in which Ishiuchi's approach seems to coincide with Barthes' musings on photography. Ishiuchi has a strong sense of the way that persona is inscribed in and emanates from the surface of the body, its clothes (which she refers to as a second skin) and its accessories. She characterises this emanation as an 'aura' (although, as will be noted, there are also connotations of reliquary in the personal objects that she photographs).[26] Moreover, this notion of aura again seems to agree directly with Barthes' thoughts on the mimetic power of the photograph, which he sees not as a physical resemblance but as the capturing of the 'air' of the thing or person. For Barthes, this air is not 'a simple analogy – however extended – as is "likeness". No, the air is that exorbitant thing which induces from body to soul – *animula*, little individual soul, good in one person, bad in another.'[27]

However, there are clear differences as well as correspondences between Ishiuchi's *Mother's* series and Barthes' writing in *Camera Lucida*. While Barthes seeks out his mother through a meditation on photography, Ishiuchi uses photography as a medium of remembrance. And, where Barthes' relationship with his mother is unequivocally loving, *Mother's* began as part of a process of reconciliation between Ishiuchi and a mother who she had had difficulty communicating with over a period of many years.[28] In fact, Ishiuchi was only to have one year left after their reconciliation to photograph her mother before she died, after which the process of reconnecting was continued by photographing objects that might be seen as contiguous with and carrying traces of her mother's body – the aforementioned clothes, underwear, shoes, hairbrush (still with hairs), used lipsticks, etc. And, as already noted, all of this – firstly her mother's body and then her bodily accessories – is rendered in close-up. In effect, Ishiuchi selects details of her mother's being and of her having been and enlarges them in a way that, like the cinematic close-up, is more emotionally connective. Here differences can also be noted in terms of Barthes' notions of *punctum* (detail, often incidental, which somehow pierces, pricks or wounds the emotions of the viewer) and *studium* (a more generic cultural response to the subject matter).[29] It might be said that Ishiuchi is both deciding upon the *punctum* and making it decisive in the work, rather than leaving it to the more 'accidental' details and responses that Barthes speaks of. Moreover, the staged nature of her photographs shows that *studium* is not necessarily the lesser order of representation or expression, as Barthes implies, but that it can arrest the viewer on another level that allows for a slower, more measured, equally rewarding response.

This brings me back to the monumental aspects of Ishiuchi's photographs. I have already described how this is achieved in formal terms: scale, frontality, symmetry, monochrome, etc. Theses are all qualities associated with traditional sculpted monuments, so that, on their formal basis alone, the photographs suggest worth in their subject matter and its right to preservation. On this purely formal level, Ishiuchi seems to be staking a claim to posterity and to commemoration in the *Mother's* photographs. But, as I have already briefly suggested, the photographs also recall other types of photography that are deeply embedded in the remembrance techniques or strategies of their time. The daguerreotype with its fetishistic associations and its commonplace function as a memento mori is an obvious example, but there are also other types of remembrance photography, such as those that acted as reliquaries through the inclusion of objects and materials (the hair of the deceased, for instance). For Sekula, the daguerreotype functioned as a fetish in the way that it seemed to penetrate and transcend appearances, acquiring magical connotations and an imaginary status as a relic when depicting the dead.[30] This definition aligns readily with the way that the fetish is understood in anthropology, as an object endowed with supernatural powers to be worshipped or appeased, or, as more appropriate to the daguerreotype, an object kept to facilitate mourning and remembrance.

As if in anticipation of Ishiuchi's *Mother's* photographs, the people depicted in daguerreotypes are usually frontal and extremely still, lending the daguerreotype easily to the notion of the photograph as a *petit mort* – the arresting of time with the photograph standing metonymically for the finality of death. And, as if to acknowledge the tradition of the photograph as fetish and reliquary, Ishiuchi isolates the objects that she photographs or isolates parts of the body that are being photographed, in many cases at the same time removing their colour. As a result of this reduction in colour, a key signifier of vitality is lost, emphasising a sense of other-worldliness – the ghostly transference or the 'marvellous' in the insignificant referred to earlier. An association with one of the driving concepts of Surrealism is, inevitably, conjured up by reference to the 'marvellous'. As Rosalind Krauss has noted, Surrealist photography exploited indexicality in the interest of representing the strangeness of the world, further noting that the Surrealists saw photography as akin to automatic writing, in that it provided a conduit for the manifestation of both the convulsive beauty of things and the marvellous.[31] Krauss also observes that André Breton characterises convulsive beauty as the arresting of movement, the stilling of the life of an object which allows its 'surreality' – or, as Breton also put it, its 'absolute reality' – to be revealed.[32] And, while I am not interested in making crass comparisons with Surrealism as practised by the early twentieth-century avant-garde, there are notable resonances in Ishiuchi's ability to render normally insignificant objects and materials uncanny. In their distillation and decontextualisation of normally mobile objects, her photographs elicit a convulsive beauty that, to some extent, recalls Jacques-André Boiffard's close-up photographs.

One key difference is that the Surrealists preferred to find convulsive beauty or the marvellous by chance in everyday objects which were not necessarily suggestible. Ishiuchi, on the other hand, focuses on the known specificities of her mother's body and personal possessions, so that there is already a weight of emotion in them. However, it is never the specificity of her mother's face that is represented but, rather, the traces of the person on the surface of the body or that remain on its clothes and accessories – the aura referred to earlier. This refusal to identify personality through physiognomy runs through other series produced by Ishiuchi, notably *Scars* (late 1980s – ongoing). Like the images of her mother's skin (which at times also show scars), the photographs that make up *Scars* are indexical renderings of yet another index (of physical wounding) that is inscribed on the body itself. Like the photographs in *Mother's*, they function metonymically, alluding to a much bigger 'picture' of that person's life. Moreover, scars left on the body have come to stand not only for memory but, in Ishiuchi's eyes, for photography itself as an agent of memory:

> I continue to take photographs of scars. I cannot stop because they are so much like a photograph. More than like, they have almost the same quality as a photograph. They are visible events in the past and recorded days. Both the scars and the photographs are the manifestation of sorrow for the many things that can never be retrieved and love for a life that is a remembered present.

Ishiuchi's memorialisation of her mother, then, is complex in memory techniques. She inflects the medium in a way that fetishises her subject matter, recalling older types of remembrance photography. But, in her close-ups of the body, she dwells on detail while eschewing the whole and, in particular, those parts of the whole that would identify the person in terms of their physical likeness. Undergarments and bodily accessories, on the other hand, may often be represented whole, but, again, they are contingent on an absent and particular person for their meaning. The most intimate clothing is treated like a second skin – in the same visual terms as Ishiuchi represents the skin itself, reduced in colour but augmented in scale. Such intimacy might threaten to overwhelm, but is offset by an aesthetics of delicacy, in the weave and lace of the garments themselves and the way they are placed and lit in order to be photographed, equivalent to the delicacy of ageing skin in other photographs. The photographic process here is silver gelatine, which lends itself not only to the aestheticisation of the image but also to a sense of the ephemeral. Less intimate objects and accessories are, by contrast, often illustrated in C-type colour prints, which, although as a result are far starker and more uncompromising in effect, still act symbolically as attributes of the body that they helped maintain. All this speaks to the complexity and delicacy of Ishiuchi's relationship with her mother, which takes another turn when it is remembered that Miyako Ishiuchi is not the real name of the photographer but her mother's full name (first name and family name), a fact that is surely not without significance and which to my mind adds another layer of haunting.

If the photographs that make up *Mother's* are part chronicle, part remembrance, until recently those produced by Nan Goldin (born 1953) were at the time of production all chronicle, but have since slipped from a diary or memoir-like practice into that of remembrance. This is especially the case when her works are brought together in the context of a photographic book or an exhibition, as with her major retrospectives, *Autour de Nan Goldin*, at the Pompidou Centre in Paris, and *Devil's Playground*, at the Whitechapel Gallery in London (both 2002). Goldin has practised photography since the late 1970s and has consistently made her peer group the subject of her work (although this way of putting it is perhaps to sell the close familial bond she established with the people that made up these groups somewhat short). In essence her work is documentary, almost reportage, which is not to say that her work is by any means a conventional example of the genre. Her 'style' is predominantly that of the snapshot, although, as has been noted elsewhere, her work is also filmic in the way that the images are 'like "frames" (in the cinematic sense) belonging to a more complex narrative', and also, of course, because they are often shown as slide shows in darkened conditions that resemble those of the cinema.[33]

The decision to display the images in the form of a slide show was at first a way round the expense of processing colour images, but it turned out to be an innovatory move, which, along with iconic soundtracks (often pop music, sometimes classical), created a unique set of conditions and added to the already powerful effect of the single images. Goldin's best-known slide show is *The Ballad of Sexual Dependency*, which began to take shape in the early 1980s (including some images taken in the 1970s) and was published in book form in 1986, and is still an ongoing project subject to continual modification. The images here show her trademark use of artificial lighting and flash, which gives immediacy to the images – a sense of being there at the moment that combines poignantly with the having-been-thereness produced by their indexical connection. Even more poignant, however, is that the *petit mort* that is incumbent on the taking of a photograph turns out to be prophetic in the case of so many of Goldin's subjects – her close friends and adopted family, who were to meet premature deaths through drug abuse or AIDS.

Goldin begins her introduction to the book version of *The Ballad of Sexual Dependency* by stating that it is 'the diary that I let people read' and she ends it by dedicating it to the memory of her sister Barbara Holly Goldin, who had committed suicide having just turned nineteen, when Goldin herself was only eleven.[34] A framework of recording and remembrance is set up in which Goldin readily speaks of the way that her suites of images equate to the processes of memory. The small story encapsulated in each single image contains triggers to the 'density and flavour of life', which, through accumulation, emulate memory's 'endless flow of connections'.[35] In *The Ballad of Sexual Dependency*, the theme is one of human intimacies and human relationships, from those between couples to men or women alone in intimate settings or personal spaces. Indeed, context, along with the snapshot aesthetic, is an important factor, whether a bar, bathroom or bedroom. The background details and settings bring a sense of inhabitation to the photographs, a sense of the person's everyday reality, which often simultaneously include signifiers of their symbolic lives. In *Trixie on the Cot, New York City*, 1979 (fig. 7), for instance, Trixie sits smoking in an austere and physically impoverished environment while wearing a potentially gorgeous taffeta embroidered frock and a (now wilted) satin ribbon in her hair. It presents as a post-party image that speaks both to the fantasy version of Trixie's life (marked by her dress and the magazine that sits next to her on the cot) and the harder or coarser conditions of the life that she actually leads (signalled by the frugality of her surroundings).

This is not to say that the symbolic realms of our lives are less 'real' than our actual lives or that the two are necessarily separate. The subcultures that formed Goldin's friends and 'family' were situated in opposition to the mainstream, bowing out of its conservative values in favour of fulfilment through difference and excess, often expressed through the tropes of glamour (striking make-up, elegant or spectacular clothes). Goldin shows all of this, covering a spectrum from the glamorous to the truly grim, with much that is tender mixed in. In addition to the testimonial and symbolic content of the images, conditions of viewing are also important to the effect that is created, works presented variously as large stand-alone Cibachrome prints, photographic books or slide shows. Each form of viewing makes different demands on the viewer and evokes slightly different cultural practices which inevitably give a different 'frame' or register to the works. Viewing large prints on the walls of galleries allows for close scrutiny but can also run the risk of creating an aesthetic distance; viewing them collected together in a book has the advantage of privacy and holds connotations of the family album. The slide show functions in the manner of cinema, simultaneously spectacularising the images and immersing the viewer. However, regardless of which method of representation is chosen, Goldin, like Ishiuchi, takes us beyond appearances and the basic existential status of the images, and she does this with great deliberation, producing 'pictures that come out of relationships, not observation'.[36] As with Ishiuchi, the images are meant to convey the 'humanness' of the person represented; as Goldin herself put it,

> My desire is to preserve the sense of people's lives, to endow them with the strength and beauty I see in them. I want the people in my pictures to stare back. I want to show exactly what my world looks like, without glamorisation, without glorification. This is not a bleak world but one in which there is an awareness of pain, a quality of introspection.[37]

While *The Ballad of Sexual Dependency* does all these things, it asks the viewer to travel through a number of lives and relationships, and the overall effect is impressionistic and kaleidoscopic, giving heightened glimpses of other people's reality that, together with the music, represent not only individual lives but also a social climate or even a set of mores. But, most overridingly, Goldin stresses that the people she represents are her 'family', begging the question of the relationship of her images to the context of family photography. As Annette Kuhn has shown in her account of her own family photographs, family photographs are never just records of the moment, whether anecdotal or formal or anywhere in between. They form part of larger interpersonal, sociological and ideological networks and are always historically and culturally specific.[38] Moreover, as Kuhn also observes, there are almost behavioural conventions that family photographs abide by, the foremost of which is to present a preferred, socially acceptable or idealised version of the family history which can often belie deep tensions and conflicts.[39] In contrast, Goldin's 'family' photographs are not made to collude with a mythical idea of family, or to perpetuate a dominant social paradigm. She constructs images of another order that might be likened to film stills from *cinema verité* (or Direct Cinema, as it is known in the United States), characterised by a hand-held aesthetic and frank naturalism.

This approach is also evident in other groups of 'family' photographs that Goldin put together retrospectively to form sets such as *The Cookie Mueller Portfolio, 1976–1990, Gotscho + Gilles, 1992–1993, Alf Bold Grid* and *The Positive Grid* – all posthumous tributes to close friends who died of AIDS in the devastating years of the 1990s, when the illness became a manifest killer in the United States. Although it includes images that go back to the mid-1970s, *The Cookie Mueller Portfolio* was conceived in response to Cookie's illness and eventual death in 1989 and is marked not only by retrospection (already a feature of *The Ballad of Sexual Dependency*) but also commemoration. Looked at in terms of the overall development of Goldin's work, *The Cookie Mueller Portfolio*, along with *Gotscho + Gilles*, *Alf Bold Grid* and *The Positive Grid*, marks a shift in emphasis from the recording of ways of living to the documentation of the processes of dying. Of these, *The Cookie Mueller Portfolio* covers the longest span in time and shows Cookie in a range of places, situations and moods, from mother with child to party girl taking a pee, bride on her wedding day and Cookie 'at rest' in her coffin, to name just a few.[40] While the images that make up *The Ballad of Sexual Dependency* can be seen cumulatively as a group portrait, *The Cookie Mueller Portfolio* is a multiple portrait in which Goldin focuses on one life, extracted from a larger context; that of 'a social light, a diva, a beauty, my idol. Over the years she became a writer, a critic, my best friend, my sister.'[41] In revealing a series of intimate moments, Goldin also reveals the way that the act of taking photographs allows an entry to the person photographed. As she put it, 'Part of how we grew close was through me photographing her – the photos were intimate and then we were – I was outside of her and taking her photograph let me in.'[42]

The notion of a multiple portrait applies equally to *Gotscho + Gilles* and *Alf Bold Grid*, except that the images cover a much shorter time span and the move from apparent health to visible illness is more pronounced. Rather than portraying an individual's life and character, the *Gotscho + Gilles* series builds a multiple portrait that memorialises a relationship (between Gilles, Goldin's dealer in Paris, and his partner, Gotscho, an artist). From 1991 to 1992 the photographs show Gilles in apparent health and are dominated by images of the couple in intimate proximity if not actually

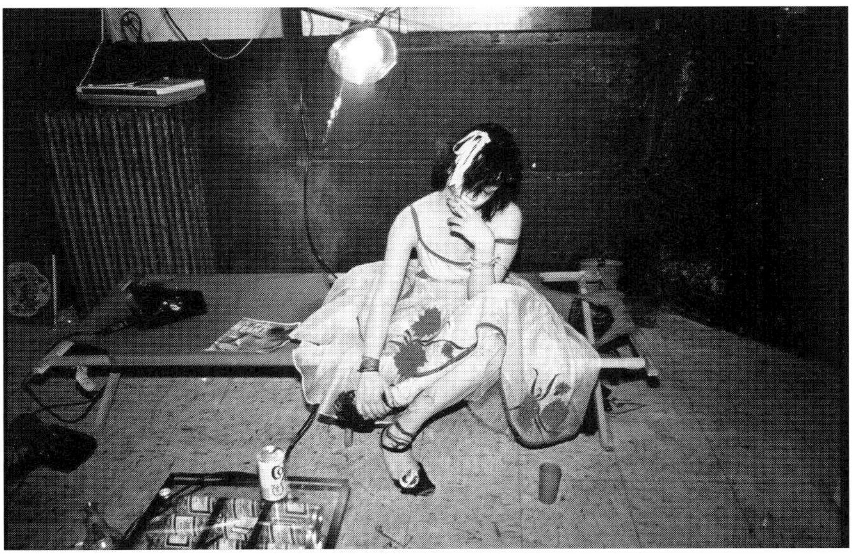

Figure 7: Nan Goldin, *Trixie on the Cot, NYC*, 1979. Cibachrome print, mounted on Sintra 27 3/8 x 40 inches (69 x 101.6 cm). Solomon Guggenheim Museum, New York. Purchased with funds contributed by the Photographic Committee and with funds contributed by the International Director's Council and Executive Committee Members, 2002.

embracing, as in *Gilles and Gotscho Embracing* (1992). By 1993 the effects of AIDS have become visible in Gilles, and the images now document his decline, and Gilles and Gotscho are more frequently photographed apart, seeming to prefigure their forthcoming final separation and making the deathbed image, *Gotscho Kissing Gilles* (1993), stand out the more poignantly. Nonetheless, while *The Cookie Mueller Portfolio* and the *Gotscho + Gilles* series can be characterised as multiple portraits, they are also built around a strong narrative thread, conjuring up a sense of the duration and development of their relationship. The grids differ in that they tend towards an iconic distillation of the subject; as Goldin says of *The Positive Grid*, it is made 'in the manner of a Renaissance alterpiece', showing 'people who are positive living positive lives'.[43] After the harrowing experience of watching and caring for friends as they died and of becoming Alf Bold's principal carer in the period leading up to his death, the grid seems to have offered a means through which Goldin could step back and give some sort of order to the overwhelming traumas that she witnessed and experienced.

Looked at retrospectively, Goldin's work moves along a trajectory from the broad spectrum of friends and 'family' in *The Ballad of Sexual Dependency* towards the representation and remembering of particular individuals in *The Cookie Mueller Portfolio*, *Gotscho + Gilles*, *Alf Bold Grid* and *The Positive Grid* until it arrives at a commemoration and tribute to her older sister Barbara Holly Goldin, who, as already noted, committed suicide in 1965, when she had just turned nineteen. This work of remembrance, *Sisters, Saints and Sybils* (2004), was Goldin's response to a commission from the French Ministry of Culture and Communication for the Paris Autumn Festival in November 2004, which was installed at La Chapelle de Saint Louis de la Salpêtrière, attached to the contemporary art centre.[44]

Essentially, *Sisters, Saints and Sybils* takes the form of a triptych, with images projected onto three screens in a slide show of thirty-five minutes' duration, divided chronologically into three related 'stories' (some of which are video/digital footage). The first part is a brief account of the life of the third-century Saint Barbara, whose martyrdom was that of being beheaded by her own father for her embrace of Christianity. The images here are reproductions of religious works of art that have depicted the saint, for which Goldin provides a voice-over narration interspersed with religious choral music. Beginning with a historical figure in this way, Goldin uses a strategy that is common in religious painting: to use one story (usually from the Old Testament) to prefigure and lend historical authority to a later event (usually in the New Testament). In doing this, Goldin puts her sister's story into a wider historical and cultural framework, drawing parallels across the ages between the victimisation of women. In this case, connections are made between two women who share the same name and who both suffered appallingly at the hands of their parents and the ideological and social constraints that governed them, so that the '*Sisters*' in the title refers not only to Goldin and her sister but to a wider sisterhood of 'women who have committed suicide or been institutionalised for their rebellion'.[45] Barbara Holly Goldin's 'martyrdom' was tied to a refusal to conform to parental control, and took the form of incarceration in a detention centre and mental institutions and, ultimately, her suicide.

For a while the second part of the slide show is made up exclusively of images from the family album, creating a perhaps misleading sense of happiness and family harmony, until the point at which Barbara was first committed to a detention centre at the age of fourteen (although I am sure that such times must have featured among the more difficult periods). The images and narrative that follow include more photographs of Barbara, but these are subsumed in a suite of images that speak to her institutionalisation, largely made up of photographs and footage that Goldin later took of the institutions to which Barbara had been committed. These are accompanied by Goldin reading extracts from institutional documentation relating to Barbara and more classical music, although, strikingly, the detached voice-over narrative is at one point dramatically punctured by a soundtrack of an emotional argument between a young girl and her mother. This second part of the work comes to a close with images of the scene at which Barbara's suicide had taken place, and with Goldin reading a newspaper report of the death. There is momentary blankness and the sound of a male voice screaming (Goldin's father's response) and a female voice asking the policeman to 'tell the children it was an accident' (repeating the words that Goldin heard her mother say).

The account of Barbara's life finally comes to a close with shots of the King David cemetery where she was buried, after which photographs of Goldin taken in the 1960s appear, against which she comments: 'My sister told me her psychiatrist said I would end up like her. I thought I had to kill myself at eighteen.'[46] In reality, however, it is difficult to say exactly where this second part ends and the third begins, perhaps because the second part necessarily haunts the third and recurs graphically at the end of the whole slide show with more footage of the graveyard and an image of Barbara's gravestone. However, after the images of the teenage Goldin, the emphasis is on Goldin's life after leaving home aged fourteen, her new 'family', drugs and photography. In this Goldin takes the viewer through her own two periods of hospitalisation and self-abuse, accompanied this time by sound tracks from such experts in introspection and mental anguish as Nick Cave, Leonard Cohen and 'the late, great Johnny Cash'.

Various mnemonic devices feature in the work as a whole. The religious images of Saint Barbara are devotional but also serve to preserve her legend.

The photographs of Barbara Holly Goldin are from the family album and, given the actualities of her adolescence, constitute a poignant example of the desire for normalcy and idealisation that underpins this form of record. There are the readings from newspaper accounts of the death and archival material from the hospital records as well as the photographs and footage of the detention centre and hospitals (these are of the institutions as they appear today, but nonetheless they are reminders of the past). There are the images of Goldin's adult life, many of which are familiar extracts from other bodies of work, and there are the images of her sister's graveyard and tombstone, including a headstone with 'sister' carved into it. A further device is that of the music and songs that Goldin attaches to the images. Here, I would argue that the rhythmic and emotional charge of music and lyrics has a particularly tenacious hold on memory, which, as with photography, is due in a large part to its indexical nature. The emotion generated by music is a direct trace of a bodily movement on an instrument or the voice, relayed to the ear and body of the listener. And, even when it is recorded music that is heard, it has, as Walter Benjamin asserts, the ability to reactivate the original experience.[47] As noted earlier, the result is highly immersive when orchestrated in the viewing conditions of an audio-visual slide show.

There is a sense that the revisiting of the past brings some sort of redemption from its suffering as the work makes its essentially painful journey towards the present. In *Sisters, Saints and Sybils*, Goldin assumes the role of '*Sybil*' – the third element of the work's title. Yet she is not so much a female prophet but a seer who has looked back at her formative past (governed in essence by her sister's conflicts and suicide) and carried it through to review the experiences of her adult life. That Goldin comes out at the other side of the loss and pain that she has witnessed (despite a further stay in hospital in winter 2002–2003) is perhaps symbolised in her written commentary to *Sisters, Saints and Sybils*, in which she notes that she discovered daylight during her first recovery from drugs in 1998. As she states elsewhere, this realisation of daylight brought with it that a realisation of the outside world and set her thinking about her relationship to nature.[48] Among the memories in *Sisters, Saints and Sybils* are images and footage of landscapes and sky, through which Goldin lets in both light and grace and which, to me, are major signifiers of the redemptive trajectory of the work.

Less personal, but deeply evocative in their remembrance of the past, are a number of historically grounded works by US sound artist Bill Fontana (born 1947). Although Fontana's works are often realised in the public realm and sometimes occupy a vast amount of space, he categorises them as sound sculptures – thinking of sounds as 'volumes of space that existed in time'.[49] In other words, there is a formal integrity to his works, which are situated within the coordinates of space, volume and time that condition material sculptures, and perhaps puts them on a scale that can be likened to that of major land artworks of the late 1960s and 1970s by Robert Smithson or Michael Heizer, for example. But this is not to say that Fontana's works are formalist or only preoccupied with the physical properties of the site. On the contrary, they are very much to do with his perception of the lived world – 'a way of listening to the world'. Fontana works with the actual sounds of a place or places, using them as a basis for his compositions, ultimately connecting the listener to the place by way of sound traces. These places are often already culturally and historically 'resonant' and already serve as anchors for social or collective memory.

An obvious example is *Sound Island* (1994), commissioned by the French Ministry of Culture, which in its commemoration of the D-Day landings in Normandy might be classified as a monumental work. In fact, a pre-existing war monument provided the setting for the work, which was sited at the Arc de Triomphe in Paris. In itself, the Arc de Triomphe follows an ancient classical formula of triumphal architecture, and, as Fontana notes, it is one of the most frequently visited war monuments.[50] Located at this particular monument, the sounds that make up *Sound Island* become situated among a number of heavily loaded signifiers and symbols related to warfare. For instance, heroism and patriotism are embedded in the sculpted programme, in particular *The Departure of the Volunteers of '92* by François Rude (more popularly known as *La Marseillaise*), and a reminder of the sacrifice of the common man for the greater good exists in the tomb to the Unknown Soldier at the base of the arch, where an eternal flame burns. Yet, spectacular as all this is, Fontana managed to offset the heavy symbolism of the monument by wrapping it in a sea of sound, literally formed from the sounds of the sea that he had previously recorded on the Normandy coast, stating that 'the sound of the sea is acoustically like an eternal flame, because it's a timeless sound, a sound that's been going perpetually for millions of years'. Fontana not only brought the actuality of Normandy to the Arc de Triomphe but both subverted and redefined the iconic visual presence of the monument by cloaking it in the simulated presence of the sea. As Fontana has said, the advantage of the invisible is that it has the ability to alter our perceptions of the visible. In the case of *Sound Island*, Fontana was able to take memory from the circumscribed realm of programmed commemoration to the more expansive realm of sensation and association, so that the 'memory-work' becomes more subliminal.[51] This is also a realm of emotional arousal that is fed in two intertwined ways: by capturing and reconfiguring actual traces of the past and, at the same time, by opening the mind up to the myriad possibilities of involuntary memory.

A similar transposition of the sounds from one location to another to create a complex and dense memory experience is at the heart of an earlier work, *Distant Trains (Entfernte Züge, 1984)* (fig. 8). But, whereas the sounds that were wrapped around the Arc de Triomphe formed a noticeable contrast to the normal traffic noise of the site and to the architectural character of the work, the sounds in *Distant Trains* were taken from one (functioning) railway station and transposed into another (defunct) railway station, creating a simulation that was at once at home in its setting but which at the same time rendered the already uncanny feel of the ruin even less homely. The sound sculpture was installed in the ruins of Anhalter Bahnhof, which had served as a major railway station in Berlin (and at one time the largest train station in Europe), near to which Checkpoint Charlie, the famous crossing point between East and West Berlin, had been situated. Again, the site was loaded with significance, having twice been bombed by the Allies in World War II and left as wasteland. For Fontana, the empty field that was left surrounding the remaining bit of façade was 'a space haunted with sound and acoustic memories' that he wanted to reactivate.[52] He did this by making recordings in the main station at Cologne, the busiest contemporary German station, and playing them on hidden loudspeakers in the grounds of the Anhalter Bahnhof. The acoustics worked in such a way that the sounds, which were already carrying the weight of their indexicality, seemed real to the abandoned station. As Fontana remembers, 'It became a very emotional

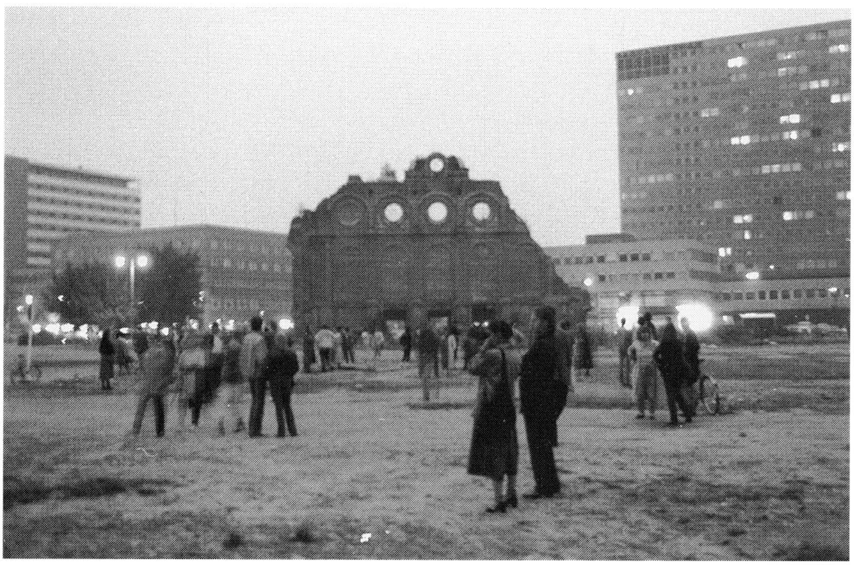

Figure 8: Bill Fontana, *Distant Trains*, 1984. Sound Installation, Anhalter Bahnhof, Berlin. Courtesy of the artist.

space, because in 1984 there were still a lot of people alive who had memories of the station.'[53]

For me, the emotive effect of Fontana's sculptures lies in the combination of the site and its associations. Sound permeates the environment but also intensifies the environment, through the doubling up of the real and the simulated. However, this doubling is also made intense by the fact that the sound is indexical, derived from pre-existing sounds in the environment. This was certainly the case with both *Sound Island* and *Distant Trains*, in which memory was intensified by the layering of past and present. It was also the case with a more recent work, *Pigeon Soundings* (2005), which was aimed at preserving the memory of a ruined church, St Kolumba, that had become the site for the building of the new Diocesan Museum in Cologne. Fontana began this work in 1994 by recording the sounds of the pigeons that flew in and out of this space in order to capture an acoustic memory (backed, of course, by other ambient sounds, such as traffic and bell-ringing). But, interestingly, the installation of the piece did not take place until 2005, when the sounds had indeed become historical, a sort of time capsule that Fontana had to reconfigure to regain their sense of actuality and maintain their fluid relationship with the actual sounds of the building and its outside.[54]

Throughout this chapter, I have foregrounded works that have an indexical tie to that which is remembered. With Whiteread the traces left on her casts are at once intimate and anonymous. The photographic traces in the work of Ishiuchi and Goldin are both intimate and personalised. The sounds captured and redistributed by Fontana intensify the historicity of the site in which they are played but provide an emotive sensory experience. In my next chapter, I move the emphasis away from this sort of intimate connection, although it still figures prominently in the work of one of the artists concerned, Doris Salcedo. Instead, the focus will be on the recovering and reconfiguring of social and political histories as a form of counter-memory. To do this, I have selected examples of historical revision in which the methods and cultural politics of historicisation are as important for my discussion of the workings of memory as the histories or counter-memories themselves.

3

Revisions: The Reassembling of 'History'

The emphasis in the last two chapters has been on personal or intimate memories, although, as has been noted and shown, the personal inevitably sits within a public or collective framework of some sort and, for some, such as Gonzalez-Torres and Whiteread, broader cultural issues and history are expressly a part of that which is addressed. In this chapter I intend to shift the emphasis to artists who take political or social histories as their starting point, although it will come as no surprise that individual histories will sometimes be seen to intertwine with the wider histories that I foreground. Moreover, the issue of traces that underpinned chapter 2 is not entirely left behind, although there is a shift from the indexical trace to the notion of history as an act of tracing. As historian Keith Jenkins argues, history is dependent on there having been a past and that there is evidence of some sort to prove it. Importantly, Jenkins has also noted that the past, which is gone, can only ever be partially reconstructed within the ideological and discursive frameworks of the present – that history is not the same thing as the past, which are 'ages and miles apart'.[1] It is now well established that history exists in many versions and forms, and that all these are relative to the context in which the history is produced. This broad view includes versions of history which openly declare themselves as fictionalised, such as the historical novel or drama, which begins to demonstrate the elastic relationship between history and artifice that underpin this chapter. Accordingly, the works discussed in this chapter are as much works of history as they are works of art, even those of Yinka Shonibare MBE, which are so full of historical incongruities that they seem to stretch the notion of history as a tracing or reconstruction of the past to its limit.

It is also important to note that recognition of the contingency of history reflects a more widespread understanding of the ownership and production of knowledge as a power base that works on several levels in the culture – psychical, social, political and economic. That knowledge gains particular power and particular inflexions through its institutionalisation forms the basis of this awareness and has been largely told by French philosopher Michel Foucault, who devoted the best part of his academic career to studying the ways that institutions produce dominant paradigms of knowledge and the ways in which these paradigms are consistently implicated in a set of hierarchical power relations.[2] Following this recognition of the political and ideological role of institutions, a discussion of the institutional practices of the art world will be part and parcel of my account of the counter-histories and counter-memories that are the central concern of this chapter.

In speaking of the institutional power of knowledge, Foucault also speaks of the production of discourse, the ways in which knowledge is framed, spoken and transmitted, so that Foucault's overall project was equally concerned with the contingency of discourse – that it is never disinterested while often presenting itself as intact and objective.[3] The relationship between the production of knowledge, discourse and art institutions is exemplified historically by the genre of history painting, which emerged with the classification of painting into a hierarchy of types in 1667 by André Félibien of the French Academy. Of these (others being portraiture, landscape, genre and still life), history painting, as a didactic and moralising representative of human achievement, held sway as the 'highest' form until rocked by Charles Baudelaire's championing of the painting of modern life and its realisation in the works of nineteenth-century painters such as Edouard Manet (1832–1883). Typical of history painting and highly regarded by their contemporaries are Jacques Louis David's paintings *The Oath of the Horatii* (1784), which shows a pledge on behalf of the Horatii family to fight for Rome against Alba, which meant the men would be fighting the family of one of their wives, and *Brutus* (1789), in which the revolutionary leader has had his own son executed for betrayal of the republic. In both these works, painted just before and at the time of the French Revolution, the message is clearly programmatic and didactic – to put the interests of the state before personal concerns, no matter the sacrifice involved.[4] Here, the production of art and the representation of history is demonstrably not disinterested, sitting clearly within the two frameworks of the classificatory discourse of the French Academy and of the political discourse leading up to the French Revolution.

The French Revolution was, additionally, the point at which previously dominant social and political ideologies were radically challenged and uprooted, inaugurating a paradigmatic shift in the notions of who makes the rules in society and on what basis, thereby setting a precedent for later challenges to the values and practices of the Establishment. Art, for instance, would no longer always tread the path prescribed by the Academy, nor would it always conform to dominant social and political ideologies. This departure from the preferred artistic programme of the Academy occurred in the time frame of the Revolution with Romanticism and its cult of the individual and of subjectivity, and recurred later in the nineteenth century with Realism and its regard for social issues and inequalities. Realism, as represented by the painter Gustave Courbet, also inaugurated an avant-garde that opposed the status quo in terms of what should be represented in art and how it was to be represented. It is not necessary here to trace the development of this avant-garde over the last hundred and fifty years, just to note that its inauguration opened the way for numerous alternative and oppositional viewpoints and practices (most of which, admittedly, have subsequently been diffused and appropriated into the mainstream). At present, the institutions of art tolerate a plurality of approaches and standpoints, often, although not always, welcoming dissent from mainstream values and ideologies, including the dissents from and challenges to previously dominant versions of history that are the subject of this chapter.

The works that I have chosen to discuss all formulate counter-histories and/or counter-memories of those that have been socially and politically oppressed (through gender, political belief or race). Before commencing, however, I think it important to draw attention to the problematics of using such closely related terms as 'history' and 'memory', which intertwine, sometimes to the point of fusion and possibly confusion. Despite the recognition of the contingency of historical knowledge, academically endorsed methodologies remain the principal means by which the ideas and events of the past are established and authorised. In academic historical research, the ideas and events of the past are usually of collective interest, seen as verifiable and situated within a logical framework of time and space. This does not apply so readily to memory, which is not necessarily bound to collective interests, logic or the precise chronology or location of ideas and events, although it is often bound to genre or convention, as is traditionally the case with the production of commemorative monuments.

Nevertheless, to distinguish between history and memory in this way places them in a binary relationship in which memory can be seen as a less legitimate means of establishing the past, or, conversely, history can be seen as the 'destroyer of a more authentic, existentially rich, living memory'.[5] As Dominick LaCapra argues, memory is nether the opposite of history nor is it identical to it. For LaCapra, memory, despite its often fickle nature, is a crucial source for history, and history reciprocally provides a means by which memory can be critically tested. History and memory are in supplementary relation to one another, with history functioning as a (perhaps more regulatory) form of memory that interprets and authenticates the testimonies of primary witnesses and sources.[6] On the other hand, if, as sociologist

Barbara A. Misztal has observed, memory is often a social activity or even a means of socialisation, historical research or recall can in turn be seen as providing essential material not only through which memory can be figured more elaborately but upon which human understanding and relationships are modelled or formed.[7] It is this understanding of history as an aspect or function of collective memory that will underpin my use of both terms as I proceed through this and subsequent chapters.

Among the now numerous works through which contemporary artists have sought to re-evaluate history and rework memory, *The Dinner Party* (1979) (fig. 9) by Judy Chicago (born 1939) is of pioneering significance, calling attention to the highly selective versions of history that were taught in the United States in the 1970s (in this case, to the omission of women's histories).[8] In doing so, it encapsulated some of the key issues of feminist art and became representative of the preoccupations of the movement at a certain point in time, particularly those related to essentialism and the notion of a female aesthetic.[9] And it captured them in no uncertain way. *The Dinner Party* takes the form of a huge installation which is as monumental, programmatic and didactic as any history painting. That Chicago consciously positioned herself in relation to this sort of tradition is evident in her call upon Last Supper paintings as both a thematic and art historical reference point. As she recalled, 'I began to think about meals, most notably renditions of the Last Supper, which of course included only men. It was at this time that I titled the work *The Dinner Party* and began referring to it humorously as a reinterpretation of the Last Supper from the point of view of those who've done the cooking throughout history.'[10]

The tables in *The Dinner Party* form an equilateral triangle. Each side is thirty-three feet long on the outside and is set with thirteen dinner places (the number of attendants at the Last Supper), thirty-nine places in all, the settings serving to iconise women that were known of but undervalued in history and mythology. As a result of the large dimensions and open-centred triangular configuration of the tables, there is a large expanse of floor space around and inside the tables, known as the *Heritage Floor*. This is clad with triangular tiles upon which the names of a further nine hundred and ninety-nine women who have been neglected in history are inscribed (one thousand and thirty-eight women in all). If commanding in scale, *The Dinner Party* is stunning in the quality of its craftwork. In addition to celebrating women of achievement, Chicago also wanted to honour materials and techniques that were the traditional preserve of women. Each setting has an individualised ceramic plate, chalice, knife, fork and spoon, arranged on top of an individualised embroidered runner which lies from back to front of the setting, rather than following the length of the table. The choice of craft techniques traditionally associated with women was, of course, as significant as that of the subject matter itself, serving to reinforce the message of the undervaluing of women's achievements and to challenge patriarchal associations that go with high art materials. But the result is by no means domestic, the chalices and the use of ecclesiastical methods of embroidery in particular giving a sense of sacrament, the quality of the materials (linens, gold threads, rich glazes etc.) and the exquisite finish on all parts signifying that which is precious. As well as its now mythical status as a piece of feminist art, all of this is what made seeing *The Dinner Party* special for me when I eventually got to it over twenty years after its first showing. I found it a tour de force, was moved by the many hours of women's dedicated unpaid labour that had gone into it and, despite the criticisms that follow, derived satisfaction from the restitution of women who had been previously marginalised in history.

While *The Dinner Party* can be judged successful in terms of calling attention to historical exclusions and in commemorating some of the excluded, it hoists itself by its own petard by attempting a universalising history. From the start and throughout its travels to venues around the world, *The Dinner Party* met with vehemently adverse criticism, particularly

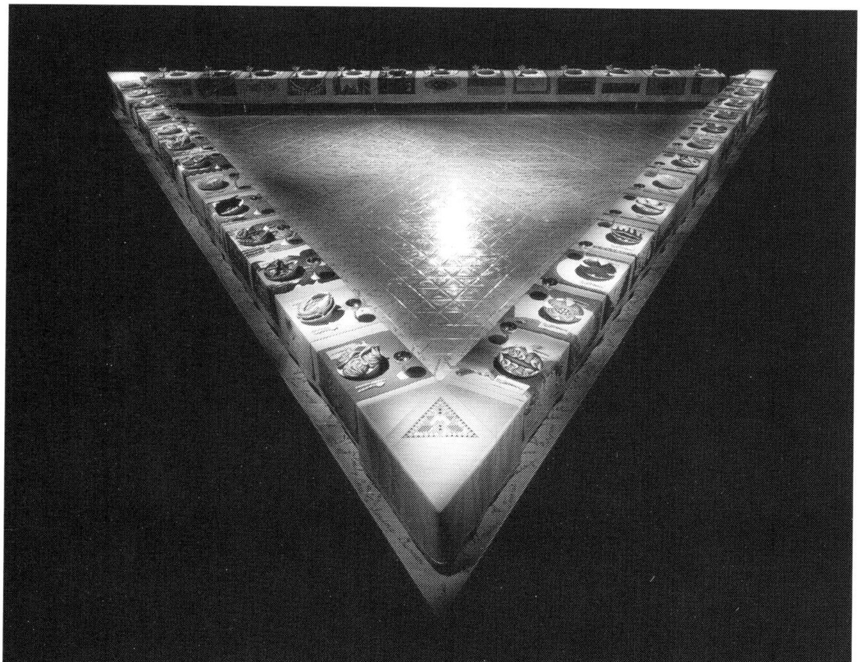

Figure 9: Judy Chicago, *The Dinner Party*, 1979. Courtesy: Through the Flower. Copyright © DACS 2007.

from fellow feminists, for its attempt to universalise and essentialise women's experience.[11] An early example is the response of black American writer Alice Walker to the Sojourner Truth place setting, which she felt set black women apart from the larger community of women of achievement that the work represented. The Sojourner Truth setting differed noticeably from other settings by depicting two weeping faces either side of an African-style mask instead of using the central core/vaginal motifs that characterised almost all the other place settings.[12] The absence of the vagina in Sojourner's setting not only signified difference within what was supposed to be unification but, in denying Sojourner her embodied history, reduced the fullness of black women's lives and experiences.[13]

As Anette Kubitza has noted, feminist critics in the United Kingdom mounted an attack on several fronts: the work lacked theoretical rigour, was hierarchical while seeking to challenge hierarchies and reduced women to the lowest common denominator of their vaginas, potentially encouraging the sexual objectification of women.[14] Similar criticisms were raised in Germany, with additional connotations brought by that country's particular history of fascism, seen in the work's inherent 'irrational spirituality' and 'biological determinism'.[15] In short, what was meant to be an unequivocal avowal of women's achievements quickly became contested for its claims to universality and essentialism, and was ultimately and perhaps justifiably denigrated for its single-mindedness. Chicago attempted to do what history painting had done in the past and deliver a grand universalising message for the edification of her viewers, but she did this in a political climate when such overarching histories, or 'grand narratives', as French philosopher Jean-François Lyotard has named them, were being discredited and when such an approach could be construed only as conservative, even retrograde, by radically committed historians and critics.[16]

So, although Chicago had sought to redress history and offer a counter-discourse to that which privileged male achievement, her grandiose vision failed to connect with some of the very women on whose behalf she was working. As a programmatic piece of didactic art, *The Dinner Party* was simplistic and out of tune with the more mobile and personalised sensibilities of the time. Yet, in its defence, for many women outside the inner core of feminism *The Dinner Party* was thought-provoking at the very least, and at best revelatory and inspiring. *The Dinner Party* has been seen by thousands around the world, has prompted a number of participatory spin-off events, stirred a volume of debate and is still seen (not necessarily uncritically) as an educational tool for women's studies, all of which seems to indicate that the retrieval and restitution of women previously 'lost' to history was not and is still not without purchase.[17]

However, despite the evident popularity of the work (100,000 visitors at its first showing at the San Francisco Museum of Modern Art), institutional recognition for *The Dinner Party* from the art world was to wane rapidly, and when the work toured in the 1980s it was mostly seen in alternative venues.[18] As Misztal has argued, institutional recognition given by the museum and, by extension, major art galleries is significant not only for the authorisation and legitimisation of collective memory but also for its production.[19] From the start, Chicago had wanted recognition from the art world, and her bitter disappointment at not receiving it signalled an Establishment-mindedness for some feminist critics.[20] But this lack of support from the art world is not to say that *The Dinner Party* was unable to partake in the production of collective memory, only that it had to do so by locating spaces in which 'communities of memory' could come together rather than the institutions of art. As Misztal has also noted, mnemonic communities 'socialise us as to what should be remembered and what should be forgotten'. She further notes that each 'community' is marked by a 'cognitive bias' which expresses some essential truth about the group and its identity and sets the emotional tone of its remembering.[21] In the end, it is perhaps more fitting that *The Dinner Party* did not sit within a framework of institutional authorisation but, in its alternative venues, was able to meet the needs of its 'community' more directly. After some years without a permanent home, *The Dinner Party* is now kept at the Brooklyn Museum in New York and occupies a dedicated gallery in the Elizabeth A. Sackler Center for Feminist Art at the Museum. Here it is exhibited within the context of the history of feminist art and is central to the educational ambitions of the Center, which aim to 'present feminism in an approachable and relevant way'.[22] This seems to me an appropriate context. In authorising and legitimising feminist art, the Elizabeth A. Sackler Center aims both to document and preserve the memories of a movement and, within this, *The Dinner Party*, which began as a work of historical redress, has now gained the status of a both a historical document and a collective memory.

After Chicago's *The Dinner Party*, artists who challenged or attempted to reveal neglected or repressed histories did so in less ambitious terms, which does not mean that they were any less ambitious in their political messages, just that the forms they employed have, for the most part, been less didactic, less totalising and more open to extrapolation. The hybrid furniture and clothing sculptures of Colombian artist Doris Salcedo (born 1958) provides a suitable case in point, which also serves to advance my discussion of the themes of counter-histories and counter-memories and their relationship to the institutions of the art world. Salcedo's work derives from personal memories of the dead and disappeared that she has collected first-hand from the politically oppressed in Colombia. While the memories that she represents are told to her directly, Salcedo relays them in forms and materials that are allusive rather than explicit. At the same time, however, the sculptures contain parts or details that connect almost directly to the actuality that is behind the work. This is most obviously the case in works that incorporate items of clothing, which Salcedo began to collect in Colombia between 1987 and 1989 as a way of evidencing the stories of atrocity that she was gathering. The display of shoes which were once worn by those who have disappeared in the *Atrabiliarios* installations (1992–1993) are the most representative example and return us to the notion of indexicality discussed in the previous chapter. The direct imprint of the wearer in each shoe harbours an accumulative trace of that person and, for those left behind, a presence of the missing person. In other words, memories are quite literally connected to the reality of the person, so that '[a]rt sustains the possibility of an encounter between people who come from quite distinct realities'.[23]

Nevertheless, the shoes in *Atrabiliarios* are not openly displayed and the indexical connection is muted by the method of display. The shoes are placed in niches in the wall of the gallery that are roughly the size of shoe boxes (they differ according to the dimensions of the shoe and whether it is one shoe or a pair that is shown). The niches are set in a horizontal band in the walls roughly at eye level and the open or visible side of the niche is veiled by translucent animal skin that is stitched with surgical thread to the edges of the wall. The effect is occlusive, in that memory is obscured and rendered latent within a set of secondary associations (those of veiling, suturing, fetish, reliquary, for instance). For art critic Nancy Princenthal, this clouding of vision is necessitated by the inherent unspeakability of trauma and the impossibility of properly representing the experience of pain, whether one's own or that of another.[24] As Princenthal also notes, the very title of the work, *Atrabiliarios*, also obscures by way of its arcaneness.[25] This is the case in both Spanish and English (atrabilious), where the word, an adjective, is practically out of usage but can most usefully, although approximately, be defined as 'melancholic'.[26] Princenthal also locates the origin of the word in the Latin term for 'melancholy' that is associated with mourning, *atra bilis*, which, in turn, invokes Freud's definition of melancholy as a pathologised form of mourning, characterised by a severe crisis of identity concomitant with the loss of the loved 'object', although *Atrabiliarios* speaks to the repression of the identity of the loved one as much as to the crisis of those left behind.[27]

The memory work in *Atrabiliarios* is thus closely allied to the process of grieving. Salcedo evokes the losses that have taken place in a country pathologised by the violence of civil war and drug trafficking, which perhaps can only ever produce a pathologised or disfigured form of grieving: 'My work speaks of the continuation of life, a life disfigured, as Derrida would say. Memory must work between the figure of the one who has died and the one disfigured by death.'[28] This choice of the word 'disfiguration' to describe the lives those who have suffered the trauma of loss resonates with the sculptures themselves, which are literally disfigurations of found objects. The disfiguration of the object is not so prominent in *Atrabiliarios*, but can be seen in earlier untitled works of the late 1980s, in which the shoes themselves are tightly stitched inside animal skin and then simply hung from the wall. However, it is the furniture sculptures produced for and around the *La Casa Viuda* installations (1992–1995) (fig. 10) and the three *Unland* pieces (1995–1998) that best exemplify the process of disfiguration that Salcedo imposes on her objects.

La Casa Viuda translates as 'the widowed house', signifying the way that loss becomes ingrained in the space left by the absence of its inhabitants, so that the space becomes 'a home grieving for its lost occupants'.[29] The way that furniture is deployed in the installation space is of key importance in all the furniture sculptures, evoking a sense of displacement and discontinuity, or, as historian Andreas Huyssen has suggested in relation to *Unland: The Orphan's Tunic* (1997), the uncanny or the unhomely.[30] The *La Casa Viuda* installations are largely made up of doors that have been fused with other pieces of domestic furniture that are often strategically placed in the gallery in a way that transforms it into a room space, although also in a way that inhibits easy circulation within the space.[31] Rather than move between discrete but related objects of art, visitors are asked to inhabit the space and relate to the works almost as if inside a theatre set, becoming a part of the tensions set up between themselves, the objects in the installation and the installation space.[32] The physical engagement of the body is symptomatic of Salcedo's overall approach, which is to involve viewers affectively, positioning them at a sensory or intuitive level. However, as Jill Bennett notes, the experience of the work does not remain at the level of affectivity. Rather, the affective nature of the work lays the ground for more distanced critical reflection, and an active recognition (re-cognition) of its content.[33]

While much of the affectivity of the works lies in the way that the spaces they inhabit are made 'strange', this is also true of individual pieces, whether part of an installation or stand-alone. Just as the installations are choreographed to discomfort the viewer, the furniture itself is treated in a way that conjures up feelings of unease rather than comfort.[34] The furnishings are disfigured by alterations that Salcedo imposes on their surfaces and structures. Often these disfigurations rob the items of their potential for use, impairing them, seeming also to stand for the notion of impaired mourning and, by extension, the impairment of memory. However, the disfigurements are neither violent nor grotesque but a partial erasing of form and anonymisation of the object. Just as the shoes in *Atrabiliarios* are masked and distanced by screens of animal skins, so the furniture is veiled by the

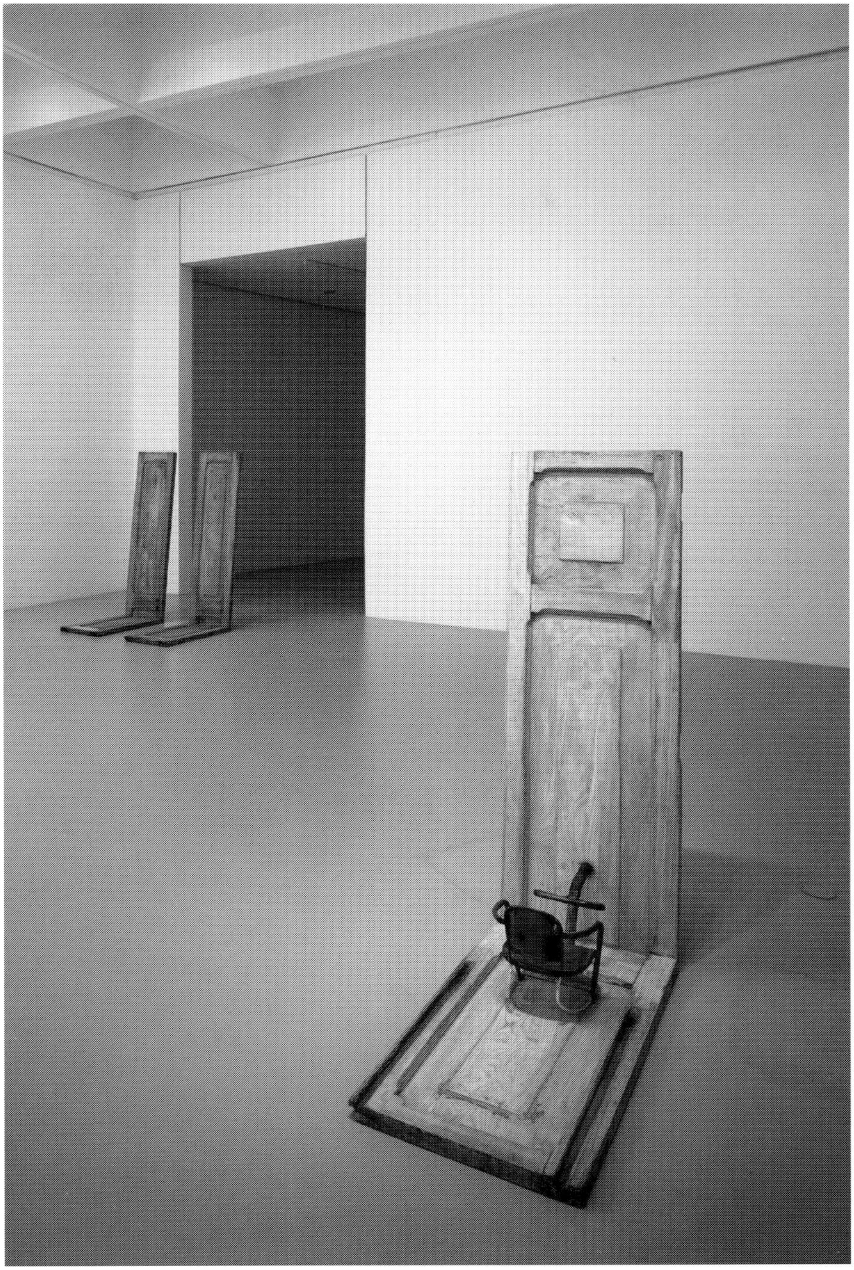

Figure 10: Doris Salcedo, *La Casa Viuda VI*, 1995, wood, bone, metal 3 parts. Installation: Distemper: Dissonent Themes in the Art of the 1990s, Hirschorn Museum and Distemper Garden, June 20–September, 1996. Courtesy: Alexander and Bonin, New York. Collection Israel Museum.

application of concrete over recessed surfaces. In the early 1990s the concrete was left rough and the effect was one of distress; later in the decade the concrete was applied more smoothly and the effect one of erasure or ghostliness. This is the case with the items of furniture in the 1999 installation at the Anglican Cathedral in Liverpool, in which wardrobes, chests of drawers and chairs were both stilled and somehow distilled by the effect of the concrete. Grouped, yet standing in isolation from one another, these pieces were not only partially divested of signs of their temporality but given a sense of sacrament, of ceremonial grace that relates to the associations with reliquary and fetish already noted in *Atrabiliarios*.

The furnishings can be said not only to be disfigured but also to have been mutated. This applies both to works whose surfaces have simply been altered by concrete, as described above, and to those which have also been combined or fused with other pieces of furniture or fabric, creating hybrid objects that are neither one thing nor the other but have become absurd (in the existential sense of the word) reminders of a world marked by violence and atrocity which no longer makes any sense.[35] A frequent inclusion of fragments of clothing or even bones not only adds to the incongruity of the furnishings but also reminds us that the furnishings are a conduit for remembering the fate (the specifics of which were often unknown) of actual people, the relatives and loved ones of those who Salcedo interviewed while researching the works.

The processes and techniques that are employed are also an important factor in the effects produced by the disfiguration, mutation and reconfiguration of form. Objects and materials are transformed from their ready-made states by time-absorbing and meticulous hand labour, which at times reaches almost obsessive-compulsive proportions, especially in the stitched works. In *Unland: The Orphan's Tunic*, uneven lengths of two kitchen tables of similar width have been joined together to form a makeshift whole. The shorter and slightly higher end has been covered with a piece of finely woven silk that is stuck onto the table end and its legs, as if to dress the table in a tunic. The piece marks the loss experienced by a young girl who Salcedo had interviewed who had witnessed the death of her mother and who, poignantly, always wore a dress that her mother had made for her. Once this is known, both table and garment become fairly obvious but no less tragic signifiers of melancholia, despite the deciphering work that has to be done in order to make out the 'tunic'. However, beyond this, there is a further component that demands even closer and more enduring attention, which is the hundreds of individually stitched-in human hairs that form a seam between the table ends. The stitching-in process involved both the drilling of numerous small holes through the table surface and the weaving of the hairs in and out of these holes to form a thin netted band that crosses the width of the table. As with items of clothing or fragments of bone that are embedded in other sculptures, the hair and 'tunic' have the effect of anthropomorphising the furniture, inviting the sort of intimate scrutiny that we might (surreptitiously, perhaps) give to a person in unusually close physical proximity, especially if that person has marks or wounds that 'disfigure' his/her appearance.

When asked by Charles Merewether about the significance of the elements of duration and proximity involved in the viewing of her works, Salcedo replied that it is important to find ways of forming a bridge between the viewer and the lives that are seen in her works. To do this, she sets up conditions of silent and extenuated contemplation which allow such lives to reappear, reflecting her belief in Gilles Deleuze's claim that '[d]uration is essentially memory, conscience and liberty. It is conscience and liberty because it is primordially memory.'[36] Duration plays a major part in the conditions of affectivity referred to earlier, allowing attenuated conditions in which contemplation is extended into what might be seen as a form of meditation. Referring to Salcedo's belief that her work comes into being ('forms itself') through objects that are related to the person that is remembered, Bennett suggests that the long and meticulous process of making (up to four years) is a way of encountering the objects that renders the process as symbolic as the objects. More specifically, the process is a symbolic enactment of trauma in which, according to Salcedo, '[t]he world made strange by death – the alienating and disorienting experience of loss – is thereby slowly revealed to viewers in their own encounters with the objects in transformation'.[37]

On a wider political level, what is being produced is a set of counter-memories that, for all their obfuscation, bring notice to the disappeared or deceased. The works are acts of resistance that relate to what Misztal (following Foucault) refers to as 'popular' memory, as opposed to 'institutionalised' or 'hegemonic' memory (in this case, the memories of the disenfranchised, oppressed and bereaved).[38] That Salcedo's work embodies popular memory is indisputable, given its grounding in numerous stories of individuals who have suffered at the hands of the state. To be heard outside their immediate communities, however, the counter-memories of the populace also need a context of representation, which is sometimes to be found in the media, increasingly on the internet, but also in the arts. And, as noted at the start of this chapter, contexts and the discourses produced by institutions are neither disinterested nor ideologically neutral. Edlie Wong, for instance, argues that US mainstream media representation of Colombia tends to see the violence there almost as a given, a condition of its ideological otherness, whereas violence occurring in other countries outside the frame of US political and economic interest is held to be more shocking, even when the statistics of that violence are remarkably lower, as is the case with Chile.[39] Here Wong quotes from Salcedo herself, who states that the dead in Colombia have no status. From this, it becomes clear that Salcedo's status as an international artist is an especially important factor in gaining not only recognition for but also appreciation of the depth and extent of violence in her country. As Wong observes, Salcedo's recognition by the art world gives limited but nevertheless influential public exposure to the dead and the disappeared in Colombia.[40]

Essentially, Salcedo's suggestive and empathetic approach is governed by the precariousness of speaking out in her native country and by the aesthetic preferences of the art world, and she has had to find a means of expression which works in both contexts. She also has to work against a problematic background of American neocolonial relations in which, Wong argues, the United States allows forms of human terror and human rights abuses to perpetuate under the cloak of international drugs control legislation.[41] Salcedo has 'to reckon not only with the violence that is internal to Colombia, but also the US's intimate involvement in sustaining violence in Colombia', and much of her achievement is in her ability 'to renegotiate the institutional site of the US art museum into an alternative, albeit limited form of a public sphere incapacitated in her native Colombia'.[42] However, while Salcedo has admirably and discerningly found an approach that both fulfils her political mission and sits within the aesthetic requirements of the museum or gallery, some recognition has to be given to the changes in outlook in those institutions since the 1980s and the willingness of many to embrace politically charged work, and in some cases to actively support oppositional politics.

I will come back to the issue of museums and galleries briefly when concluding this chapter. For now, however, I want to continue by looking at examples of postcolonial art in the UK, in particular the work by British/Nigerian artist Yinka Shonibare MBE (born 1962), who, for me, tests the extent to which memory and history have to rely on the specifics of the past in order to historicise and form counter-memories. The historical figures in complex ways in terms of the inner historical references or content of Shonibare's work, which also needs to be read in relation to the history of contemporary black art in the United Kingdom. What constitutes black art and who exactly produces it has been a matter of debate and shifting claims for at least twenty years.[43] But, as was demonstrated by curator and artist Rasheed Araeen's landmark exhibition *The Other Story* (1989), black artists (African, Afro-Caribbean and artists from the Asian subcontinents) have a history of production in the West following World War II that related directly to Western modernism but lacked the recognition given to the work of European and North American modernists. However, while Araeen's agenda was to showcase these artists and redress the history of modernism in terms of its exclusion of black artists, the exhibition also included the work of a younger generation of black artists, who were more politically motivated and who put more emphasis on issues of black identity and postcolonial politics. This generation of younger black artists have been seen by critic Kobena Mercer as carrying a particular 'burden of representation', as indeed has the exhibition itself.[44]

Impelled by the need to make their politics visible, the younger generation of black artists of the 1980s were effectively required to represent black issues in an almost monolithic and totalising way.[45] As black photographer, critic and curator David A. Bailey noted in his introduction to Keith Piper's exhibition *A Ship Called Jesus* (1991) (figs 11 and 12), the fact that black artists were being perceived as 'a homogeneous representative group', had led to a 'form of crisis and poverty', and the time had come to recognise and build upon the diversity and multiplicity of practice in black art.[46] Black art in the United Kingdom in the 1980s had, indeed, been characterised by its strong ideological commitment, anger, didacticism and use of simplistic or propagandist methods of representation.[47] Typical of the more confrontational, single-minded and, indeed, passionate approaches of this time are works such as Eddie Chambers' *Destruction of the National Front* (1980), a collage in four panels which simply shows a simple progressive disintegration of the Union Jack. By the end of the decade, and in the early 1990s, David A. Bailey and Kobena Mercer's call for a less singular and less confrontational approach had seemingly been heard.[48] The result was a more complex engagement with issues of black identity and postcolonial history that has found its place in the competitive world of contemporary art, as witnessed by the Turner Prize successes of Chris Ofili and the Turner Prize nomination of Yinka Shonibare.

Keith Piper's *A Ship Called Jesus* serves as a pioneering work from this point of view. Consisting of three sequential installations that incorporate photographic images, video and text, *A Ship Called Jesus* was an epic rendering (I remember it taking up both of the large floors of the Ikon Gallery in Birmingham) of the epic transportation of African slaves on the British slave ship *The Jesus of Lubeck* in 1564. In addition to its historical role in the slave trade, Piper took *The Jesus of Lubeck* to stand synonymously and symbolically for another 'ship' that, he argues, black people have sailed ever since – that of the institutions of the Christian Church. In revisiting the journey made by *The Jesus of Lubeck* in 1564, Piper divided it into three stages that could stand for three particular historical phases in the relationship between peoples of African descent and the Christian Church: the original journey, Christianisation and its effects, and the hope of retribution and end of purgatory for black people.[49] In charting 'the multiple effects which that

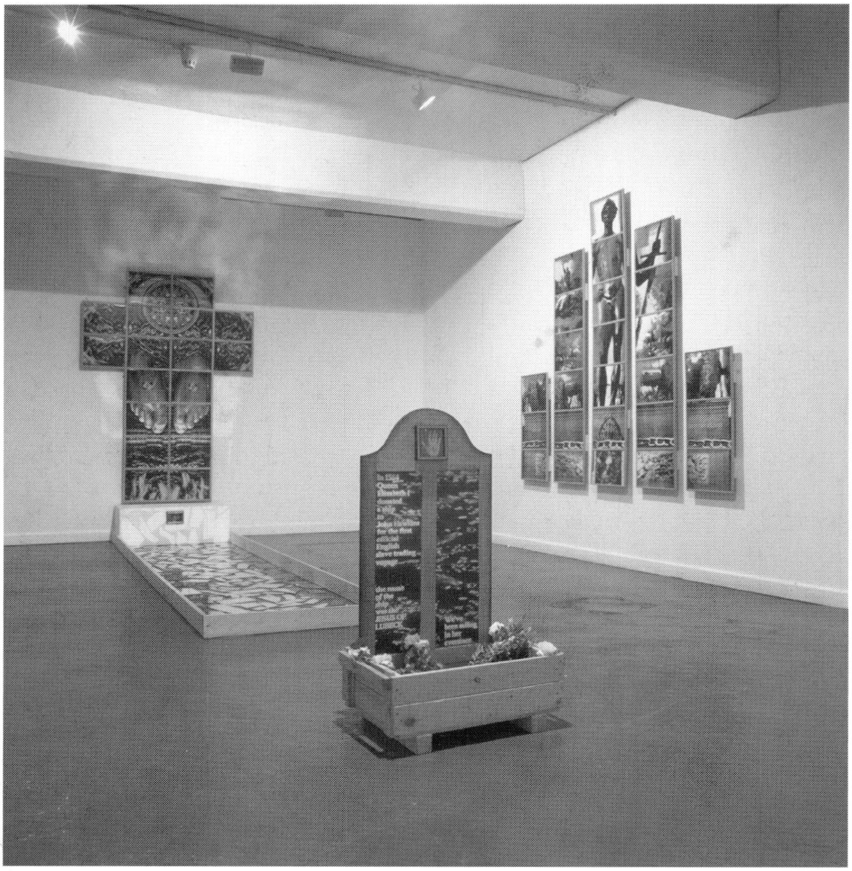

Figure 11: Keith Piper, *A Ship Called Jesus*, 1991. Mixed Media, Installation view, Ikon Gallery, Birmingham, 1991. Courtesy: Ikon Gallery. Photography: Keith Piper and Spring Heel Jack.

relationship has had on the lumbering progression of that ship out of colonial histories into the bedlam of the modern world', Piper traced Christianity's colonisation of the hearts, minds and souls of black people.[50] Significantly, given Mercer's call for a shift in 'language', he did this by combining the advanced technologies of the late twentieth century with the deconstructionist principles of collage and assemblage that had been so important for the radicalism of the early twentieth-century avant-garde. As Chambers' *Destruction of the National Front* and Piper's own early work shows, collage had been an oppositional strategy for disrupting mainstream ideologies in the 1980s. In *A Ship Called Jesus*, however, Piper was to take collage to another level, not only through the use of sophisticated technology but also in the construction of complex formats and intricate iconographic schemes.

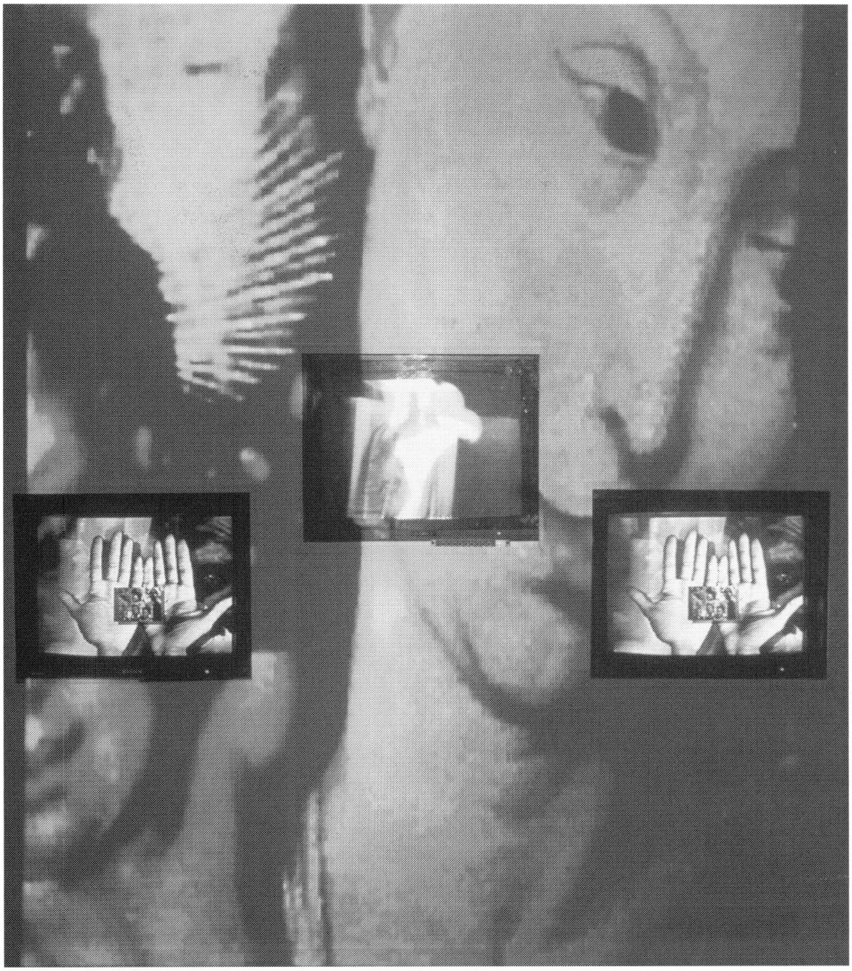

Figure 12: Keith Piper, *A Ship Called Jesus*, 1991. Video projection with TV monitors, Installation view, Ikon Gallery, Birmingham. Courtesy: Ikon Gallery. Photography: Keith Piper and Spring Heel Jack.

A Ship Called Jesus, like Chicago's *The Dinner Party* and Salcedo's sculptures, offers a counter-history in which the artist seeks to redress previous versions of the past that have served to reproduce a dominant ideology. The work of Yinka Shonibare departs from this approach in a way that tests the boundaries of what it means to historicise. Rather than revisit the past, Shonibare uses historical signifiers for an exploration of identity and social positioning as well as a vehicle for fantasy. In doing this, however, he creates a number of historical and political subtexts. Take, for example, *Diary of a*

Victorian Dandy (1998), in which Shonibare imagines a day in the life of a well-known Victorian social type in five photographic tableaux vivants. Although set in the nineteenth century, an early eighteenth-century art historical precedent is invoked in the form of William Hogarth's *The Rake's Progress* (1733–1735), a tale of a young man's descent into vice and madness (although Shonibare omits the moral sting that Hogarth delivers). While Hogarth's series is set in his own time, Shonibare's tableaux are deliberately anachronistic and historicising, reconstructing a previous period in history and almost parodying the fake period room settings found in museums such as the Geffrye in London or the Brooklyn in New York. Moreover, the fictionalised nature of the images is made immediately obvious, not only through the apparent anachronism of the colour photography but also through Shonibare's casting of himself in the central role of the dandy, the only black protagonist in the scene.

In insisting on the centrality of the black dandy, the power relations of nineteenth-century British colonialism are overtly parodied, reversed and ironised, and the viewer is required to rethink and remember those relations rather than attempt to reconstruct the colonial past as such. History is therefore implicit in the work and an aspect of it, but the actualities of the past that are invoked haunt rather than occupy the stage. As Angela McRobbie suggests, the central figure of the black dandy raises the spectre of exploited African or Asian labour behind the conspicuous consumption of the Victorians, but, at the same time, Shonibare 'muddies this picture and avoids didacticism by putting himself in the picture as luxuriating in these worldly goods'.[51] McRobbie also notes that our perceptions of the period are inevitably mediated by its popular representation in cultural products, such as the historical drama or the bodice-ripper.[52] Similarly, we relate to the figure of the black dandy through our experience of contemporary versions such as Chris Eubank, or certain Versace-toting rappers.[53] What this amounts to is a work of art in which the artist seems to be acting out a fantasy of privilege, decadence, vanity and the erotic, which at the same time seems to invite questions concerning those issues and values and their ideological context. For all its artifice and fantasy, *Diary of a Victorian Dandy* demands reconsideration of the past social and political relations, and, on that basis, can be considered as a postcolonial revisionist work.

A similar combination of art historical precedents and incongruous motifs that indirectly reference the political and economic past of colonialism is found in many of Shonibare's major works, most famously those which incorporate 'Dutch wax' textiles. Well-known examples include *Mr and Mrs Andrews without their Heads* (1998) (fig. 13) and *The Swing (After Fragonard)* (2001). *Mr and Mrs Andrews without their Heads* is a very obvious appropriation of Gainsborough's double portrait of an eighteenth-century landowner and his wife, *Mrs and Mrs Andrews* (c. 1750), rendered life-size in three dimensions. The positioning of the figures and the clothes that they wear are as depicted in Gainsborough's painting, except that Shonibare has substituted 'Dutch wax' cloth for the plain silk, lace or cotton worn in the original and rendered the figures headless. It is important to understand the complicated history of these textiles, because they represent a hybridity that relates not only to postcolonial identity but also to Shonibare's colonial historicisations and fantasies. Indeed, the story of the 'inauthenticity' of what have commonly believed to be characteristic west African textiles has been told many times in relation to the postcolonial content of Shonibare's work.[54] 'Dutch wax' prints were, first, an early nineteenth-century attempt by Dutch textile merchants to mass-reproduce Indonesian hand-made batiks and sell them back to their country of origin. The attempt failed, because the industrial

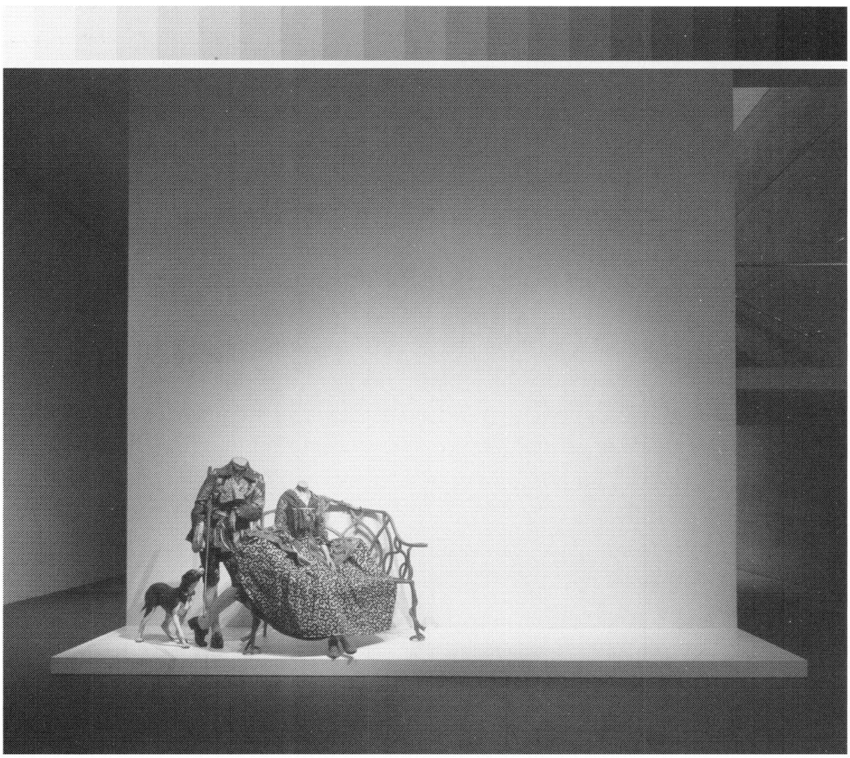

Figure 13: Yinka Shonibare MBE, *Mr and Mrs Andrews without their Heads*, 1998. Wax-print cotton costumes on armatures, dog mannequin, painted metal bench, rifle, 165 x 635 x 254 cm with plinth. Photo © National Gallery, Canada. Collection National Gallery of Canada, Ottowa. Copyright © Yinka Shonibare MBE, courtesy the artist and Stephen Friedman Gallery (London).

process distorted the design and randomly variegated the coloured surfaces of the fabric, rendering the product unacceptable to traditional Indonesian taste and discernment. However, an alternative market was found in western Africa towards the end of the century, when British producers began to foreground motifs that symbolised the identity, values and aspirations of the Gold Coast. The textiles are the products of Western economic expansionism and are cultural appropriations, and as such they carry associations of exploitation that go with the era of Western imperialism and colonialism in which they were produced – associations that are readily carried over into Shonibare's work. Indeed, the fact that the lineage and cultural identity of the textiles is hybrid makes them especially suited to the hybridity of Shonibare's work, in its juxtapositions of apparently disparate cultural signifiers.

As is the case with *Diary of a Victorian Dandy*, Shonibare trades on obvious incongruities that call attention to the political and economic conditions of production and consumption that lie hidden behind the textiles. Interestingly, Gainsborough's painting has already served as an example of the ideological importance of the materials and forms in which works of art are produced in John Berger's groundbreaking book and television series *Ways of Seeing* (1972). For Berger, ownership and property were signified not only by the way the figures are dressed or the way they command the (their) landscape while looking confidently towards the viewer but also by the fact that the work is in oil paint – a medium that can so readily simulate the material signs of wealth.[55] Gainsborough's *Mr and Mrs Andrews* are presented for posterity, wishing to be remembered in terms of their social and economic position, which, from the expressions on their faces, is not to be taken lightly. In his version, Shonibare undermines their power and status simply by removing their heads and raises questions concerning the socio-economic system they inhabit by dressing them in fabrics that allude, albeit obliquely, to the dependency of that system on the exploitation of other cultures and peoples.

In mixing historical and cultural signifiers in this way, Shonibare plays not only with history but with its conventional modes of delivery. As Piper did with *A Ship Called Jesus*, Shonibare has performed an elaborate collage, which, following Max Ernst, can be seen as a method by which two incongruous elements produce a third meaning (reality or 'plane') when brought together.[56] While Shonibare is not concerned with developing counter-histories as such, his imagined and incongruous conjunctions and adaptations of historical artefacts make an appeal to our sense of history and require us to infer a third meaning based on the historical references in the work. The onus is shifted onto the viewer, and the result is a very different method of historicising in which imagination plays with and on the past. Shonibare's work not only sends us back to the past but demands that we make our own critical, and potentially creative, leaps between the contexts and artefacts that he brings together. In this, Shonibare's work sits at the edge of history. Because of its call upon the imagination the work qualifies not so much as counter-history as a very particular form of counter-memory, in this case characterised by discontinuities and paradox.[57]

In his recent review of the successes and failures of black art, Rasheed Araeen (replicating a similar shift in feminist thinking noted earlier) clearly argues the necessity of entering the system in order to change it – that 'that entry requires an understanding of history and how one deals with it, and how one locates within it'.[58] Araeen's recommendations resonate with Shonibare's own stated position, which was to adopt a strategy which involved a return to history and the origins of his own dual identity.[59] This was a complicated and ambitious return, because it involved not only negotiating the contemporary art world but also engaging in a dialogue with selected 'masterpieces' from the history of European art. It has also involved the co-option of iconic cultural figures, as in *Henry James* (1843–1916) and *Hendrik C. Anderson* (1872–1940) (both 2001), and several digs at European privilege and power (*Gallantry and Criminal Conversation*, 2002 and *Scramble for Africa*, 2003). A particularly interesting example of the latter is *Yinka Shonibare Dresses Britannica* (2001), for which Shonibare clothed the statue of Britannica that sits above the front entrance to Tate Britain in 'Dutch wax' printed fabric. This exploitation of the Tate's exterior decorative scheme might be seen as part of an ongoing challenge to the exclusivity of the museum and gallery space that began in earnest in the late 1960s, but, in Shonibare's case, it also challenges museums and galleries as privileged spaces in which history and memory are constructed.[60] As Divya Tolia-Kelly and Andy Morris observe, Tate Britain's commissioning of *Yinka Shobibare Dresses Britannica* signals a significant (although limited) institutional shift in which the Tate shows willingness to confront previous ideological failings.[61] After all, the Tate's first benefactor, Henry Tate, built his fortune on colonial exploitation, slavery in particular.

The role of institutions such as museums and galleries has been a recurring issue in this chapter, and it seems appropriate to conclude by tying this issue into Pierre Nora's notion of *lieux de mémoire*, sites or repositories 'where memory crystallises and secretes itself'.[62] For Nora, *lieux de mémoire* are numerous and varied in form, symbolic value and function, some more normalising than others (they can be as intangible, for instance, as a two-minute commemorative silence).[63] By Nora's very broad definition, artworks in themselves constitute *lieux de mémoire*, and, indeed, all the works discussed in this book are repositories of memory in one way or another, given that the memories and histories that are figured or suggested belong to different contexts. But artworks also have to be housed in one way or another, so that they become *lieux* within *lieux*. This points to a larger web of history and memory, which Nora speculates is held together by 'an invisible thread, linking apparently unconnected objects' and which he has described as 'a differentiated network to which all of these separate identities belong, an unconscious organisation of collective memory that it is our responsibility to bring to consciousness'.[64] One of the ambitions of this book is to map the wide range and variety of *lieux de mémoire* in contemporary art and examine the memory-work that they perform. So far I have followed a trajectory that has led from personal memories to rememorisations of social and political history. This foregrounding of social and political histories continues in the next chapter, which deals with ways of remembering the atrocities of World War II and continues to examine ways in which art and history meet to form counter-memories. Issues concerning traditional museum practices are taken up again in my final chapter, which returns to the themes of the institutionalisation and organisation of knowledge, and the ways in which contemporary artists have challenged them or offered alternatives.

4

Postmemory: 'The Ones Born Afterwards'

In this chapter I want to move from notions of counter-history and counter-memory to a type of memory characterised by Marianne Hirsch as 'postmemory' – secondary memory that has been constructed by the next generation rather than by primary witnesses.[1] While counter-history and counter-memory provide ideological and political alternatives to previous historicisations of the past, postmemory is the inheritance of past events or experiences that are still being worked through. Postmemory carries an obligation to continue that process of working through or over the event or experience and is not yet a process of reply. However, as with counter-history and counter-memory, postmemory is still a type of social memory, although often one that articulates that which has been inhibited in the memories of the primary witnesses of the previous generation. The relationship between societal and politically inflicted trauma and memory has already surfaced in my discussion of Doris Salcedo's work in the last chapter, when I wrote of collective memory in her work as a form of resistance to contemporary or recent events in Colombia. Placing more emphasis on protocols and limits in the representation of extreme human atrocity, this chapter continues to examine secondary memories of human abuse, in relation this time to the Nazi Holocaust of World War II.

However, while victims of the Holocaust experienced the traumas of abuse and atrocity en masse, it is not really possible to speak of them as 'collectively' experienced. As Lawrence L. Langer has shown, victims were systematically reduced to such basic day-to-day strategies of survival that norms of social responsibility, kinship and mutual support disintegrated into their general absence. Indeed, the damage to personhood was so extreme for victims of the Nazi Holocaust (and, by extension, the survivors of other catastrophic events) that an integrated recall of degradation and suffering by individuals, let alone a shared recall, has scarcely been possible.[2] But this does not mean that former victims' voices are heard in isolation or that memorisation cannot take a social or collective form.[3] Projects such as the Fortunoff Video Archive for Holocaust Testimonies at Yale University (established 1982) and the Shoah Foundation Institute at the University of Southern California have now amassed hundreds of thousands of former victims' testimonies that, in their accumulated view of depersonalisation and degradation, gain the force of collective memory. Nor does it mean that the events and experiences cannot achieve some form of integration and collective meaning in or through postmemory and its articulation in works of art (although the immediacy and specificity of the events and experiences felt by individuals is, of course, necessarily lost).

Through his analysis of former victims' testimony held at the Fortunoff archive, Langer demonstrates that extreme trauma makes particular demands on memory and representation. Following Freud, psychologists have characterised trauma as the overwhelming and normatively unconceivable nature of an event which the person or people involved find inassimilable. As literary scholar Cathy Caruth notes (also citing Freud), recall of a traumatic event may not be admitted to the consciousness until a safe period of time after its occurrence, signalling the unpreparedness of the person/s involved at the time of its occurrence and their consequent inability to integrate the experience. For Caruth, trauma is experienced belatedly and invokes the unknown as much as, or even more than, it can reveal the known.[4] It seems, therefore, that the magnitude of extreme trauma is so great that it can only ever be partially told. As noted above, this is demonstrated by Langer's analysis of former victims' testimonies, in which he observes a fragmentation of the self that led to incomplete or conflicting accounts. The people testifying would constantly struggle with their own incomprehension, not only towards things that were done to them but actions that they, themselves, felt they should or should not have taken. Time and time again, Langer produces primary witness accounts which show a conflict between the complete objectification of the situation and the (usually only partially) recovered subjectivity of the former victim. For me, this in-between state invokes Julia Kristeva's definition of the 'abject' as that which is neither subject nor object – a term which signals both the utter abasement of the camps and its legacy in the split psyche of the former victims.[5]

Langer attributes some of the inability to speak comprehensively of the Holocaust to the inadequacy of a normative narrative framework that can accommodate the psychological extremities of the former victims' experience. The extremity of this experience, for instance, cannot be appropriately expressed through familiar tropes such as redemption and closure. But Caruth argues that there are new ways of listening to the primary witness ('the other', as she terms him/her) and new forms of address through which trauma can nevertheless be articulated in literary and artistic production, which I would deem to be specialised forms of secondary witness. As Dominick LaCapra observes, secondary memory is not just the work of an 'observer-participant' but a meeting of the primary participant and the secondary witness, who is better able to do the critical work on primary memory.[6] The notion of secondary memory is not to deny or devalue primary testimony, without which trauma becomes an abstraction, but to recognise the struggle that the primary witness has in relying on pre-existing forms of representation which are inadequate to his or her needs (let alone the problems he or she might have in formulating new ones). With the advantage of greater distance, the secondary witness is perhaps better equipped to develop much-needed new forms of expression.

Nonetheless, opinions as to who is entitled to represent what and how with regard to the Nazi Holocaust are divided. For example, the Hungarian writer Imre Kertész, a former victim of Auschwitz and Buchenwald, admits to a certain amount of possessiveness with regard to the Holocaust accompanied by a fear of the appropriation of its ownership by secondary witnesses. But these primary instincts give way to an understanding that if the Holocaust is to be known then a price has to be paid, which he characterises as the 'stylisation' of the Holocaust. In the best of cases (Kertész lists a number of literary figures, including Paul Celan and Primo Levi), the artist can achieve a vital catharsis, but in the worst (here Kertész names Steven Spielberg's 1993 film *Schindler's List*) the Holocaust is sentimentalised and commodified.[7] However, moving away from Kertész's concerns about high art forms versus popular and trivialising forms, art historian Ernst Van Alphen notes an opposition between history and imagination, between a drive towards uncovering the hard facts and a desire to represent it figuratively. As Van Alphen further observes, this opposition carries moral overtones that stem from Theodor Adorno's condemnation of the aestheticisation of suffering, which he saw as yet another violation of the victim that not only offers him/her up for aesthetic pleasure but, in doing so, removes some of its proper horror. For Adorno, there is a danger of detraction even in the 'highest' art forms, such as the poems of Celan, which may also undermine the unspeakable reality of the Holocaust, bringing a sense of redemption through art to that which cannot be redeemed.[8]

Van Alphen himself argues in favour of a more sophisticated understanding of figurative representation: that it is a form of cognition, not just a matter of aestheticisation,[9] as cognitive processes, figuration or stylisation have a much better chance of getting to the heart of trauma or atrocity than so-called 'literal expression'. Indeed, Van Alphen goes on to dismantle the opposition between figurative and more literal forms of representation by showing that all representation draws upon available symbolic possibilities which are not immutable but hold the promise of a new representational mode – a mode which is not available in the so-called 'factual reconstructions' of the historian, which, as Van Alphen convincingly demonstrates, tend to construct the past through recognisable and graspable plot lines which gloss over its unimaginable aspects. Modes developed in art and literature, on the other hand, make use of alternative methods and approaches and are better suited to the task:

> History brings with it more responsibilities than only knowing and remembering the facts, especially when that history concerns the Holocaust. Other responsibilities that are poignantly imposed on us involve the working through of the traumatic intrusion of an unimaginable reality, and the foregrounding of the cracks and tears that are concealed by the coherence of the stories being told. It is in relation to those responsibilities that the imaginative discourses of art and literature can step in and perform functions that, though historical, cannot be fulfilled by the work of the historian.[10]

This recognition of the greater potential of art and literature resonates with my discussion in chapter 3 of the ways in which a number of contemporary artists have reframed history, not only stretching the boundaries of historical practice but also subverting conventional distinctions between history and memory. At the end of that discussion, a figure emerged who might be described as the artist-historian, who had found new ways of redressing and historicising the past. To my mind, this figure chimes readily with the notion of the artist as secondary witness and carrier of postmemory. Although Hirsch initially speaks of postmemory in terms of her own experience of inheriting her parents' stories of exile and loss, later she moves into a broader characterisation of postmemory as separate from the primary event or experience, but based equally on the need to (re)build and mourn, which is the way that the term will be used in this chapter.[11] The artists to be discussed in this chapter have presented distinct alternatives to conventional narrative modes and tropes and, following Hirsch, they can all be seen as part of an ongoing articulation of Holocaust memory taken up by the next generation of witnesses and, as such, are exemplary as producers of postmemory.

The Holocaust-related works of French artist Christian Boltanski (born 1944) are often singled out as a positive response to the issues of Holocaust representation, and they have also been firmly placed within the category of postmemory by Hirsch.[12] Boltanski is best known for his installation works, which, in the regularity of their composition, betray origins in Minimalism, to which the artist readily admits. But they are also post-Conceptual works that address central ideas or themes, most often those of memory and death. These themes are activated in his early works, which create fictive biographies, build up 'archival' data and construct inventories. The stuff of these 'archival' pieces is made up of personal possessions and photographs, though not all the possessions are genuine in origin, which sets up an ironically deceptive juxtaposition of fiction and authenticity. Early examples include autobiographical material (photographs, documents and fragments of clothing) relating to his childhood, brought together in three books, and the installations *Attempts to Reconstruct Objects that Belonged to Christian Boltanski between 1948 and 1954* (1971), for which he made crude reconstructions of artefacts from his childhood and displayed them in a series of drawers covered with wire mesh. These early parodies of archival practices were followed by a series of display cases, *Reference Vitrines* (begun 1970), that featured bits and pieces taken from his previous works. Other works of the early 1970s, such as *Photo Album of the Family D. 1939–1964* (1971), show his growing preoccupation with the found or appropriated photograph as a medium for (fictionalised) documentation and inventory.

Photo Album of the Family D. 1939–1964 also makes a disingenuous play on the authenticity of the document, which was to become a central strategy in Boltanski's later works, including those which have referenced the Nazi Holocaust (and to my mind this is one of the reasons why they are successful at representing the repressed, denied or evaded truths that haunt primary witnesses). *Album de Photos de la Famille D.* is a photo-diary made up from boxes of unsorted family photographs that had been given to Boltanski by his dealer, Michel Durand-Dessert. Boltanski did not know the people in the photographs but nevertheless constructed a family history, giving names to them and a chronology of events. Although Boltanski at first saw the piece as a record of the family's existence and the significant events of their lives, he later stated that, rather than teaching about the family D., they sent the viewer back to his or her own past.[13] In this, he recognises that associative value is perhaps more important than authenticity. Nevertheless, whether the story they tell is authentic or not, the photographs still have an existential purchase, despite that fact that they represent an absent, possibly dead, person. This invokes the having-been-thereness of the photographic index talked about in chapter 2. But, as indexical signs, Boltanski's found photographs are substantially degraded by the fact that they have been rephotographed and have lost some of their definition, and by the way that they have been standardised in size and format to occupy the walls of the gallery in a serialised arrangement (in five vertical tiers of landscape format images that are ranged across the whole length of the walls). As Hirsch points out, they seem to be 'icons masquerading as indices, or, more radically, symbols masquerading as icons and indices' (increasingly the case with Boltanski's later works).[14]

Boltanski recognises 'a direct relationship between a piece of clothing, a photo and a dead body, in that someone existed but is no longer here'.[15]

Moreover, indexical objects such as clothing and photographs represent what Boltanski terms 'small memory', the sort of object which distinguishes people's lives from each other's and harbours memory but which is lost with each individual death. But Boltanski is also aware of 'large memory', and simultaneously translates the specificity of the clothes having been worn by a particular person into a larger abstraction on the themes of death and memory. The *Canada* installations are typical of such large-scale renditions. In the Ydessa Hendeles Art Foundation version (1988) an overwhelming number of clothes (six thousand) are crowded onto the gallery walls, on top of one another in tiers and lit at regular intervals from above by the sort of unrelenting institutional lamps associated with offices and hospitals. Significantly, 'Canada' was the name given by the Nazis to the warehouses in which items of clothing belonging to the victims of the gas chambers at Auschwitz were collected and sorted. For me, six thousand representatives of small memories not only add up to a much larger one but provide a way of articulating an aspect of the Nazi Holocaust that cannot easily be told at an individual level. The difficulty of expressing individual horror is demonstrated by one of the testimonies that Langer singles out in his research, that of Chaim. E., who recalls sorting clothes in the 'Canada':

> But you cannot tell how I felt when I found the clothes of my brother, for example. Now if you ask me what I was thinking about, I wasn't thinking at all. I was horrified – things like that you know. But I can tell the story, and it sounds – well, another story. But it is more than a story. It is more some feelings that you cannot bring out, you know. Or all these kinds of things – what happened.
>
> Sometimes I hear telling back a story that doesn't sound at all the same what I was telling, you see; it doesn't sound the same. It was horrified and horrible, and when you live once with this tension and horrification – if that is the right word – then you live differently. Your thoughts don't go too far. In normal life, you think about tomorrow and after tomorrow and about a year, and next year a vacation then, and things like that. Here you think on the moment what it is. What happens now, on the moment. Now is horrible. You don't think 'later.'[16]

Boltanski does not attempt to replicate this horror. His strategy as a post-Holocaust artist is one of allusion, which does not even demand the authenticity of origin that characterises the shoes in Salcedo's *Atrabiliarios*. In fact, the inauthenticity of the garment is often openly declared (they are usually of a much later manufacture and style and bought in bulk from second-hand sources). Boltanski relies on our ability to treat arbitrary items of discarded clothing as surrogates for the garments sorted in the 'Canadas', knowing that their function as memento mori carries through regardless of origin. This use of randomly collected garments allows the distance of the secondary witness to become an overt feature of the work, placing it firmly and overtly in the realm of postmemory. More than this, it allows Boltanski to achieve a balance between monumentality and specificity. The volume of clothes and the scale of the installation accumulate into the sort of large-scale abstraction associated with the monument, but, at the same time, each garment carries the trace of the person who wore it, returning something of that person and effecting 'a kind of resurrection'.[17]

A similar effect of monumentality is produced in the installations based on pre-Holocaust photographs of Jewish high school children that Boltanski has appropriated, such as *The Chases High School* (1987–1990) and *Reserves: The Purim Holiday* (1987–1990).[18] As with most of Boltanski's work, the layout of the installation of these two pieces tends to vary from venue to venue, but the installations always share the same iconography and tropes of death and memory. As with earlier pieces, such as *Photo Album of the Family D. 1939–1964*, found or ready-made photographs are rephotographed and resized, but this time the faces of the photographed have been enlarged into close-ups, losing the specificities of the features. Contrary to the intimacy and lingering detail of the cinematic close-up, the face is made spectral, and the blurring of the features tends to emphasise the underlying skull, perhaps the most familiar symbol or reminder of death in the West. Some of the photographs are stored in biscuit tins, which form a plinth or base around or above which more photographs are openly displayed (the piece may be free-standing or arranged against a wall). For the generation of young people represented in these installations, biscuit tins were a commonplace method of keeping family documents in one place, where they would be easily locatable and free from damage. In respect of this, Boltanski deliberately aged the tins that he used, imbuing them with a sense of lived history that acts as a counterpoint to the abstractions performed on the faces. While the photographs are ghostly reminders of those who have lived, continue to live or have perhaps died in the Holocaust, the biscuit tins mimic the function of memory as a storehouse. The third component to these installations was that of the (again institutional) lamps around or in front of the openly displayed photographs (although in some cases the photographs may be surrounded by bare light bulbs). In those installations, where there is one clamp-on lamp per photograph, the lamps are unflinchingly situated at very close range, head-on to the photographs, sometimes disturbingly positioned between the eyes or in front of the mouth, suggesting the brutalities of execution or interrogation.[19] Often the installations are given the formal arrangement of an altar, adding solemnity to these already sombre signifiers.

It is not actually known whether the people represented in the photographs of *The Chases High School* works (fig. 14) and *Reserves: The*

Purim Holiday were actually victims of the Holocaust, yet both works refer to Jewish history and culture either in their titles or in the original contexts of the photographs, clearly inviting speculation that that might have been the case. But perhaps what is also suggested by their ambiguity is that the potential for atrocity is there for all and that any one of us might become an anonymous face in such an installation. In effect, Boltanski's particular brand of postmemory is highly connected to the thematic and iconographic tradition of *vanitas* and its reminders of mortality.[20] For instance, a similar stillness and silence to Boltanski's altar and monument-like installations is typically found in Dutch seventeenth-century still lives. These paintings often carry memento mori, such as the skull or the extinguishing candle, accompanied at times by reminders of the temporariness of life such as blighted fruit that is on the brink of decay. A similar iconography of mortality seems to inform Boltanski's skull-like close-ups, his dimmed lighting effects and his use of aged biscuit tins, with the result that remembrance of the Holocaust is articulated not only in terms that create a sense of reverence but also in terms that invoke well-known and widely understood reminders of the essential vanity of life.

Boltanski's interest in the Holocaust connects to his family background and the fact that his father was a non-orthodox Jew who converted to Catholicism (his mother was Catholic). While he was not raised according to Jewish tradition, Boltanski's childhood was nevertheless marked by family discussions concerning the war and the story of his father having to live under the floorboards to avoid capture by the Nazis. The fact that the Holocaust surfaced more overtly in his work in the mid- to late 1980s may obviously signal a delayed working-through of the implications of this inheritance but it also occurred at a time when the Holocaust was undergoing a process of fairly public historical revisionism which, while largely centred in Germany, also received attention further afield in Europe and the United States.[21] The subject of Holocaust revisionism brings me to Boltanski's contemporary, the German artist Anselm Kiefer (born 1945), who had no direct family connection with former Holocaust victims but is one of a generation in Germany known as the *Nachgeborenen* (the ones born afterwards).[22] Kiefer's career as an artist developed in the context of a reassessment of national identity in Germany, and his paintings of the 1980s bear clear correlations to German interest in historical revision that emerged later in that decade and has since acquired the label of 'the Historian's Debate' (the *Historikerstreit*). While postmemory in Kiefer's work is, again, the reaction of the next generation to the silence of the previous generation of primary witnesses, it is not the personal silence of former victims that is at issue but the collective silence of the nation that perpetrated the atrocities.

As German-born historian Andreas Huyssen notes, Kiefer's critique of Nazism began in 1969 with a suite of constructed photographs called *Occupations* (published in 1975), at a time when the first post-war generation came into adulthood and began to question and protest against the values and ideologies of their parents (part, of course, of a larger phenomenon of counter-cultural and oppositional politics that emerged in the late 1960s in the West). The photographs show Kiefer giving the Nazi salute in a number of locations across Europe, so that the first point of reference in viewing these images is that of the Nazi conquest of Europe in World War II. Kiefer

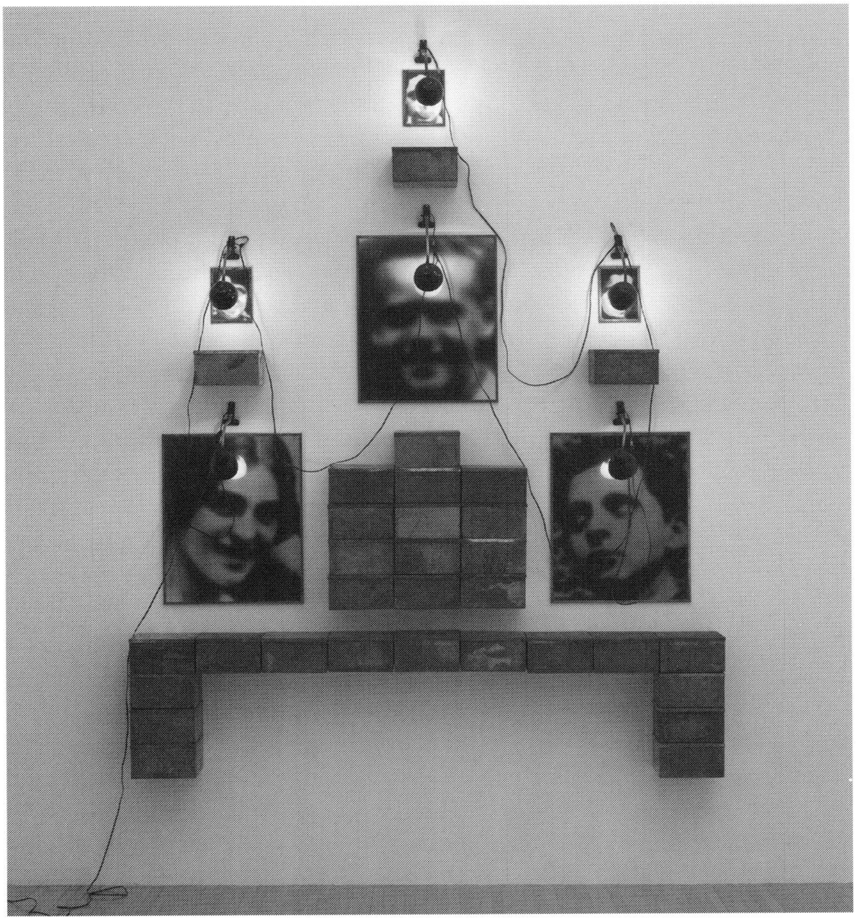

Figure 14: Christian Boltanski, *Autel De Lycée Chases (Altar to Chases High School)*, 1988. Six black and white photographs, 31 biscuit tins, and six lamps 81 x 86 inches (207 x 219.7 cm). The Museum of Contemporary Art, Los Angeles. Gift of Peter and Eileen Norton, Santa Monica, California.

references this through the incongruous motif of the lone figure in Nazi uniform, often, as Huyssen notes, diminished in scale in relation to his surroundings.[23] In this respect, Kiefer's saluting figure aligns with the Romantic leitmotif of man's insignificance in the face of nature (although in Kiefer's case it can also be in the face of monumental architecture or artworks) that he parodies in an image that makes direct reference to Casper David Friedrich's widely reproduced *Wanderer above the Misty Sea* (c. 1818). In the spirit of Romanticism, Kiefer's figure becomes pathetic or an 'anti-hero', who, as Mark Rosenthal puts it, is 'incapable of throwing off the chains of his countrymen and their memories'.[24]

However, while Kiefer's main point is not only to revive but to deflate the pomp and glory of Nazi imperialism, Huyssen also places *Occupations* in the context of the 'image orgy' or excessive visual spectacle that surrounded Nazism. For Huyssen, the Seig Heil photographs allude to the centrality of visual manipulation in the Nazi rise to power (torchlit parades, mass rallies, the 1936 Olympics, Albert Speer's floodlit operas).[25] However, it is also important to note, as Huyssen does, that the photographs follow a period in German history in which Nazism was not spoken of and certainly not represented in any visual discourse, a period that was to last from the end of the war into the 1960s, when a new German cinema began to emerge. What had dominated media representation in the meantime had been the sort of nostalgic or sentimentalised genre of the *Heimatfilm* (homeland film) or the consumer spectacle of advertising, both of which ignored the political history of the Third Reich.[26] Kiefer's Seig Heil photographs were among the first visual representations of Nazism to emerge after this period of general cultural silence with regard to the war. In drawing from the loaded symbolism of Nazi spectacle, Kiefer translated images of a repressed and reprehensible ideology into a critical weapon that contributed to the emerging reassessment of German history and identity.

But Kiefer was not content to let history rest with his ironic resurrection of Nazi imagery. He also began to make works that referenced the devastation of war and the atrocities of the Holocaust. For instance, by carbonising a series of paintings beyond recognition and assembling them in a set of eight volumes, Kiefer invoked a number of Nazi-related signifiers in *Cauterisation of the Rural District of Buchen* (1975) which referenced Adolf Hitler's scorched earth military campaigns, Nazi book burning and the Buchenwald camp itself.[27] The motif of the scorched earth was to be reiterated many times in the paintings of the 1980s, including the Margarete and Sulamith paintings (1981–1983) in which Kiefer addresses the evil of the Holocaust via a poem by Paul Celan. Kiefer's decision to revive Germany's Nazi past and its consequences in the Holocaust was not well received in his homeland, where silence regarding that period in history was the order of the day (to make

Nazism visible again entailed facing up to its abhorrent actions and values and risked reigniting them). On the other hand, Kiefer's critiques of Nazism and his references to the Holocaust were quickly appreciated abroad, particularly in the United States where his works on these themes were bought largely by Jewish dealers and collectors.[28]

This mixed reception brings us back to the issues of the how and what of Holocaust representation. The fact that Kiefer's work was liked by Jewish collectors testifies not only to its relevance but to its acceptability. Like Boltanski, Kiefer found a means of representation that both pointed to and evoked the deep tragedies of the Holocaust without reducing them in any way. Working in a postmodern climate that was beginning to reject grand narratives (not to mention the question of whether there could be such a narrative anyway after the Holocaust), neither artist attempted to produce definitive works nor to overtly moralise. Instead, they each orchestrated an already deeply embedded iconography in order to poeticise rather than narrativise. For Boltanki this has involved the development of a modern version of traditional *vanitas* imagery, and for Kiefer it involved the deployment of highly resonant materials such as straw, sand and lead, or highly symbolic motifs such as the scorched earth, the forest, history-laden buildings, the artist's palette or Biblical and mythological figures.

However, while Boltanski orders his Holocaust-related iconography in a way that is solemn and silent, creating an atmosphere that is at once hallowed and disturbing, Kiefer is rooted in the less contemplative tradition of Expressionism, deploying motifs and materials in a way that signifies the disordering and destruction of culture and civilisation. The Margarete and Sulamith paintings are typical of this approach. The poem on which the Margarete and Sulamith series is based, Celan's *Death Fugue* (1944), is a rhythmic evocation of the overriding and oppressive presence of death in the concentration camps, which places the Aryan Margarete in opposition to the Jewish Sulamith, while jointly addressing them in the refrain 'Your golden hair, Margarete, Your ashen hair, Sulamith'.[29] However, while the poem makes broad reference to the habitual circumstances of the death camps, Kiefer extrapolates the figures of Margarete and Sulamith and transforms them into emblems or archetypes that he situates against symbolically loaded backgrounds.

In *Your Golden Hair, Margarete* (1981) (fig. 15), this background is one of a vast landscape where, as in many of Kiefer's scorched, devastated or barren landscapes, the skyline is pushed almost to the top of the picture plane, so that the land occupies most of the picture surface. This allows Kiefer to exploit surface effects to the full, charging the work with expressive brushwork and loading it almost chaotically with the substance of his materials. In this version of Margarete, paint is used pictorially to figure the perspective of the landscape and expressively to create a sense of violent recession, which is superimposed with a series of large, violently executed black marks, signifying the charring of the earth. Almost centre stage in all of this, and in contrast to the more illusionistic figuration of the painted landscape, is the arc of straw that stands for Margerete's golden hair, the cultural and historical significance of which has been aptly put by Lisa Saltzman:

> Kiefer's Margarete, who is at once Celan's and Goethe's, is a blond-haired ('strohblond', literally straw blond) figure of German womanhood, embodied, corporealised, and metaphorised, in straw. For the straw is at once the German landscape, in its pure materiality, and, at the same time, strands of blond hair, the conflation pictorially enacting the ideological conceit of Nazism, namely, that German identity was autochthonous, that it was rooted in and emerged from the soils.[30]

Here Margarete can be seen in relation to German nationalistic rhetoric of blood and soil, which linked racial purity inextricably to indigenity. Already a recurrent motif in German Volk literature and art, the term was adopted by the Nazis in their anti-Semitist propaganda to justify the expulsion of the Jews from Germany on the grounds that they had no

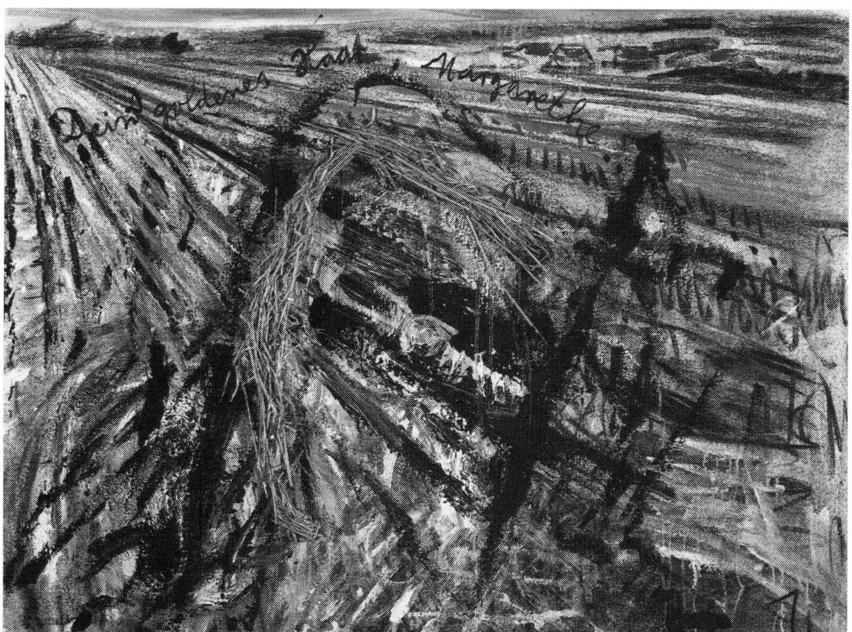

Figure 15: Anselm Kiefer, *Your Golden Hair, Margarete*, 1981. Oil, emulsion, straw on canvas 51 3/16 x 67 inches (130 x 170 cm). Private collection. Courtesy: Anselm Kiefer.

indigenous claim to the land, or, therefore, to the purity of the German race.[31] Yet, as Rosenthal observes, Kiefer figures Margarete as an emanation, 'a naïf or an ideal, then, who exists in nature, unaffected by the events of history', while the Sulamith of *Your Ashen Hair, Sulamith* (1981) is represented pictorially as an embodied figure. Like Margarete, Sulamith is also represented through her hair, which is similarly rendered in an arc shape, but, again, this is imaged in paint rather than figured through the properties of a symbolic material. Unlike Margarete, who is figured in relation to the land, Sulamith 'exists in or near civilisation', in this case the high buildings of an urban metropolis.[32] While Kiefer represents Margarete as emblematic of German soil, he seems to suggest that Sulamith is a victim of German 'civilisation'.

This interpretation is borne out in *Sulamith* (1983) (fig. 16), in which Sulamith is not given a bodily presence but represented by the inscription of her name in the top left corner of the painting. The painting represents an unrealised National Socialist building project, the interior of Wilhelm Kreis' design for a Mausoleum for German War Heroes (c. 1939). The vaulted brick hall is rendered in deep and dramatic perspective that culminates at the vanishing point in a group of flames, which Saltzman likens to a menorah or Jewish ceremonial candlestick, suggesting that Kiefer is transferring the commemorative potential of the space from Kreis' 'Great German Soldiers' to Jewish victims of the Holocaust.[33] But, as with the landscapes, effect is produced as much by the materials and materiality of the work as by its pictorial content, the sooty overlay of black pigment on brick seeming to reference, as Huyssen suggests, a giant and sinister cremation oven.[34]

Alongside the scorched earth landscapes, the interiors of National Socialist buildings serve as a major signifier for the ideologies of Nazi rule in Kiefer's work. But, again, Kiefer uses his materials or develops his imagery in a way that signals that all is not well in the state of Germany. While imposing in the grandeur of their architecture and vast in scale (the same almost melodramatic use of one-point perspective), the interiors are usually unpeopled and always rendered in Kiefer's now signature fractured technique, invoking a sense of disrepair or ruin. Edifices that were meant to celebrate a new reign in German history have become sites of decay, suggesting that what Kiefer wishes to inscribe in these buildings is the inherent decadence of Nazi ideologies. However, the emptiness of the interiors and the absence that is signalled by it can also be read on another level, as Huyssen has done, as standing for repressed memory and the inability to mourn.[35] Saltzman further argues that Kiefer's perspectives pull the spectator into the very spaces of Nazism and, in doing so, remind him/her of the dangers of the spectatorial dynamic that these buildings thrived on, which ended in the 'inassimilable trauma' of their historical consequences.[36]

Kiefer also recognises that the artist is made complicit in processes of spectacularisation and aestheticisation, as is demonstrated by his palette paintings, which can also be seen as a contribution to the debate over the representability of the Holocaust. The palette occurs as a central motif in both Kiefer's landscape and interior architectural paintings and is read as a metonymic sign for the figure of the artist, if not Kiefer himself. An early example is *Nero Paints* (1974), in which the palette hovers over a blackened landscape that features a row of menorah-like candelabras on the horizon at the top right of the image. While the painting obviously speaks to the relationship between the rhetoric of blood and soil and the Nazis' attempted extermination of Jews, a further implication is that the artist can do no more than Nero wilfully did, which was, of course, to fiddle while Rome burned. But, more specifically, the hovering palette also suggests limitations in the capacities of the artist as witness of atrocity. If *Nero Paints* is taken at face value these capacities are remote, as the artist seems able only to hover at a distance, or, as is the case with *Icarus: March Sands* (1981), fall from the heights. In *Icarus: March Sands*, the artist's palette persona gains wings and becomes conflated with Icarus, who in Greek mythology is granted the power

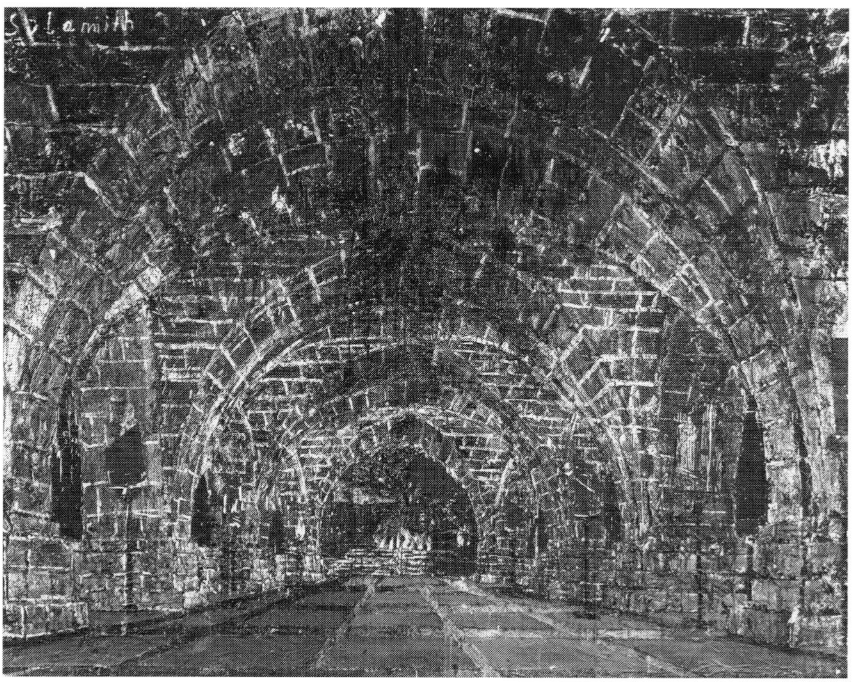

Figure 16: Anselm Kiefer, *Sulamith*, 1983. Oil, acrylic and straw on canvas, with woodcut 114 3/16 x 145 11/16" inches (290 x 370 cm). Private Collection. Courtesy: Anselm Kiefer.

of flight but, ignoring his father's warning not to fly too close to the sun, melts the wax on his wings and falls to earth. Saltzman reads this fall from grace as Kiefer falling victim to the paternal legacy of Germany, and as a symbolic move towards a position of victimhood.[37] Identification with the actual victims of the Holocaust apart, Kiefer and his generation of German artists have not only had to position themselves against the post-war interdict but, as *Nachgeborenen*, they have had to make their representations of the atrocities of war from a distance and in reaction to their 'fathers'.

If the artist aligns himself with a generalised sense of second-generation victimhood in *Icarus: March Sands*, his role as victim is further specified in the works which place the palette in an architectural interior as a surrogate for the Unknown Soldier. In the series of works *To the Unknown Painter* (1980–1983), Kiefer equates his proxy, the palette, with a more specific type of victim, or martyr, even: that of the common foot soldier. In the series, Kiefer often presents the palette as an impaled head, stood in the centre of a vast fascist architectural interior, placed, as Saltzman suggests, in spaces of repressed memory that emphasise the position of the unknown soldier as 'a victim of a burdensome historical legacy, a deferred trauma and the loss of ability to be unselfconsciously German'.[38] However, this acknowledgement of victimhood and loss does not necessarily mean that Kiefer fails in his project of remembrance and redress. As Saltzman also suggests (and I am summarising mercilessly here), the traumatised landscapes and ruined buildings can also be read as standing for psychical wounds that may never heal, that, captured in his distressed surfaces, are distilled in time, never to be resolved but also never to be forgotten.[39]

Clearly, Boltanski and Kiefer have each inherited the Holocaust in different ways. As members of the post-Holocaust generation they are both *Nachgeborenen*, but they grew up in very different contexts, which led to very different approaches. As Boltanski put it in a 1989 interview for *Parkett* magazine, Kiefer speaks of a world of great pain, where armies clashed and where the Jews of his (Boltanski's) culture lived: '[H]e is the army, present by a sort of physical weight... And I am the Jew who flees... My activity is always derisory, phantasmagorical...'[40] And, indeed, as I have shown, Kiefer asserts physical presence by the density of his materials, whereas Boltanski often creates a sense immateriality or even spirituality in the altar-like arrangement of many of his installations and the use of spectral images. The result is two different but complementary forms of representation that have helped shifted the debate on the representability of the Holocaust from Adorno's question of whether it should be represented at all to that of how it can be appropriately represented – a point made by Huyssen in relation to the last artist whose work I want to discuss in this chapter on postmemory.[41] Art Spiegelman (born 1948) is, again, one of 'the ones born afterwards', but more literally so, as the son of two former Holocaust victims, and thus even more closely connected to the atrocities of the Holocaust. But, far from the fine art context in which Boltanski and Kiefer produced their work, Spiegelman worked as a comic illustrator and chose to figure his father's memories through the medium of the comic book, produced in two volumes: *Maus: A Survivor's Tale* (1986) and *Maus II: From Mauschwitz to the Catskills* (1991).[42]

Given all that has already been said about the difficulties of finding an appropriate means through which the Holocaust can be represented, a comic book, with all its associations with the popular and the vulgar, would seem to be the least suitable choice. Yet *Maus* won a Pulitzer Prize in 1992 after the publication of *Maus II*, and was greeted as a primary example of ethical postmodernism by Todd Gitlin in the *New York Times Book Review*. So, the comic book is not necessarily a 'lowbrow' or a reductive medium but one that is also capable of psychological complexity and introspection. This was amply demonstrated by the underground comic movement that emerged in the late 1960s, later examples of which include Harvey Pekar's *American Splendor* (begun 1976) and the better-known *Uncle Bob's Mid-life Crisis* (1982) by Robert Crumb, both of which represented the interior lives of their characters.[43] Recognising that the comic strip and its associated forms are generally regarded as inferior art forms, Spiegelman offered a redefinition of the terminology in an article for *Print* magazine in 1988. A major problem for Spiegelman was the use of the word 'comic' to describe storytelling through image and text because of the connotation it has of humour, which he does not see as intrinsic to the medium. Spiegelman offers the word 'commix' as a better alternative, 'because to talk about comics is to talk about mixing together words and pictures to tell a story'.[44] In this he draws attention to the structural qualities of the medium and its potential to produce 'meaningful works of art and literature'.

Nonetheless, there is little that is innovatory or sensationalist about the comic book style that Spiegelman adopts, especially when compared to contemporaries such as Robert Crumb or Harvey Kurtzman, who are often given to visual exaggeration and caricature. Like Pekar, Spiegelman sticks to a fairly static arrangement of frames, with very few departures from a standard rectangular format. Actions and interactions are generally observed from a middle distance, neither too intimate for a critical distance to be struck nor too far away for meaningful emotional engagement with the characters and the story. However, this seemingly non-manipulative approach is tempered by the 'reverse anthropomorphism' of the characters, who are classified as animal types according to their ethnicity (Jews are mice, Nazis are cats, Poles are pigs, Americans are dogs, and so on). While anthropomorphism is a familiar trope in comic book illustration, with its origins in animal fables, Spiegelman explains his use of animal ciphers as a way of owning up to the ultimate inauthenticity of his representations, while creating an accessible way of dealing with the extremely sensitive and problematic content of the story.[45] Rather than breaking new ground in the conventions of comic book illustration, Spiegelman brought changes at the level of genre and narrative form. As Joshua Brown argues, *Maus* is neither a fictional comic strip nor an illustrated novel; it is, as Spiegelman himself has insisted, a carefully researched historical work.[46] As a transcription of oral history, a biography and an autobiography that centred on Holocaust memories all rolled into a comic strip, *Maus* is both extraordinary and unclassifiable.[47]

The complexity of *Maus* lies in the overlaying of several 'stories'. Spiegelman's master plot attempts to retrieve his father's memories of the war and his interment at Auschwitz, but at the same time he develops a narrative of Spiegelman's present-day relationship with his father, Vladek. The story proceeds in the present with flashbacks to the past whenever Vladek is persuaded to volunteer a memory, so that past and present intertwine in a battle for control between father and son. Vladek is recalcitrant, trading memories off for filial attention, and Artie (as Spiegelman designates himself in *Maus*) reverses this, trading his attention to his father off for his father's memories, all of which is shot through with the tensions of their relationship and Artie's struggle with his father's obstinacy and crankiness. As LaCapra notes, there is a 'sitcom' feel to the work which plays on a sort of gallows humour, 'the plight of the intellectual, sensitive, vaguely inept and overwhelmed son confronting an impossible but necessarily iconic survivor father'.[48] Moreover, in addition to these two master narratives, there are references to other related stories that are not as fully told: that of Artie's mother, Anja, another 'survivor', who committed suicide in 1968; his brother, Richieu, who was killed by a relative to spare him from Nazi deportation; his daughter, Nadja, to whom he dedicates *Maus II* (along with Richieu); and his wife, Françoise Mouly.

All these ongoing narrative relationships and tensions are strikingly punctuated towards the end of the first Maus book by an insert, *Prisoner on the Hell Planet: A Case History* (fig. 17), a strip that Spiegelman had produced in 1973 in response to his mother's suicide.[49] For Hirsch this insert, along with two photographs that appear in *Maus II*, 'protrude from the narrative like unassimilated and unassimilable memories'. The insert not only fractures the cohesion of the narrative but also provides a 'more pronounced version of the insanity he lives through every day of his postmemory'.[50] Spiegelman not only introduces another layer of memory with *Prisoner on the Hell Planet* but demonstrates the extent to which his parents' identity as Holocaust 'survivors' had permeated family life and attitudes. For example, while *Prisoner on the Hell Planet* depicts events around his mother's funeral, Spiegelman dresses himself in the striped uniform of concentration camp internees and, in a moment of reflection after the funeral, he visually foregrounds the thought that 'Hitler did it' (slightly in front of and more centrally placed than 'menopausal depression'). The style in which *Prisoner on the Hell Planet* is drawn is noticeably more dramatic than that of *Maus*, causing the insert to stand out jarringly, reminiscent to my eyes of the German Expressionist woodcuts of Karl Schmitt Rottluff (1884–1976).

This reminder of the persistence of his parents' traumatised past in the present reinforces the fact that Spiegelman's father is trapped by his memories. Spiegelman alerts us to this at the very beginning of *Maus*, where, by way of prelude, he tells and illustrates an anecdote from his childhood. A young Artie goes in tears to his father after being rejected and taunted by his friends for losing his roller skate – to which his father's response is: 'Friends? Your friends? If you lock them together in a room with no food for a week... then you could see what it is, friends.'[51] Although Vladek is reluctant to speak directly of his memories, his experiences of the Holocaust are simmering away just below the surface and prevent him from exercising conventional parenting skills when his young son is in distress. Indeed, there is as much buried memory in *Maus* as there is retrieved memory, most of which was destined to remain lost due to Vladek's reluctance to confront the past. This reluctance is acted out at a later point, when Vladek eventually reveals that he has destroyed Anja's memoirs, forcing the exclamation 'God damn you! You – you murderer!' from Artie (fig. 18). In a typical example of the tensions in their relationship, Artie is then obliged to forgive Vladek, who immediately instils guilt by reminding Artie of his own depression after Anja's death.[52]

As Hirsch notes, *Prisoner on the Planet Hell* is a work of memory situated within a work of postmemory.[53] But it is equally a work of absent memory, signalled by the loss of the memories that Anja had stored in her notebooks and the absence of memories of an older brother, Richieu, who was killed before Spiegelman was born. Indeed, Richieu features only briefly as part of Vladek's narrative, when we learn the bare facts that he was put under the protection of his aunt and subsequently killed by her as part of her own suicide.[54] But, while given a low profile in the narrative, Artie's brother forms a parenthesis around *Maus II* – invoked right at the beginning in the dedicatory photograph and again in the very last frame, when Vladek ends the narrative by mistakenly referring to Artie as Richieu: 'Let's stop, please, your tape recorder. I'm tired from talking, Richieu, and it's enough stories for now.' Born some time after the death of Richieu, Spiegelman could have no actual memory of his brother and inherited very little by way of postmemory from his parents, yet his brother comes to frame the bulk of the postmemory related in *Maus II*. In effect, Richieu existed as a 'ghost

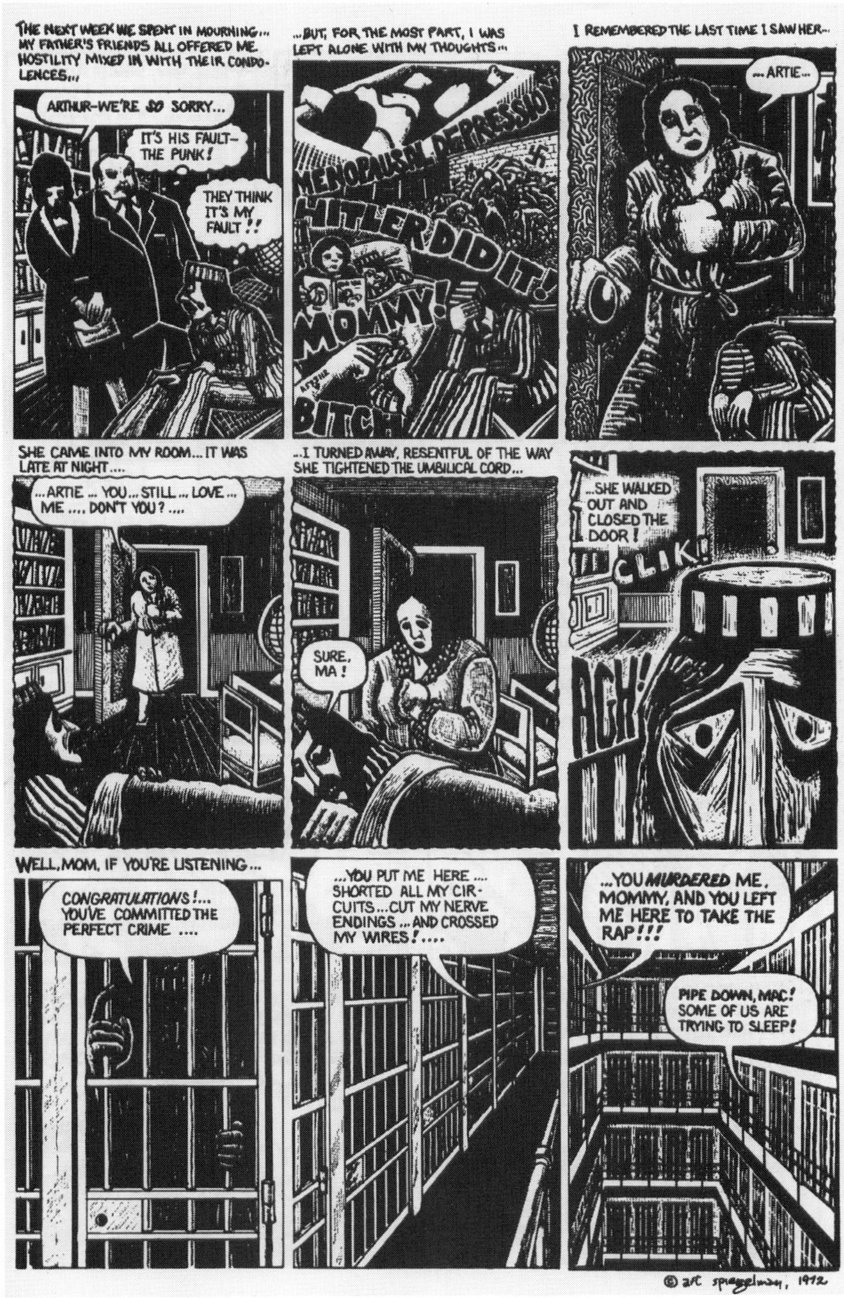

Figure 17: Art Spiegelman, from *MAUS I: A SURVIVOR'S TALE/MY FATHER BLEEDS HISTORY*, copyright © 1973, 1980, 1981, 1982, 1984, 1985, 1986 by Art Spiegelman. Used by permission of Pantheon Books, a division of Random House Inc.

brother' for Artie, a figure who occupied his parents' memory in a photograph hung on their bedroom wall – a deceased sibling that Artie nevertheless had felt in competition with as a child: 'The photo never threw any tantrums or got in any kind of trouble... It was an ideal kid, and I was a pain in the ass. I couldn't compete... They didn't talk about Richieu, but that photo was a kind of reproach...'[55] In the end, no matter how much or how little Artie manages to get out of his father by way of recollection, the past, of course, can never be fully reconstructed, but remains ultimately haunted by its ghosts and losses.

Artie has been left not only with the task of managing the relationship between his father's past and the present relationship between himself and his father but also with that of integrating loss and absence into that account. As an example of Holocaust representation, *Maus* embodies the complexities of telling, but never really being able to properly tell. It is a complex rendering of family history, in which Spiegelman has also to manage the subjectivities and the contradictions in the lives of those involved in its reconstruction (Vladek, Artie, Françoise and Vladek's second wife, Mala). In Vladek's case, contradiction often manifests itself as contrariness. A simple example is when he returns, and expects a refund for, left-over food, including a half-eaten packet of Special K to Shop Rite, oblivious to the protocols of returning used goods, driven only by his memory of hunger and the consequent need for thrift.[56] But a more complex and ironic example of what seems at first sight a contradictory, if not contrary, gesture is in the souvenir photograph that he has had taken of himself posing proudly in a spruced-up concentration camp uniform (later given to Anja as proof of his survival).[57] As Hirsch notes, this photograph is particularly disturbing because it '*stages*, *performs* the identity of the camp inmate', a bit of theatre which most of us would see as a travesty of the truth of the camps. But, as Hirsch also reminds us, the staging of the photograph calls attention to inherent conceits of representation that are inevitable in the telling of a history that can never be or has never been properly absorbed.[58]

In foregrounding the work of Spiegelman, Kiefer and Boltanski in this chapter, I have so far omitted any discussion of the most obvious form of post-Holocaust commemoration, which is the memorial and which, to my mind, relates only distantly to the notion of postmemory and secondary witness.[59] Nevertheless, I want to end this chapter by noting two innovatory public memorials that I feel can be aligned with works of postmemory – as opposed to the institutionalised or formalised memory of conventional monuments. The first is Christian Boltanski's *The Missing House* (1990) and the second is the *Harburg Monument against Fascism, War and Violence – and for Peace and Human Rights* (1986) by Jochen Gerz and Esther Shalev-Gerz. Both works eschew the formal autonomy of memorial statuary and can be

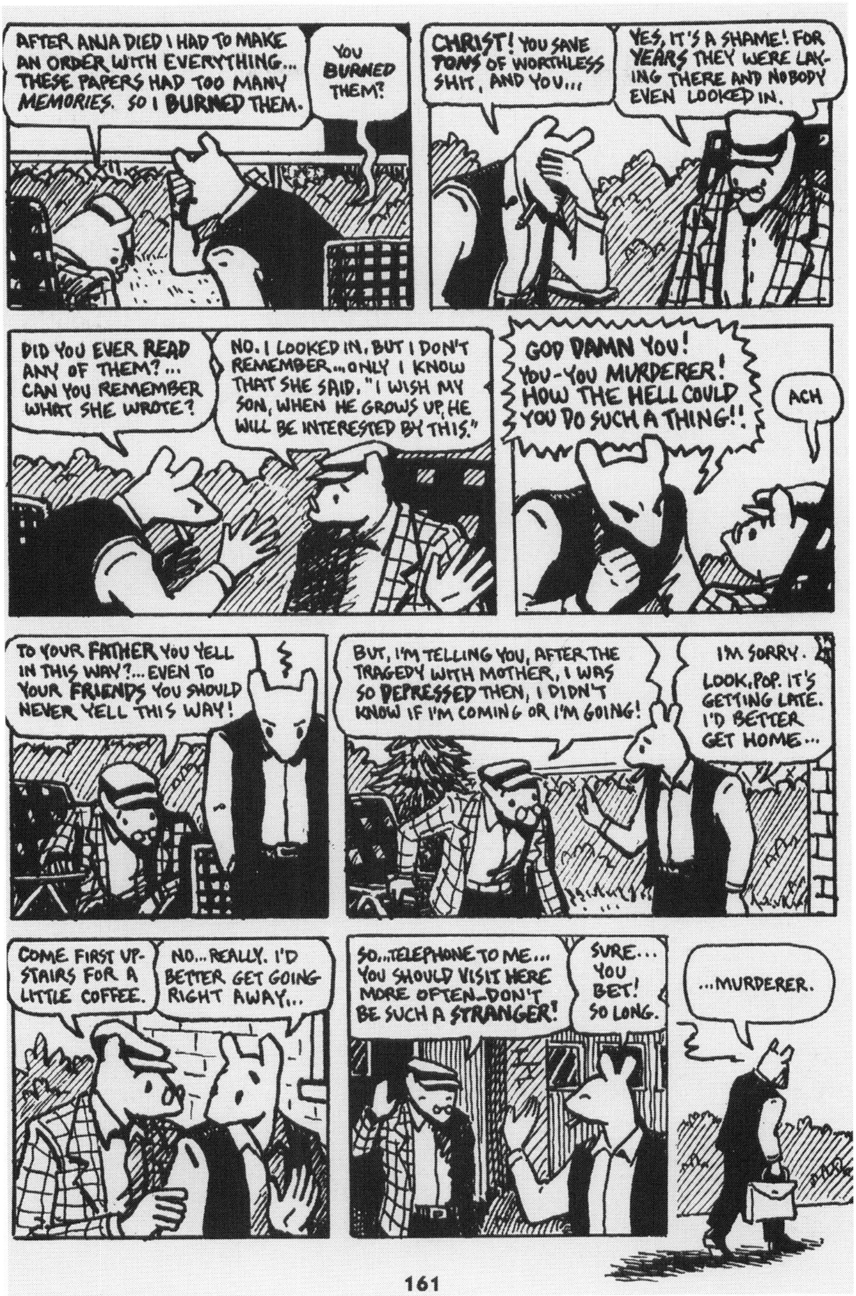

Figure 18: Art Spiegelman, from *MAUS I: A SURVIVOR'S TALE/MY FATHER BLEEDS HISTORY*, copyright © 1973, 1980, 1981, 1982, 1984, 1985, 1986 by Art Spiegelman. Used by permission of Pantheon Books, a division of Random House Inc.

considered anti-monuments, and both introduce elements of site specificity and preformativity, which are key to the experiential memory practices that will be discussed in my next chapter.

One of the events that Vladek remembers in *Maus* is that of having to move from the family home into cramped accommodation in the district of Stara Sosnowiec, an area that had been cordoned off in order to regulate the movements of Jews, which in turn conveniently allowed for the appropriation of Jewish property.[60] Boltanski's *Missing House* refers to this very practice. As the title implies, the work is constituted by a gap in a row of houses in Grosse Hamburgerstrasse (numbers 15–17) which had been left after Allied bombardment of Berlin in 1945. Boltanski heard that the former house had been occupied by Jews until their removal by the Nazis, and, with the help of the local archives, he also discovered the names of the previous Jewish inhabitants, which he then used as the basis for the memorial content of the work. This was done by installing nameplates on what would have been the party walls of the adjacent buildings (still carrying structural reminders of the inner walls of the missing building), with each plate giving the names, occupations and dates of residency of previous inhabitants. Significantly, however, the names are not exclusively those of past Jewish residents but also those of the non-Jewish occupants who lived there between 1943 and the bombing in 1945, pointing towards more complex issues with regard to who lived there and under what terms. As with Whiteread's *House*, absence becomes the primary means through which that which has been lost is signified, but, rather than giving that absence material form, Boltanski leaves the void caused by the bombing, which had become a passageway between streets. The result is an experiential work that unobtrusively incorporates the passer-by while he or she travels through the city – a far cry from the plinth-bound autonomy of the traditional sculpted monument.

Like *Missing House*, the Gerzes' *Monument against Fascism, War and Violence* in the Harburg district of Hamburg is essentially an experiential rather than contemplative work, which subverts the conventions of traditional monuments. Basing their approach on the premise that there are already too many monuments, the Gerzes decided to make a monument that would disappear over a period of time, thus challenging the notions of permanence, authority and fascist tendencies that they believe to be inherent in traditional monuments.[61] This desire to run counter to traditional memorial practices extended into the choice of site. Having originally been offered what might be considered a prime location in a city centre park, the Gerzes chose the busy arena of a suburban shopping mall for their 'monument', a utilitarian rather than a symbolic space.[62] Made of aluminium sheeting and clad with a thin layer of lead, *Monument against Fascism, War and Violence* started out in 1986 as a three foot by three foot square column that rose to a height of forty feet. The column was then gradually allowed to sink into the ground until, seven years later, it became flush with the surface of the paved area around it. However, there was more to the column than a simple disappearing act. The inscription it bore was not commemorative as such but an invitation to passers-by to write their names on the lead surface (steel styluses were provided at each corner), committing themselves to remain vigilant to injustice. The inscription also warned that the monument would gradually disappear as the writing gradually filled up the lower part of the shaft, again making the point that it is not monuments as such but people who are 'able to rise up against injustice'.

Unlike traditional monuments, *Monument against Fascism, War and Violence – and for Peace and Human Rights* demanded both reflexivity and participation from its viewers. As with *Missing House*, memorialisation was achieved by the incorporation of the viewer into the work, who, this time, made an active contribution towards the completion of the project (the final form was achieved when the top surface of the column reached ground level, which read 'Harburg's Monument against Fascism'). As James E. Young notes, *Monument against Fascism, War and Violence – and for Peace and Human Rights* undid many cherished conventions of the monument:

> Its aim was not to console but to provoke, not to remain fixed but to change, not to be everlasting but to disappear, not to be ignored by passers-by but to demand interaction, not to remain pristine but to invite its own violation and desanctification, not to accept graciously the burden of memory but to throw it back at the town's feet.[63]

Disappointingly, public participation turned out to be less than ideal and the 'monument' became a site for graffiti of all sorts, including swastikas, not so much returning the burden of memory but becoming a reflection of the mixture of ignorance and knowledge, self-preoccupation and lack of understanding that made up the constituency in which it was placed.[64] This reaction not only reinvokes the question of appropriateness of form that is at the heart of this chapter but also introduces issues of audience and context. While I will be shifting key considerably in terms of subject matter, these are issues that apply to the works of enactment and re-enactment that are to be discussed in my next chapter, which looks at ways in which memory figures in relational and participatory works.

5

Enactments, Re-enactments and Episodic Memory

I ended the last chapter with examples of two commemorative works which are sited in the public realm and which exemplify a conceptual, performative and participatory ethos in public art that came to the fore in the late 1980s and 1990s. As Arlene Raven observed in 1993, 'Public art isn't a hero on a horse anymore', but had become a range of practices that included oral history, protest actions and guerrilla theatre alongside sculpture, painting and craft.[1] Moreover, the more enlightened producers of public art recognised a duty towards the communities or constituencies that occupied the spaces for which it is made, leading to their inclusion and participation. Art theorist Suzi Gablik characterised this turn towards inclusion and participation as relational practice which 'embodies more aliveness and collaboration, a dimension excluded from the solitary, essentially logocentric discourses of modernity'.[2] This relational model of practice was then more famously developed by performance artist Suzanne Lacy into 'new genre public art', in a similar recognition of the foregrounding of issues of social engagement and audience involvement in non-gallery-based art.[3]

However, while Gablik and Lacy had various community-based art projects in mind, this notion of a relational dynamics has been applied more widely by Nicolas Bourriaud, who uses the term 'relational aesthetics' to describe a tendency in contemporary art towards personalising the engagement of the audience in the work, whether gallery-based or in the public realm. Also contrasting this relational approach with Modernism, Bourriaud argues that artworks enter into 'ways of living and models of action within the existing real'.[4] Accordingly, relational art addresses the realm of human interactions and is predicated on the notion of an encounter or of artworks which either constitute 'moments of sociability' or are 'objects producing moments of sociability'.[5] Examples that Bourriaud gives include Gabriel Orozco's installation of a hammock in the MoMA Garden in New

York (1993), Jens Hanning's broadcast of Turkish jokes in Copenhagen Square (1994) and Braco Dimitrijevic's *Casual Passer-by* posters (1968 ongoing), which portray the faces and names of normally anonymous people on billboards. A feature of this preoccupation with intersubjectivity, interaction and encounter that will surface in the following discussion is conviviality – something which Bourriaud (following Félix Guattari) sees taking place principally in the micro-politics of society, at the level of the community and the neighbourhood.[6]

The works to be discussed in this chapter are all relational, albeit in different ways. As will be seen, some are more participatory and convivial in form than others, but they all carry a sense of encounter and, one way or another, make a call on intersubjective relationships. Pertinent to the context of the first works to be discussed, Bourriaud sets the development of relational aesthetics in the context of the development of a growing urbanism on a world scale that has brought increased social exchange and mobility.[7] This contextualisation also serves as a reminder that memory is always formed at specific times and in specific places, a mental image of which assists in the recall of an event, experience or fact (even learning by rote happens in particular conjunctions of time and place).[8] Some of the enactments and re-enactments to be discussed in this chapter are urban in location and some are not, but the specificity of place is a significant feature of them all, whether imagined, virtual or actual. Moreover, they are all contingent on the sort of social exchange and mobility that urbanisation has brought with it, whether literally or through the media that help maintain that exchange and mobility. In their emphasis on experience as the basis for memory, the works of enactment and re-enactment (even if virtual) fall into line with the category of episodic memory, used in the psychology of memory to distinguish between knowledge that is acquired directly and experientially, as opposed to conceptual or reflexive knowledge, known as semantic memory.[9]

For instance, several new media psychogeographic projects have been based on memories of the inhabitants of a particular part of a city or town and have involved a subjective mapping of the locality. The term 'psychogeography' was coined by members of the neo-avant-garde group, the Situationist International, who in the 1960s advocated a radical reconfiguration of the city and drew their ideas and practices of an alternative cartography directly from the Surrealists. The Surrealist's *Map of the World*, 1929, is the seminal example of politically alternative mapping. The Pacific Ocean is placed in the centre, flanked by Russia, China and a disproportionately large Alaska, against which Europe is diminished in scale, the United States completely absent and the South American continent labelled as 'perdu', or lost. In terms of memory, this alternative mapping of the world is a clear exposé of the 'slipperiness' or compromise of data of any sort, official or alternative, and, in particular, of the essential non-objectivity of maps. Alongside the remapping of the world, the Surrealists also reconfigured the city in their literature. For instance, Louis Aragon's *Le Paysan de Paris* (1926) privileges the 'non-places' of the flâneur and 'a geography of pleasure' (for example, the shop displays in Le Passage de L'Opéra), and André Breton's *Nadja* (1928) gives an account of his obsessive roaming of Paris in pursuit of the sort of elusive love or erotic longing that he later recounted in *L'Amour Fou*, 1937. The memories generated by 'a geography of pleasure' are not only subjective but essentially embodied and localised, and, as phenomenologist Edward Casey says of all memories, have necessarily to '*take place in place*'.[10] This contingency of place for memory has already been noted in relation to the mnemonics of the ancient art of memory as well as in relation to Nora's notion of *lieux de mémoire*, but also becomes pressing in works of art that are enactments or re-enactments – works that are dependent on specific locations or types of location in order to be realised.

The Situationists conflated the political imperative behind the Surrealist *Map of the World* and the subjective imperative behind Aragon's and Breton's walks in Paris by developing a psychogeography which entailed both a remapping and re-experiencing of the city. Their psychogeographic approach to the city subverted prescribed or preconstructed ways of experiencing or knowing the city, replacing them with more open, creative ways of negotiating the urban landscape. For instance, key concepts in Situationist psychogeography were: *dérive* (drift) – signifying the unplanned journey; and *détournement* (diversion/re-routing) – signifying the surprises that the unplanned might bring.[11] A recent example of the pursuit of the surprising and the unexpected through psychogeographic walking projects is to be found in the use of algorithmic programming by the Dutch artists' collective Social Fiction. In the spirit of *dérive* and *détournement*, Social Fiction have devised a number of applets upon which a walk can be based, one of which is based on the Fibonacci system that, when followed to its logical conclusion, 'soon becomes surrealistic, if not downright absurd'.[12] True to the tenets of psychogeography, the emphasis here is on exploration, the production of new experiences and new knowledge, rather than a reliance on prefabricated data.

In contrast, the three examples of contemporary psychogeography that I want to introduce in relation to memory also clearly hark back to Situationist practices, but their social agendas are more evident and the urban wanderings that they propose are related to particular places and their history. These are *Urban Tapestries* (central London, 2002–2004), *[murmur]* (Toronto, 2003) and *One Block Radius* (New York, 2004). *Urban Tapestries* is a research project which was conceived and realised by Proboscis, who describe themselves as a creative studio and think tank for culture.[13] The studio, led by Alice Angus and Giles Lane, does not make any claim to public art, but, for me, their work qualifies, defined as it is by Proboscis as creative practice that is played out with public participation in the public arena. *Urban Tapestries* is one of several Proboscis projects that tap into participants' memories, such as the ongoing *Topography and Tales*, for instance, a 'liquid geography' project which incorporates storytelling and memory as devices to study the relationships and boundaries and borders between people, language and identity.

Urban Tapestries is firmly rooted in the notion of public authoring, with the aim of enabling people to become authors of the environment around them:

> Like the founders of Mass Observation in the 1930s, we are interested creating opportunities for an 'anthropology of ourselves' – adopting and adapting new and emerging technologies for creating and sharing everyday knowledge and experience; building up organic, collective memories that trace and embellish different kinds of relationships across places, time and communities.[14]

Using a combination of geographic information systems and mobile technologies, the idea was that participants could 'annotate' their responses to a designated area of London in order to represent its social fabric. The weaving of this fabric was achieved with the help of wireless technology, through which annotations were shared with other participants – producing a form of networked blogging that instantly calls up Bourriaud's notions of encounter and intersubjective exchange. Participants could 'embed their own content into geo-specific locations' out of which threads would emerge to form 'an organic, accretive tapestry'. The feasibility of the project was tested through a number of preliminary 'bodystorming' experiments in which groups annotated large-scale maps of their neighbourhood (floor maps or table top) with Post-its. The participants in the public trial were issued with PDAs (Hewlett-Packard iPAQs), through which they could annotate their responses to Bloomsbury (an area of London that Proboscis considered heavily weighted with cultural memory in the form of blue plaques and association with the Bloomsbury set). This was then repeated in a field trial covering a larger area of central London, this time using Sony Ericsson P800 mobile phones.[15] For Proboscis, these technologies provide a platform that 'enabled people to better define their own sense of place and space', a platform that could enable them to maintain a sense of presence, could reinvigorate the public domain and augment and assist in everyday life. They also note the potential for generating collective memory out of this shared knowledge – some of which has, of course, already been gathered in the 'tapestry', which can also be seen as a databank or archive of participants' annotations.

Similarly, *[murmur]* is an archival project in which memory is site-specific. The project, conceived by Shawn Micallef, James Roussel and Gabe Sawhney, was launched in 2003 in Toronto's Kensington Market but has recently spread as far as Edinburgh (fig. 19). Like *Urban Tapestries*, *[murmur]* was dedicated to collecting stories from the residents of the area and disseminating them publicly (although slightly differently) through the use of mobile phones. People's stories are matched to the actual place in which they experienced the events that they recall, which are marked by street signs in the form of green ears. *[murmur]* maps show the locations of telephone numbers displayed on the signs, and upon dialling the number a story is related about that particular part of the neighbourhood by someone who can make the listener feel less of a tourist or stranger and more connected to the area:

> We've gone around and recruited people, regular Torontonians telling their stories about places and in those places we've put up signs so that you can kind of walk around the neighbourhood and hear those stories as if you are standing right next to the person. So, it's like taking a tour of the city, but from a really intimate point of view.[16]

While personal, the stories contribute to Toronto's identity and are meant to add 'yet another layer to the city'.[17] By dialling into a *[murmur]* story the participant steps out of routine and sees the city from another point of view. Writing for *eye weekly*, Abigail Pugh has noted that the stories are often low-impact, dealing with 'small' events or occurrences, said to range from 'historical to hysterical, from embarrassing to esoteric'. Yet, as Roussel commented to her, these events are 'not a majestic, feel-good, technicoloured moment, but simply a sense that this is a human being, like me'. As with *Urban Tapestries*, the *[murmur]* project privileges the public authoring of the site or place, and, as Roussel has also put it, 'offers an alternative, one-of-a-kind, popular mythology of the city at a citizen level'.[18] It also serves as an agent for the retrieval, collecting and sharing of memories associated with particular places, and, in this, also remaps the city according to individual lived histories rather than its topography.

As in the previous two projects, *One Block Radius* simultaneously entails the retrieval and production of data.[19] This data is again subjective, as is the mapping of the block that emerges from it. The project involves a detailed psychogeographic mapping of an area between the Bowery and Christie Street, Stanton Street to Rivington Street, which forms the block where the New Museum of Contemporary Art was to be relocated in New York, and, indeed, the project had the support of the museum (originated by Christina Ray and David Mandl of Glowlab, a Brooklyn-based artists' collective). The idea was to produce a guidebook of the area or block that would in its own way be as detailed as a city guidebook. In other words, the size of the locality was much smaller, just a fraction of the city, and the density of information much greater – and, of course, of a different order from the tourist-type information given in city guidebooks.[20] The information in the *One Block Radius* guidebook is, again, based on personal perspectives, including those of long-term residents, children, workers, children, street performers as well as the architects of the New Museum, and is recorded in a variety of ways:

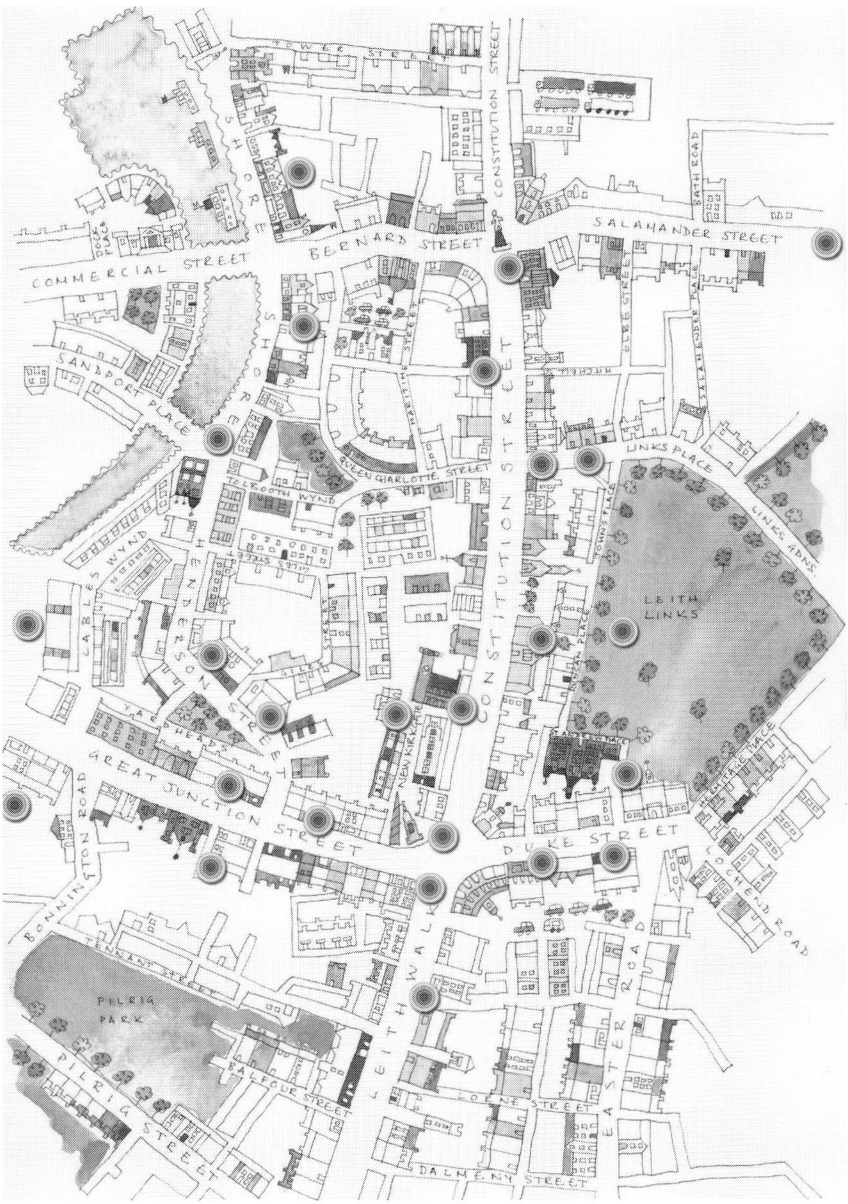

Figure 19: *[murmur]* Edinburgh, 2006. Courtesy of New Media Scotland.

field recordings (smells as well as sounds), video, interviews and blogs. As Jonah Brucker-Cohen writes for Rhizome,

> The project is a vivid example of psychogeographic cartography, where objects in urban spaces (such as fire hydrants, signs, graffiti) are documented and placed on an evolving map that reveals the emotional character of the city. The website also includes audio and video interviews with residents and the New Museum's architect. Since museum construction begins later this year, One Block Radius could be the last collective reminder of a neighbourhood in temporal and physical transition.[21]

For me, all three projects again call to mind Walter Benjamin's thoughts on memory and history and the methods he used to chronicle his native city of Berlin. In advance of contemporary thinkers such as Andreas Huyssen and Pierre Nora, who note the shift from history to memory in the charting of the past, Benjamin privileges knowledge or data that has been retrieved subjectively, rejecting official versions of history.[22] Benjamin conceives this retrieval in terms of archaeology, in which the archaeologist-historian's task is to retrieve or 'redeem' the commonplace, the everyday and the unremarkable. As already noted in chapter 1, Benjamin's notion of excavation is important for this kind of memory-work, in which memory is not an instrument for exploring the past but the soil that has to be dug and turned over. Importantly, this act of digging not only reveals deeper hidden strata in the past but also necessitates a renewed awareness of the strata which first had to be broken through.[23] Furthermore, I see this sort of memory-work as akin to Freud's notion of dream-work, an aspect of which is the processing of the events and emotions of the day for relegation to the unconscious – except that memory-work retrieves from the unconscious and takes experiences and emotions that have been stored back to the realm of the conscious.

Stories have been excavated and told in the three projects that I have described, and, in so doing, memories have been 'redeemed' and places have been remapped in new and unexpected ways. The relationship between place and memory has been foregrounded and the places of memory have become situational and interpersonal. As French cultural theorist Michel de Certeau has observed, it is not so much the city itself but the people of the city – those that travel through and interact with the city – that are not only repositories of knowledge but also the 'actualisers' of the city. Even when they are routes that have been prescribed by city maps, these paths and trajectories can only ever refer to 'the absence of that which has passed by'. De Certeau notes that the editing procedures of conventional city maps are little more than a way of forgetting, I would add that projects such as *Urban Tapestries*, *[murmur]* and *One Block Radius* are a means by which the forgotten is restored.[24] The memories unearthed in the sort of psychogeographic projects I have described are often unashamedly personal, subjective and experiential. And rightly so, for, as de Certeau also notes, the more numerous stories (rumours) made public by the media are far too pervasive (and persuasive) and take the ownership and status of information away from the individual, the family or the neighbourhood.[25]

The work of Janet Cardiff (born 1957) relates to the psychogeographic walking projects described above in that it uses new technology, is location-specific and incorporates the subjective memory of her participants. However, it differs in important respects. The memories are supplied by Cardiff as part of a master-narrative, which may include references to the historical past but may as easily be fictional or imagined. Cardiff's works are more self-consciously aesthetic, produced and received as works of art, and she is a recognised figure in the contemporary art world in a way that the producers of *[murmur]*, *One Block Radius* and *Urban Tapestries* are not.[26] While the producers of *[murmur]*, *One Block Radius* and *Urban Tapestries* use new technologies in a facilitatory manner, as a medium for reminiscence and remembrance, Cardiff uses technology suggestively, not only to map out a walk but to create atmosphere and organise narrative content. Moreover, Cardiff's walks are informed by her own thematic preoccupations, which are (often subliminally) passed on to the participants through her audio and audio-visual 'guides'.

Each of Cardiff's walks is pre-planned according to a recorded narrative, which unfolds in relation to the sound of Cardiff's footsteps and the objects, people and landmarks that she notices. The soundtrack is composed not only of Cardiff's voice but of other voices, background noises and sound effects, all of which work in concert to immerse the walker in an altered reality that the artist likens to a filmic event.[27] While conventional audio guides provide an exposition of the place in which the journey takes place, orientating the walker and familiarising him or her with the environment and the things encountered, Cardiff's are often uncanny or unhomely in effect. As Cardiff herself describes the process:

> The format of the audio walks is similar to that of an audioguide. You are given a CD player and told to stand or sit in a particular spot and press play. On the CD you hear my voice giving directions, like 'turn left here' or 'go through this gateway,' layered on a background of sounds: the sound of my footsteps, traffic, birds, and miscellaneous sound effects that have been pre-recorded on the same site as where they are being heard. This is the important part of the recording. The virtual recorded soundscape has to mimic the real physical one in order to create a new world as a seamless combination of the two. My voice gives directions but also relates thoughts and narrative elements, which instil in the listener a desire to continue and finish the walk.[28]

In effect, Cardiff's narratives are not built around prescribed linear storylines but are formed initially by a process of intuitive association with the location. Nonetheless, despite this more spontaneous beginning, the narratives are meticulously worked through, and, as Carolyn Christov-Bakargiev notes, the result of on-the-spot improvisations that may have been edited or rewritten several times before the final version is reached.[29] Cardiff talks her listener/fellow walker through the walk as if she is at his or her side, indicating, for instance, that she is tired and this might be a good time to stop and look, as in *Münster Walk* (1997), or pointing out details in the environment and small events that catch her interest or imagination. In this, Cardiff is inviting what might be seen as the kind of collusion or companionship in an event that Casey attributes to commemoration, where an absence of direct recollection is compensated for by a grouping together of co-rememberers ('com-memorisers').[30] The walk in Central Park commissioned by the Public Art Fund in New York, *Her Long Black Hair* (2004), demonstrates the way in which Cardiff co-opts her participants into a web of associations with the past, which are mentioned elusively and allusively but which nevertheless ask that her 'companion' in the walk share in the commemoration of historical figures associated with the park. In this walk, Cardiff guides her fellow walker though Central Park, tracing the footsteps of a mystery woman whose found photograph has prompted the excursion. But, while following a geographic route, the walk wanders temporally and culturally from the present-day Central Park to the period in time in which the park was constructed.[31] The range of associations are wide and complex, including quotations from Søren Kierkegaard (on the significance of the accidental and insignificant), a poem by Charles Baudelaire (on his black-haired mistress and mortality), the words of American slave Harry Thomas (on the abuse he suffered and his epic escape from enslavement) to the invocation of Orpheus' last look at Eurydice (on the way that memories disappear or dissolve on looking back).[32]

These 'com-memorations' are always experienced performatively and are integral to the present circumstances of the walk. The voice-over gives directions, and various aspects of the day-to-day business of the park are remarked upon – casual observations of the weather, the traffic noise, peanut sellers, squatters, the zoo, for example. But the continuity of the walk is interspersed with the wider associations that Cardiff wants to build in, which are made to occur as if they have been subliminally triggered. Characteristically, the associations that are conjured up in the spoken narrative vie not only with one another but also with a number of sound effects (arranged and edited by Cardiff's partner, George Bures Miller). Some of these sounds are the immediate noise of Cardiff's footsteps and the daily comings and goings of the park – traffic, children's voices, a dog barking. But, at one point, the more unusual sound of a shot occurs: 'Do you hear that? They're shooting the scavengers – the wild goats and pigs who are supposed to eat the garbage in the city streets but they keep coming into the park to eat the grass, so they have to shoot them.' Then, in a typical shift of register from the actual to the suggested, this sharp interruption is swiftly contrasted by a shift of attention to an organ grinder (and the sound or organ music), which immediately leads on to thoughts about Kierkegaard: 'At this very moment there's an organ grinder in the street – it is wonderful. It is the accidental and insignificant things in life that are significant – Kierkegaard wrote that... He was a walker. Every day he would wander through the streets of Copenhagen.'[33]

This juxtaposition of actuality and association mimics the way that the mind works organically to process information and connect it to its pre-existing reservoir of knowledge and experience. But the demands on the walker's ability to integrate this process of knowledge-building are stretched by yet another overlay, that of the simulations of Cardiff's recorded walk onto the actuality of the participant's actual walk, resulting in a sense of immersion into more than one reality. As Cardiff notes, her voice is recorded with microphones close to the body, a method that causes the listener to feel as if the recorded body and voice are almost inside the listener's body, but which, at the same time, can act as a disorienting mechanism:

> In this type of work synchronistic events play with the listener's understanding of reality. There is a sense of wonder and shock when events and scenes described on the audiotape coincidentally happen in the physical world. On the other hand, when something you hear is not there, the viewer is given a sense of displacement, as though they have been transported into someone else's dream.[34]

On top of all this, the enormous amount of visual imagery that Cardiff includes in her narrative creates a cinematic effect. But, while cinema requires the suspension of disbelief by a seated audience that allows itself to become immersed in the virtual world of the film, the virtual and the actual become integrated in to the performative engagement of the walker/listener in Cardiff's walks. Add to this the use of binaural sound, which Cardiff describes as 'an incredibly lifelike, 3-D reproduction of sound' through which it is possible 'to suggest the presence of physical phenomena that aren't actually there', and the experience becomes even more hyperreal, again easily comparable to the hyperreality of cinema.

Not only this, Cardiff also references a particular type of cinema in many of her works: that of film noir. In *Münster Walk* (1997), for instance, she created the story of a man intent on tracing his dead daughter's movements in the town (inspired by a similar attempt to capture memory by a real-life friend who poignantly rephotographed photographs that had been taken by her dead son, looking vicariously through his eyes).[35] At an early point, Cardiff frames the narrative in the knowing but detached style of film noir voice-over: 'Sometimes you just fall into a story but sometimes, you just have to take steps to unravel it.'[36] This convention has been used in noir classics such as Billy Wilder's *Sunset Boulevard* (1950), and indicates that the narrator has been involved first-hand with the events that are to be unfolded. Referring largely to Cardiff's filmed installations, Alex Ohlin has noted many other characteristics of film noir in Cardiff's work – suspense, mystery, desire, danger and loss.[37] These themes are present in several of the walks, such as *Münster Walk* and *The Missing Voice (Case Study B)* (1999). In *Münster Walk*, suspense, mystery and danger are there from the start. The walk begins at night, immediately suggesting danger and mystery, more pointedly invoked by Cardiff at a later point when she refers to the place (the church) as 'spooky'. But 'spookiness' has also been introduced from the start, when the older man begins to count in synchronicity with a child chanting a skipping rhyme about Cinderella (conjuring up the unkind and often sinister world of fairy stories), and is later heard counting while following Cardiff, as if to align himself with her footsteps.[38] Desire and loss are manifest in the way that Cardiff intersperses her walking instructions with references to the past: 'I'm taking the route we used to walk, waiting to hear him beside me again (to weird repetitive piano music)... [B]efore I left we lay on the couch together. I remember the smell of him, my nose buried into his neck, his arms around me.' Here a younger man's voice interrupts, mimicking the effect of a cinematic cut: 'I had a dream about you last night. You were in a market beside a church and someone was following you.' This coincidence between a dream and the actuality of the walk again shores up the effect of 'spookiness', and suggests a presentiment of danger for the woman (Cardiff) walking alone at night.

Suspense is maintained by enigma and ambiguity. The characters in the walks are only ever generically identified and both walk and narrative depend on turns that are made into unknown or forgotten territory (both physical and mental). *The Missing Voice (Case Study B)* (fig. 20) begins with a conflation of fiction and memory when the participant is asked to note an extract from crime novelist Reginald Hill's *Dreams of Darkness*, after which Cardiff comments, 'Sometimes when you read things, it seems like you are remembering them.'[39] The intertwining of fiction and memory is maintained by the introduction of another disembodied voice, that of a detective who is looking for a missing woman. It transpires that the female narrator has found a woman's photograph in the tube station: 'A woman with long red hair staring out at me... I put it in my pocket. I don't know why. She reminded me of my sister. It didn't seem right to leave it on the ground.' The female narrator impersonates this woman, but at times also seems to become her, as signalled by the ad hoc statement 'I've a long red-haired wig on now. I look like the woman in the picture. If he sees me now he'll recognise me.' There are further hints that the narrator might be the woman who is being sought, especially when the detective seems to be following her: 'As far as I can tell she's mapping different paths through the city. I can't seem to find a reason for the things she notices and records.'[40] So, it is not clear whether the thoughts voiced by the narrator are her own or those of the red-haired woman she impersonates, or, later, whether it is her body or the body of the mystery woman that the listener is told has been retrieved from the river.

As is the case with many of Cardiff's walks, the walker/listener in *The Missing Voice (Case Study B)* struggles to differentiate between the real narrator and the fictional woman, the narrated walk and the real walk that they are mutually engaged in. The result is a vacillation between imagination and memory that transports the walker/listener psychologically, geographically and temporally way beyond the physical confines of the walk. However, the walks are not simply highly imaginative guided journeys through a particular location; they are, essentially, re-enactments of walks that have already been trodden by Cardiff. As a device for recreating past events, re-enactment relies on simulation – a strategy which brings a sense of immediacy, which is not only present in the sound effects of Cardiff's recordings but which also, in different ways, underpins the work of the next two artists I will discuss, Pierre Huyghe (born 1962) and Jeremy Deller (born 1966).

The relationship between reality and its simulations is unquestionably at the crux of Huyghe's two-screen video piece *The Third Memory* (1999) (fig. 21).

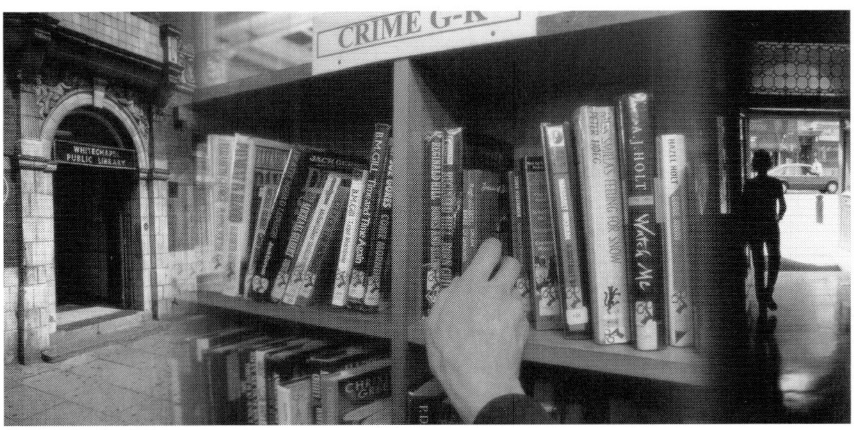

Figure 20: Janet Cardiff, *The Missing Voice (Case Study B)*, 1999. Commissioned and Produced by Artangel. Images by Stephen White.

One screen shows Sidney Lumet's feature film *Dog Day Afternoon* (1975), based on a failed real-life bank robbery that took place in Brooklyn in August 1972. Its companion shows one of the original bank robbers, John Wojtowicz (played by Al Pacino in the film), retelling, re-enacting, and to an extent reliving the original event (with the help of actors) on a set that is based on the film set, not on the interior of the original bank. However, the restaging of the robbery does not have the seamless narrative of Lumet's film, but is broken up by news footage taken at the time of the original robbery, news clippings and the inclusion of Wojtowicz' reaction to the fictionalisation of the robbery in film, written while still in prison. Although the title specifies three memories, there are in effect only two screens, which correspond to two sets of memory. The first is that of the filmmaker, who transported the event into the realm of fiction and playacting (in fact a piece of second-generation storytelling, as *Life* magazine had already reported the event as a narrative with dialogue in September 1972).[41] The second set of memories, of course, is that of Wojtowicz, a primary participant in the original robbery who retrospectively play-acts the event.

The key to the how and the what of the third memory in this piece lies in Huyghe's recognition of representation and narration as that which is temporally separated from the event or displaced in time. For Huyghe, the distance between the event and its representation opens up a gap – a non-mediated space that he attaches to Roland Barthes' notion of the third meaning.[42] According to Barthes, the third meaning manifests as an 'accent' and forms a critical metalanguage to the conventions of film language. For Barthes, the third meaning is obtuse, occupying a fold outside the purposeful encoding or the 'language system' of the representation, often (as is the case with the *punctum*, discussed in chapter 2) expressed in supplementary signifiers and contextual details that are extraneous to the consciously or methodically built narrative of the plot.[43] However, the notion of a third meaning is perhaps better understood by going back even further to the incongruous juxtapositions of Surrealism, described by Max Ernst as 'the chance meeting of two distant realities on an unfamiliar plane' which throw up a third reality. This third reality invoked by Ernst equates neatly with Huyghe's elusive third memory, which sits between the simulated reality of Lumet's film and the remembered and re-enacted reality of Wojtowicz' actual experience. In effect, the third memory of *The Third Memory* emerges only through the juxtaposition of two different memories, in what Huyghe refers to (in a close paraphrase of Barthes) as the 'fold' between them.[44] This in-between memory (or reality) then provides a place (or plane) that the viewer can inhabit and actualise. And, following Ernst, it opens up a 'space' that prompts new associations and new meanings, a 'space' that could be seen as the meeting of memory and imagination.

This 'space' that produces the third memory in *The Third Memory* is nevertheless contingent on the specific relationship and discrepancies between the two memories depicted on-screen. And, 'asked' to compare and contrast the two re-enactments, the viewer is left in a critical position, faced with questions concerning the nature of representation itself and the hold that particular forms such as film have on the culture. The effects of lens-based media have been a concern for cultural theorists for some time, enunciated in Situationist Guy Debord's critique of capitalism and the consumer society in *Society of the Spectacle* (1967), but preceded by earlier allegations of the stultifying or alienating effects of the mass media and the entertainment industries offered by Theodor Adorno and Max Horkheimer in *The Dialectic of Enlightenment* (1947).[45] However, it is French cultural theorist Jean Baudrillard who has directed most attention to the ubiquity of lens-based or electronic images in contemporary society. For Baudrillard, the media have formed a self-sufficient, self-governing, self-cannibalising world that no longer has an obligation to the real. This image world is caught in a trap where it is impossible to isolate the process of simulation and just as impossible to 'prove the real', so that the only hope for a recovery of the 'real' lies in iconoclasm.[46] It could be said that Huyghe achieves iconoclasm with *The Third Memory* when he exposes the

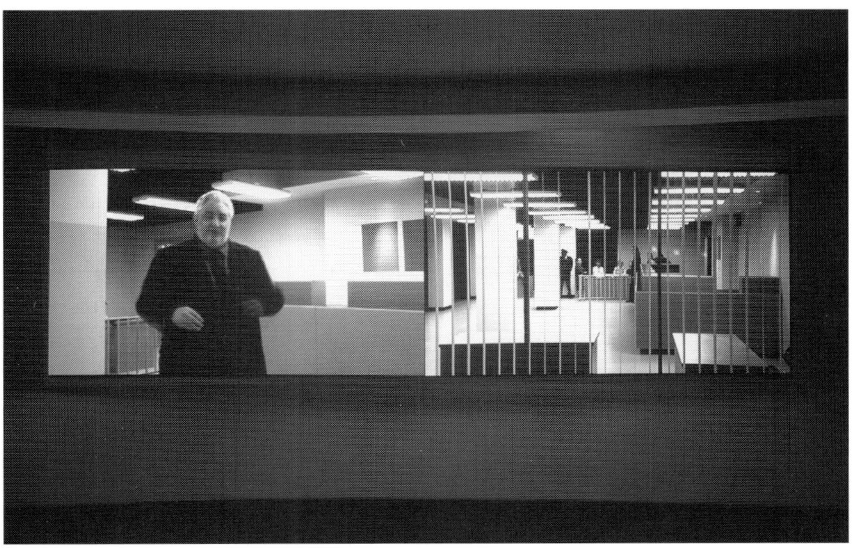

Figure 21: Pierre Huyghe, *The Third Memory*, 1999. Two-channel video and sound installation, 00:09:32. Dimensions variable. Solomon Guggenheim Museum, New York. Gift, the Bohen Foundation, 2001. Photograph by Ellen Labenski © The Solomon Guggenheim Foundation.

artifice of *Dog Day Afternoon* by screening it alongside Wojtowicz' re-enactment of the film, in which 'the subject represented – or figured – is invited to take back his place at the very heart of the spectacular machinery that has disposed him of his own identity... [A]n invitation to comment on his own gestures and deeds, to reappropriate them, to speak up once again, to regain his own image.'[47]

Ultimately, *The Third Memory* poses sombre questions concerning the mediatisation of past events that centre on the relationship of past events to cinematic representation, with all its association with visual pleasure and voyeurism, to a tragic lived experience (the other bank robber died, those present suffered a prolonged period of trauma and Wojtowicz failed in his mission to obtain money to pay for his partner's sex change). By contrast, Huyghe's inauguration and enactment (rather than re-enactment) of an American small-town celebratory festival presents its narrative in more straightforward terms and is light with the amateur charm of the occasion. *Streamside Day* (2003) is the name given to the event that Huyghe staged in Streamside Knolls, a new village created by estate agents in upstate New York on the River Hudson. The celebration created by Huyghe was filmed and shown, in the first instance, as an artwork with an interactive festive opening night at the Dia Foundation in New York, under the name of *Streamside Day Follies*. Informed on the one hand by the notion of conviviality that is central to relational aesthetics, *Streamside Day* was also conceived in relation to theories and experiments in utopian societies, such as Charles Fourier's (1772–1837) *Phalanstères*, self-sufficient communities organised on cooperative principles.[48] Significantly, Fourier influenced the founding of several such communities in the United States in the nineteenth century, such as la Reunion in Dallas (1855–c. 1860) and the North American Phalanx (1841–1856), which can be seen as the predecessors of the present-day community town of Celebration in Florida (founded in 1994), a Disneyfied, middle-American travesty of the earlier experiments.

To me, there is a strong sense of nostalgia for the ideals that underpinned these historical communities in Huyghe's choice of Streamside Knolls for the location of his 'celebration', which he explains as follows:

> And I was sure about another thing: with this community, they were coming to this specific place because of nature, an attraction to something like that old, old American idea of the wilderness. *Streamside Day Follies* wasn't really about the new home developments; it wasn't Dan Graham's Homes for America (1966–67). The community here was attracted to ideas of ecology, ecotourism, environmental issues. They were interested in going backward – it was in a sense postmodern. The homes in *Streamside Day Follies* were being

> advertised as 'postmodern housing.' It was about going back to the past, tradition, nature, animals – ways of life from the past.[49]

In staging a celebratory day for the village, Huyghe invented an event which inaugurated a sense of tradition, a sense of collective memory that invoked the past almost by virtue of its connotations, as Huyghe further comments:

> A celebration is supposed to be something that we have in common, that we share, and that we celebrate because of a common basis. It is like a monument. But unlike a monument, an event can be renegotiated each time it is repeated, although this is rarely the case. Mainly, planting a custom is about setting up a stable repetition. It is a marketing strategy, and all you need is to fill the year with traditions, to create a permanent celebration.[50]

To stretch this understanding of celebration as renewable to its logical conclusion, it is both plausible and possible to organise a new celebratory event without actually having something specific to commemorate. This view is corroborated by Paul Connerton in *How Societies Remember* (1989), in which he notes that, when a social group makes a concerted effort to begin with a wholly new start, the new beginning will inevitably contain an element of recollection. Experiences, however new, are always founded in predispositions and prior contexts so that the new experience is, in effect, an 'organised body of expectations based on recollection'.[51] Drawing from social scientist Maurice Halbwachs' seminal work on collective memory, Connerton further notes that these expectations are not necessarily conscious but a matter of 'habit memory', customs that are subliminally inbuilt in the culture rather than in personal histories or consciously acquired (cognitive) knowledge.[52] For me, this notion of 'habit memory' is at the heart of *Streamside Day*, which Huyghe appositely characterises as 'the celebration of a custom invented for a new place'.[53]

The film of *Streamside Day* was shown as part of *Celebration Park*, Huyghe's major solo exhibition at the Tate Modern in 2006. As the title suggests, the exhibition itself was organised in the spirit of a theme park, with individual works acting almost as sideshows and agents of spectacle within the whole.[54] *Streamside Day* occupied the last space in the exhibition, room 10, and it is no small token of the charm of the work that, after what seems like an epic journey through the other nine installations, the piece still held the attention of visitors (at least, that was the case when I saw it). The event encapsulates familiar aspects of community festivals – a parade, fancy dress, games, a speech, a rock band – producing the sort of quirky mix of the ceremonial and the homely that characterises such occasions. At the same time, however, there are moments and passages in the film that invoke wider cultural constructs, from the already mentioned mythic wilderness to that of an anthropomorphised nature. For instance, an ambivalent and slightly uneasy relationship between nature and culture is set when small girls are enigmatically filmed from behind in an unspoilt countryside setting – on a scale that suggests the Romantic notion of overwhelming nature, while also hinting at the fairy story caution of wandering from the path. This intrusion into nature is later counterbalanced by the opposite intrusion of a (Bambi-like) faun into the village and inside one of the houses, so that at different points in the film nature and culture are seen to overlap and interpenetrate. In addressing the relationship between nature and culture in these ways, *Streamside Day* becomes more than the instigation of a repeatable celebratory event in a newly formed community; it also addresses quite mighty themes, which have a long throw in history and which haunt the beliefs and rituals of many cultures.

The last piece by Huyghe that I want to discuss, *A Journey that Wasn't* (2005), is narrower and more specific in its thematic scope. Rather than inaugurate new memories through an enactment of 'habitual memory', as is the case with *Streamside Day*, Huyghe here stages an event which in spirit re-enacts the great voyages of discovery of the past (in a quest to discover a mythical albino penguin) – calling to mind Christopher Columbus' late fifteenth-century journey to the Americas, Captain James Cook's eighteenth-century exploration of the Antipodes and Robert Falcon Scott's early twentieth-century excursions into the Antarctic, to name the most obvious. Huyghe's project was commissioned collaboratively by the Public Art Fund in New York and the Whitney Museum of American Art in New York, with a view to producing a work that would initially occupy the public arena and subsequently be exhibited in the Whitney Biennial in 2005. The project began with an actual journey in February–March 2005, in which Huyghe and a number of other artists set sail for the Antarctic in search of the albino penguin, 'a unique solitary creature'. The journey then became the basis for a musical extravaganza performed on the ice rink in Central Park, held on 14 October 2005, footage of which, added to footage of the journey, made up the installation at the Whitney, also shown more recently in the Tate's *Celebration Park*.

Based on rumours of 'a singular white animal' that was thought to live on one of the islands that had emerged as a result of the shrinking of the ice mass of Antarctica, *A Journey that Wasn't* was made in the scientific spirit of verification (although it has to be said that the title of the work does cast doubt on its status as an actual event).[55] As such, it calls attention to the desire for factual knowledge that underpins conventional history and science and pays lip service to the type of memory that Connerton describes as cognitive, which is concerned with the remembrance of facts and data.[56] But, once again, there seems to be a strong element of nostalgia in this project, not only for the rare phenomenon of an undiscovered creature and uncharted territory but also for a time when the quest for knowledge was a grand adventure – a situation that contrasts vividly with the ready availability of knowledge and the saturation of information in today's technologically advanced societies. But, of course, Huyghe also uses the technologies of our time to present his adventure, which is received in virtual form through the film and in spectacular form through the musical. And, in doing so, he relegates the 'fact' of his journey and scientific origins of his quest to the realm of simulation and spectacle, in which fact and artifice either vie with or underpin one another. For example, the music composed for the spectacle in the park (by Huyghe's musical collaborator, Joshua Cody) translated sound data based on the island's topography into an instrumental score that lasted as long as it took to 'hear' the whole of the island.[57]

A Journey that Wasn't celebrates a thirst for knowledge and desire for the unknown, but it is also a reminder of the disappearing physical resources of the planet, reflecting the contradictions of a consumerist society that tries to live in conscience with the environment but continues a lifestyle trapped in spectacle and simulation. One response, as Huyghe shows, is in turning the language of spectacle into a critical medium and making spectacle itself a critical practice. This is also the case with the last work of re-enactment that I want to discuss in this chapter, Jeremy Deller's *The Battle of Orgreave* (2001), which commemorates a bitter confrontation that took place between police and miners in the miner's strike of 1984–1985. Anchored to a highly charged act of organised violence, *The Battle of Orgreave* is a re-enactment of a different order from Huyghe's performative projects, although similar issues of spectacle and artifice in relation to the 'real' obviously apply.

This is not to say that all Deller's work as a whole lacks the celebratory and socially benign characteristics of Huyghe's projects, but to note that it is often more pointed in its response to current political policies and their effects on small communities. As with Huyghe's projects, Deller's work is often centred on an event or performance, which is then preserved in film. Examples of performative and interactive works which demonstrate Deller's affinity to the traditional working classes in the United Kingdom are *Acid Brass* (1997) and *Unconvention* (1999). *Acid Brass* was an exercise in cultural fusion in which Deller persuaded the Manchester-based William Fairey Band to perform reworked acid house anthems. In doing this, he brought together two musical genres that represented different constituencies in the working classes of northern England, both of which sat firmly outside the more elitist cultural legacy of Thatcher's Britain, which was only seriously brought into question in 1998 when New Labour began to embrace notions of access and inclusion.[58] *Unconvention* addressed the politics of the day through an exhibition of source material used by the Welsh alternative rock band the

Manic Street Preachers (the Manics), which had been collected by Deller as part of his project *The Uses of Literacy* (1997). *Unconvention* was remarkable for the event that was staged for the opening weekend of the exhibition at the Cardiff Centre for Visual Arts, which specifically featured artworks that had inspired the Manics. True to the socialist leanings of the band, Deller invited contributions from the local community and organisations such as Amnesty International, The Samaritans, Reclaim our Rights, the Welsh Language Society and Blaengarw Workman's Hall to set up stalls. Again, this invokes Bourriaud's notions of encounter and conviviality, but this time with added socialist underpinning. In terms of performance, the leader of the National Union of Mineworkers, Arthur Scargill, gave a speech and the Pendyrus Male Choir sang in front of Andy Warhol's self-portrait.

But, while these projects demonstrate Deller's commitment to a politically aware, social engaged art, it is *The Battle of Orgreave* (fig. 22) that takes this involvement into the realm of commemoration. The work received the support of commissioning agency Artangel, after Deller's proposal had been selected through an open competition (one of around seven hundred submissions). Initially conceived as a performance, Artangel quickly decided to additionally realise the project as a documentary film, gaining further important financial support from Jan Younghusband of Channel 4 and collaboration from film director Mike Figgis.[59] But the collaboration in the production of *The Battle of Orgreave* extended beyond this, to include ex-miners who had taken part in the strike as well as members of various battle re-enactment societies from around the United Kingdom (there was only one professional actor, Simon Kirk, who played the part of Arthur Scargill). The project was based on Deller's own memories of newsreel portrayal of mass police intervention in the strike, which was so startling that '[i]t seemed a civil war was taking place all but in name'.[60] The image of mounted police in pursuit of strikers stayed with Deller, who subsequently researched the confrontation closely with a view to a commemorative re-enactment. The results of this research fed into Figgis' film and were collated as an anthology of statements, photographs and documents (including songs from the strike, one written by my children's paternal grandfather, folk singer Ian Campbell) entitled *The English Civil War Part II: Personal Accounts of the 1984–1985 Miners' Strike* (2001). These accounts and documents confirmed the deep social and political significance of the confrontation for Deller, who states in the foreword:

> It would not be an exaggeration to say that the strike, like a civil war, had a traumatically divisive effect at all levels of life in the UK. Families were torn apart because of divided loyalties, the union movement was split on its willingness to support the National Union of Mineworkers, the print media

> especially contributed to the polarisation of the arguments to the point where there appeared to be no space for a middle ground. So in all but name it became an ideological and industrial battle between two sections of British society.[61]

Through his research Deller was also able to expose the systematic way in which the Thatcher government went about breaking the unions in the United Kingdom by focusing on the coal industry. For instance, he reproduces a coercive letter to miners sent in June 1984 from Ian McGregor, chairman of the National Coal Board, entitled 'Your Future in Danger'. The letter threatened job losses and made its point literally in capital letters: 'AT THIS TIME THERE ARE BETWEEN 20 and 30 pits which are viable WHICH WILL BE IN DANGER OF NEVER REOPENING IF WE HAVE A LENGTHY STRIKE.'[62] This was followed intermittently by various notices which sought to bribe the miners back into work, for example 'Beat the Tax Man, Come Back Now' (February 1984) and 'Earn it or Lose it' (December 1984), which sported the outline of a Christmas tree filled with pound signs. Deller also reproduces the leaking of a shockingly cynical and pre-emptively confrontational government report drawn up six years before the strike by the then Shadow Secretary of Energy, Nicholas Ridley, entitled 'Appomattox or civil war?' (*The Economist*, 27 May 1978). Significantly, this report singles out the coal industry as a viable battle ground for 'the enemies of the Tory

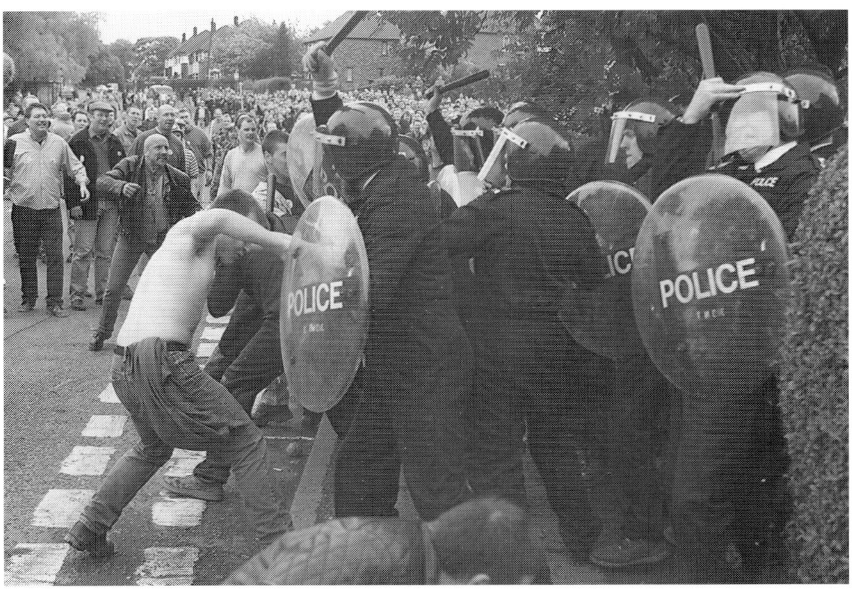

Figure 22: Jeremy Deller, *The Battle of Orgreave*, 2001. Commissioned and Produced by Artangel. Photograph by Martin Jenkinson.

government' and recommends plans to counter a future strike, including building or importing coal stocks and recruiting non-union lorry drivers to help move coal.[63]

As Deller's anthology shows, the South Yorkshire miners suffered considerable hardship to maintain their opposition to pit closure, but what is not so readily revealed in the retrospective accounts that are given is the extent to which the miners were traumatised by living through a long period of political and economic struggle and a violent confrontation which lasted four hours, which, as Deller notes, left the miners in the state of 'a defeated army returning home…where no one wants to talk about what happened'.[64] Indeed, Deller found that, although some miners have moved on, there were those who were stuck in the trauma and couldn't get over it, but who had found the re-enactment 'a healing experience'.[65] To me, this unexpectedly therapeutic effect ties in with the performative nature of the reconstruction, which Deller, using the terminology of re-enactment societies, describes as 'living history'. However, contrary to conventional re-enactments, which tend to focus on the technical aspects of reconstruction, Deller wanted to involve his participants, whether ex-miners or re-enactors, in a situation that made them part of an unfinished, messy history. Instead of the neutrality that meticulous attention to accuracy brings to conventional re-enactments, which are normally more distant in time, the re-enactors at Orgreave had to cooperate with original participants who they feared were hooligans or revolutionaries, and turn their approach to re-enactment into a critical and reflective practice.[66]

Jenny Thomas, a specialist in American studies, spent a number of years with battle re-enactors in the United States, finding it a largely closed world characterised by an obsession with accuracy and very little overt self-questioning or analysis on the part of the re-enactors. The question that she was left with at the end of her research was that of the value and cultural significance of re-enactment, or, more bluntly, what is it that re-enactors (largely men) get out of repeating the past in this way? On one level, Thomas felt that the activity could be psychoanalysed as the need for a space for a certain type of threatened masculinity and an opportunity for male bonding. But, on another and more interesting level that resonates with the re-enactment of *The Battle of Orgreave*, she drew a correlation between re-enactment and wider problems and conflicts in society: 'In the end, I felt that overcoming conflict was perhaps the strongest desire – a desire that contradicts the greater society that enshrines the ideals of peace and democracy but still carries on its own tradition of war.'[67] For me, similar contradictions inform Deller's re-enactment of *The Battle of Orgreave*, which might be further understood in relation to another of Thomas' observations (drawn from an essay by critic Christopher Hitchens), that the need to replay is connected to the inability to forgive those events in the past that transcend the norms of civilisation, such as war. According to Thomas, re-enactors feel that, while they cannot resolve war through forgiveness, neither should it to be relegated to a fantasy world (Hollywood, for instance). And, just as surely, it was not to be handed over to the official realm; rather, 'war was a subject to be personally appropriated, since reenactors feel their connection so acutely'.[68] Here, again, I see parallels in Deller's replaying of *The Battle of Orgreave*, which had been a cynical act of organised violence in the name of a so-called democratic government and which set up divisions and conflicts not only between co-workers but also in the wider society of secondary witnesses, such as Deller.

It might be said that turning re-enactment into a critical practice, in the way that Deller does, takes the unforgivable into a discursive arena in which it can be examined and debated beyond a closed cycle of repetition. I would also add, more generally, that the immediacy that characterises enactment and re-enactment is an important feature in terms of the memorisation of the events depicted. This makes enactment and re-enactment particularly effective strategies of remembrance, through which memories have the potential to become far more vivid by virtue of their experiential and relational nature. As noted earlier, the imprinting of memory through experience fits into a category known as episodic memory, which is often applied to autobiographic memory and which contrasts markedly with the methods of cognitive or semantic memorisation that underpin scholarly and institutionalised learning that have dominated the organisation and ordering of knowledge in the West. In my next and final chapter, I continue to make distinctions between types of memory by discussing the work of artists who have taken particular issue with conventional ways of managing knowledge, and draw yet more contrasts between received and alternative forms of knowledge and remembering.

6

The Ordering of Knowledge: Museums and Archives

What has become apparent in the previous five chapters of this book is not only the extent to which memory figures in contemporary art but also the sheer diversity of approaches that artists have found to address or incorporate the theme. So far this has involved examining ways in which artists have represented both personal and societal memories, recalling, retracing and giving a renewed presence to the past. In this chapter, I want to develop a rather different trajectory, which is to examine the ways in which artists have represented and critiqued methods through which knowledge and data, as aspects of memory, are ordered and stored by specialised and authoritative institutions, such as the museum and the archive. It almost goes without saying that memory is dependent on knowledge, whether in the form of cognition and re-cognition, understanding or information, and, indeed, would not be able to function without it.

I have already touched on the matter of the constructedness of knowledge in chapter 3 in which I discussed strategies that artists have developed in order to offer alternative or oppositional views of received history, noting that issues of ideology are constantly at stake. Invoking Pierre Nora's notion of *lieux de mémoire*, I noted that artworks not only serve as a location for the production and representation of memory but also that institutions such as the museum and gallery serve as locations in which already located memory in the form of artworks are often housed. As indicated at the end of that chapter, I will continue to examine the role played by such institutions, but not so much by means of museological theory (which will, nevertheless, be implicit in the discussion) but through the eyes and minds of artists who have taken the cultural politics of the museum as their subject matter. In addition to this, I develop an appraisal of the ways in which various artists have addressed the ordering of knowledge, a theme which has already been anticipated by my discussion of Huyghe's *A Journey that Wasn't*. A significant part of this appraisal will be to examine a tendency in contemporary art that critic and art historian Hal Foster has called 'an archival impulse'. In this exploration of archival techniques and strategies, Foster identifies a significant number of artists who make historical or found texts, documents or images or data a basis for their work.[1] Foster speaks of the artist as archivist as a new figure who follows that of the artist as curator, a figure who, to my mind, has not only made the processes of archiving central to his/her practice but has developed alternative kinds of ordering to those of the museum or traditional collection.[2]

An example of the artist as archivist has already surfaced in the previous chapter with Jeremy Deller's anthology *The English Civil War Part II: Personal Accounts of the 1984–1985 Miners' Strike*, an anthology of testimonies and documents related to the miners' strike in which Deller's archival interests and methodologies are vital. The same strategy of collecting personal accounts, documents and opinions also underpinned *Memory Bucket* (2003), a documentary-style film and collection of cultural paraphernalia such as souvenir T-shirts and bumper stickers. As Nato Thompson notes, the title of the work is the name of a patriotic shop that Deller visited in Hellotes, Texas, on his way to a Willie Nelson concert which 'serves as a repository for Texan Memory'.[3] *Memory Bucket* was the outcome of Deller's international artist residency at Artpace in San Antonio, Texas, and became part of the artist's winning entry for the 2004 Turner Prize. Typically, Deller was taken by the political significance of the location and the memories of those who had been affected by its political personalities and events. In his interviews, he focused on two emblematic places: President George W. Bush's home town of Crawford, and Waco, the scene of an infamous FBI siege that ended in the destruction of the Branch Davidian sect of the Seventh Day Adventist religious cult, filming, for example, a cult survivor, workers at a diner that Bush eats in from time to time and an Alamo tour guide. The result is a mixture of memory and testimony which highlights the political contradictions, prejudices and the national significance of a small town in the United States, the particularities and peculiarities of which are contrasted in an elegiac end sequence that shows an almost primeval event of three million bats emerging from a cave at dusk – the timelessness of nature as opposed to the temporality of human concerns.

While Deller takes a situation and explores its political implications in archive-based works such as *The Battle of Orgreave* and *Memory Bucket*, this is not the case with *Folk Archive* (1999–2005), which Deller and collaborator Alan Kane state to be a purely anthropological project. For Deller and Kane, the aim of the archive is twofold: to collect artefacts and document activities that have been produced by 'individuals that would not primarily consider themselves artists' and to 'engage in an optimistic journey of personal discovery'.[4] On the first count, Deller and Kane not only succeed in bringing together a range of popular activities and moving them into the arenas of high art such as the Tate Britain (as part of the Intelligence exhibition, 2000) and the Barbican (a stand-alone show, 2005), but, as art critic Waldemar Januszczak notes, have also extended the conventional scope of folk art.[5] As Januszczak further notes,

> [T]here is no fairground art here, no painted barges, no deliberately wooden toys made the way granddad made them. Instead, we get prison art about girls and psychosis, hot rod makeovers, banners waved by protesting sex workers, elaborate tattoos, cars with light shows and skull-shaped motorcycle helmets, impeccably painted to look real and determined, therefore, to beat death.[6]

So, while optimistic, Deller and Kane's journey was not utopian but confronted the differing mentalities and contexts behind the production of amateur or popular art, although, to be fair, the archive includes more familiar examples, such as flower arranging and trade union banners. In constructing what I would call an archive of the people, Deller and Kane, on the second count, present the business of archiving as a live practice that eschews the purported disinterest of institutionalised archiving practices. Typical of Deller's approach, the concern here is to connect with people in their social or political situations so that the archive serves as the material evidence of that connection, not merely as a collection of objects that are loosely tied together under the rubric of 'folk art'. This refashioning of archival practices comes back to the central questions of this chapter, which are concerned with how knowledge has been perceived and constructed through the museum and the archive and how contemporary artists have offered critiques and/or alternative models. Deller and Kane's *Folk Archive* is one of the more recent of these alternative models, which, as will now be seen, have a history in contemporary art that goes back to the 1960s.

A seminal example is to be found in the work of Belgian artist Marcel Broodthaers (1924–1976), who became a leading influence in contemporary art's critique of the museum when he created a parody of museum practices with his *Museum of Modern Art: Department of Eagles (Musée d'Art Modern: Départément des Aigles)* (1968), recently given tribute by British artist Tacita Dean (*Homage to Marcel Broodthaers*, 2002). Shown in his own home in Brussels, Broodthaers' *Museum of Modern Art: Department of Eagles* was one of several anti-institutional gestures aimed at galleries and museums that were made in the late 1950s and 1960s (others included Yves Klein's empty gallery space *Vide* (1958), Daniel Buren's *Sealed Gallery* (1968), in which the gallery door was glued shut with one of his characteristic striped canvases, and Christos' project for a wrapped museum (1969).[7] But Broodthaers' project involved more than the disabling of the gallery space; it developed a critique of traditional museum practices of display and classification. This he managed with supreme irony and characteristic wit, as is indicated by the title of the work, which is absurd and contradictory – what museum of modern art has ever had a department of eagles? This surely alludes to the classificatory system of natural history museums rather than the chronological model set by Alfred Barr (1902–1981) in 1929 at the Museum of Modern Art in New York, or the far more recent decision by the Tate Modern in London to adopt a thematic approach to their displays.[8]

The absurdity of a title such as *Museum of Modern Art: Department of Eagles* reflects a general approach that permeates much of Broodthaers' work and harks back to its origins in Surrealism, which is the setting of a rebus or riddle. This approach reflects not only Broodthaers' preoccupation with the ways in which art is framed by the ideologies and agendas of institutions but also with the institutionalistion of knowledge itself, as can be seen in many of his graphic works, which similarly highlight the absurdity and rigidity of classificatory systems. Lithographs such as *Les Animaux de la Ferme* (1974) or *Citron-Citröen* (1974) (fig. 23) debunk educational charts which attempt to define species of animal or vegetable. In the first case, the chart shows varieties of cattle, whose breed types have been changed to the names of car models. The second is an adaptation of an illustration of types of fish, into which the typographic legend *Citron-Citröen* has been incorporated in a band at the bottom of the image. The pun is obvious the sound of the French for 'lemon' being phonetically close to that of the car make, but the riddle remains: what has a lemon – or a car, for that matter – to do with the classification of fish? For Broodthaers, the rebus undermined the notion that knowledge is categorical, signalled the dangers of categorising knowledge and constituted a vital act of decoding (*déciffrage*) in the dismantling and questioning of received meanings.[9] Works such as *Les Animaux de la Ferme* and *Citron-Citröen* also implicitly question notions of how we learn to understand the world and the sort of knowledge that we are expected to retain through cognitive memory.

The Museum of Modern Art: Department of Eagles was developed in a number of installations between 1968 and its official demise (marked by a formal speech) in the 1972 Documenta.[10] The first was perhaps the most radical gesture, as it took the 'museum' right away from the institution and into the studio at Broodthaers' house at 30 Rue de la Pepinière, Brussels. This anti-institutional gesture had been prompted by his involvement with the occupation of the Palais de Beaux Arts in Brussels in May 1968, part of the wave of counter-cultural or oppositional protests that swept Europe and the United States in that year and, more specifically, a protest against the control that Belgian institutions exerted over culture.[11] Rather than mimic the layout of a museum, the installation at Rue de la Pepinière called attention to the

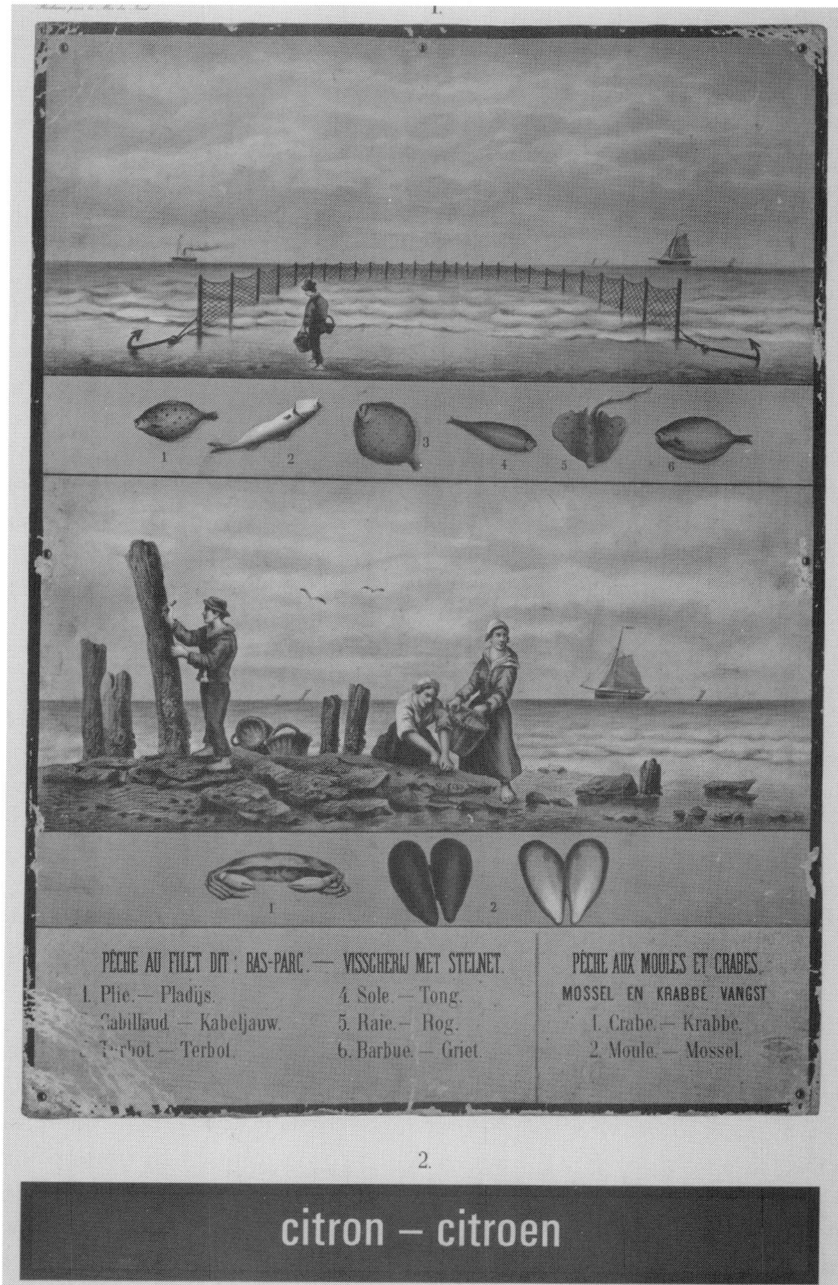

Figure 23: Marcel Broodthaers, *Citron-Citroën*, 1974. Lithograph and screenprint on paper image: 1048 x 664 mm, Collection: Tate Modern, purchased 1977. Copyright © DACS 2007.

mechanics of exhibition installation, displaying empty shipping crates, postcards of nineteenth-century 'masterpieces' and a ladder left leaning against a wall. The 'givenness' in the way that the artworks or objects are placed in museums was both undermined and underlined, as was the hype that surrounds the display of artworks. The ceremonial rituals of an opening night were mimicked, for instance, with a speech by Johannes Cladders, director of the Städtisches Museum in Mönchengladbach, and a buffet, all for something that Broodthaers described as a 'a heap of nothing' (*un tas de néant*).[12] Moreover, as historian of contemporary visual arts Douglas Crimp has noted, there is additional significance in Broodthaers' focus on the nineteenth century. As Crimp points out, 'It was in the early nineteenth century that the "romantic disposition", to which Broodthaers constantly points as the source to contemporary attitudes towards culture, took hold of art and provided it with an always ready alibi for its alienation. And it was at the same time that the museum arose to institutionalise that alibi.'[13]

Embedded in all this was Broodthaers' concern for the ways in which cultural objects and symbols are ordered in displays which frequently ignore not only their own historical and cultural specificity but also the historical and cultural specificity of the context in which they are shown. This critique was developed in more detail in the 1972 installation, which was constructed as a 'section de figures', and dedicated to the eagle as a cultural symbol that has been deployed in numerous contexts with numerous associations in history. But, rather than formulate a cultural history of eagle symbolism and its connotations, Broodthaers used the eagle as a vehicle to demonstrate the instability of cultural emblems. As Rainer Borgemeister notes, the eagle was already a symbolically overinvested figure and an ideal motif for the point that Broodthaers wanted to make.[14] Objects, documents and pictures from different periods in history that represented or bore images of eagles (including a suit of armour donated by the Städtische, Kunsthalle in Dusseldorf) were gathered together from all over the world to make up a display that had no classificatory coherence – in which objects from different times and contexts were placed anarchically alongside one another.[15] But one thing was made repeatedly clear in the labelling of each piece, which read 'This is not a work of art', a reference not only to René Magritte's *La Trahison des Images* (1929), which famously shows an image of a pipe accompanied by the legend 'this is not a pipe' (ceci n'est pas une pipe), but also to Marcel Duchamp, who destabilised the authority of 'juries and schools' by introducing the found object as a work of art.[16] The objects in the Museum of Modern Art were denied their potential status as art objects, with the labelling, according to Broodthaers, serving to disrupt 'the narcissistic projection' of the viewer onto the object of contemplation – another feature of the hype that is built around objects that are designated as art.[17]

Classification and the ordering of knowledge are also central preoccupations for American artist Mark Dion (born 1961), whose work is reminiscent of that of Broodthaers. There is common ground, for instance, in the way that Dion singles out the natural history museum as a 'very unself-critical site of the production of truth', and in the way that certain works expose or parody the hidden procedures behind the display.[18] *Ursus Maritimus* (1995), for example, is an installation which, as Carolyn Christov-Bakargiev puts it, 'is a taxonomic piece about taxonomy' – that of bears and their habitat.[19] The installation consists of a stuffed polar bear resting in an ironically *au naturel* pose on a packing case in the centre of the gallery, the walls of which display photographs of bears that are usually displayed in natural history, science and hunting museums around the world.[20] But, while the sense and atmosphere of the museum are initially conjured up, this effect is soon undercut by the fact that the bear remains on its packing case (a reminder of a prehistory of its being hunted and becoming a cultural commodity) and by the fact that the top surface of the packing case is covered in tar which seeps up into the bear's fur (bringing dual connotations: of transportation (tarmac) and of being trapped). Like Broodthaers, Dion makes us aware that, while the traditional, 'factual', displays of museums add to our general knowledge bank, they are not as innocent and plain-speaking as they pretend to be. Dion's signalling of museums' attachment to data and documentation can also be seen as a reminder of the limitations of cognitive memory, which comprehends facts and data but does not necessarily do so reflexively.

Dion employs a number of strategies in his interrogation of the ways in which natural history is investigated and represented, harking back in many cases to historical practices such as the scientific expedition. For me, there is a similar appreciation for the hands-on adventure of it all to that noted in relation to Huyghe's *A Journey that Wasn't*, coupled with a knowingness of its status as a form of cultural performativity that easily translates into fiction. For instance, Dion shows this awareness by co-opting Mickey Mouse into his installations on the themes of animal classification and extinction. To do this, he creates a hybrid character, Mickey Cuvier, a fusion of the French zoologist Baron Georges Cuvier (1769–1832) and Mickey Mouse. This character was central to a number of speaking installations, including *The Desks of Mickey Cuvier* (1990), which finds Mickey at work among the bureaucratic trappings of the expedition, providing a reference also to Baron Cuvier's way of working between eleven desks in his 'studio', each separately furnished with writing equipment, books and a bell.[21] At the crux of this fusion of zoologist and cartoon character is the issue of turning nature into culture and the way that both provide 'raw material for those coercive tidy paradigms that Disney (man and corporation) would impose on the world's past, present, and future'.[22]

Also at issue, then, is the question of who controls the knowledge to be passed on from generation to generation, or who is authorised to do it – a concern which is central to *The Delirium of Alfred Russel Wallace* (1994). This piece 'recreates' the expeditionary campsite of natural scientist Alfred Russel Wallace (1823–1913), who proposed a theory of natural selection slightly in advance of his contemporary, Charles Darwin (1809–1882). Yet, as Helen Molesworth observes, it is Darwin who has been remembered as the originator of these ideas rather than Wallace. For Molesworth, this lack of recognition can be attributed to the different ways in which the two men gained their insights into natural selection, Darwin labouring methodically over his research in a dedicated and analytical manner, as opposed to Wallace, who received his almost as a flash of inspiration while suffering from malaria in the Ternate jungle.[23] Dion's installation recreates some of the hallucinatory effect of the fever by replacing Wallace with a bespectacled fox in a hammock accompanied by a simulated rendering of Wallace's fevered ramblings. But what is at stake here is more than a matter of who owns the theory, or even the ownership of knowledge in general; it is also a matter of types of knowledge, which, for me, invokes similar issues concerning the ways in which knowledge is memorised. As Molesworth suggests, it seems that Darwin gains the authority because of his rigorous methodologies, which clearly reflected the work ethos of the nineteenth century, while Wallace's delirious insight could offer no such back-up.[24] Although not uninformed (Wallace conjures up Thomas Malthus' work on the principles of population in his autobiography as part of his hallucination), Wallace's insight was intuitive rather than the result of disciplined scholarship – running contrary to the notion of evidence that underpins conventional scholarship. In paying homage to Wallace, Dion contributes to debates over the sanctity of knowledge, but also reminds us that there is not only more than one way of knowing but more than one way of remembering knowledge. In producing his insight, Wallace reconstituted his existing knowledge (re-membered it) spontaneously in a dream-like state, and was prompted to do so by the objects that surrounded him in his fever, including the copy of Malthus' *An Essay on the Principle of Population* (1798).

In addition to reconstructing scenarios of museum display or expeditionary research and fieldwork, Dion has also retrieved the past directly through a number of internationally located archaeological digs in order to stage his own scenario of classification and display.[25] *Tate Thames Dig* (1999) (fig. 24) typifies these works and their division into three components: the dig, the cleaning and classification of the findings and their formal display (in the case of the *Tate Thames Dig*, in a large, purpose-built cabinet, in the style of traditional museum cabinets). In other words, Dion's digs appear to follow archaeological practice, but, like his installations, are parodies of these practices – in the case of *Tate Thames Dig*, a parody that is part process art, part performance art and part installation art. In turning archaeology into an aesthetic practice in this way, Dion, like Broodthaers with his parody of the museum and Huyghe and Deller with their enactments and re-enactments, again opens a critical gap between an original event and its simulation, although in this case it is only the presentation of the work in the context of the Tate Gallery that makes it readily distinguishable from a professional archaeological dig.[26] But the fact that the artwork is almost identical with a scholarly based archaeological dig also reveals something about archaeology as a way of connecting with the past, which, as professional archaeologist Colin Renfrew notes, is characterised by an immediacy of contact with its material remains.[27] In other words, there is a difference between scholarly reconstructions of history and the uncovering of history through its artefacts, which, to me, now invokes the notions of reliquaries and memento mori and the psychological as much as the academic hold that objects from the past have over us, no matter how anonymous.

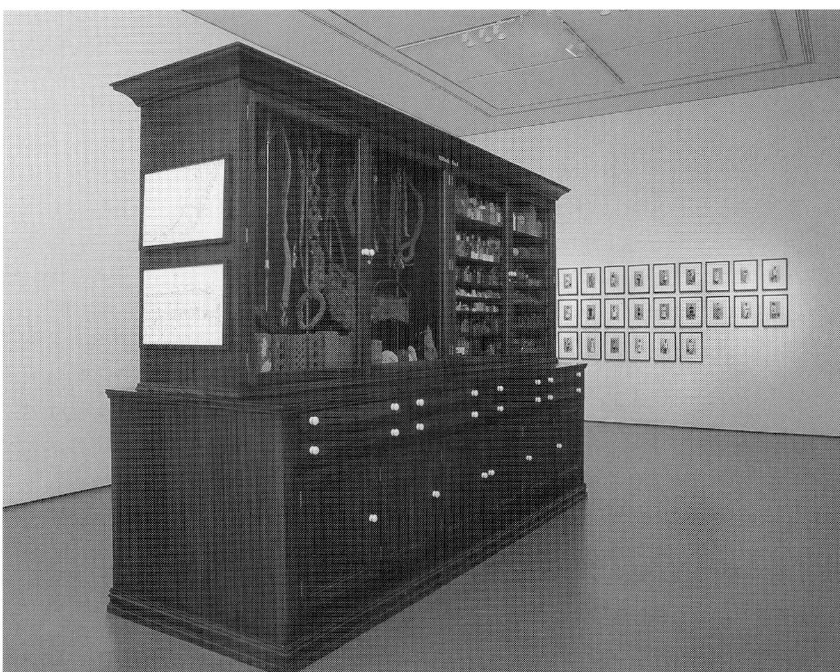

Figure 24: Mark Dion, *Tate Thames Dig*, 1999. Mixed media installation unconfirmed: 2660 x 3700 x 1260 mm. Collection Tate Modern, purchased with assistance from private benefactors 2000. Copyright © Mark Dion.

As with that of Broodthaers and Dion, the work of US-born, UK-based artist Susan Hiller (born 1940) is informed by the ways in which knowledge is constructed and transmitted, but it differs in that there is more attention paid to the development of alternative methods of knowing and remembering and less direct critique of institutional practices. After training in anthropology Hiller began to practise art in the early 1970s, initially making paintings, which soon turned into a deconstruction of the conventions of painting. These early deconstructionist pieces are significant as they introduce ongoing themes of collection and collation and display of found materials, objects and images that resurface in later works, such as *From the Freud Museum* (1991–1996 fig. 25). In these early works, Hiller undermined notions of the preciousness of the medium by transforming her own work in ways that made a significant contribution to the questioning of the medium that was taking place at that time in feminist and Conceptual art. As is well known, these movements posed vital questions about what sort of content and what sort of understanding was to be relayed in the name of art, and how this content and understanding was to be relayed.

In works such as *Collected Works* (1968–1972), *Hand Grenades* (1969–1972) and *Measure for Measure* (begun 1973), Hiller takes the irreversible step of burning her own paintings and collecting the ashes in glass containers reminiscent of the chemistry laboratory (a test tube, glass jars with stoppers and burettes, respectively). *Collected Works* is a particularly intriguing piece, providing a complete oeuvre in the form of trace evidence in a single test tube, a rebus in the manner of Broodthaers, but at the same time an indexical reminder of their previous existence (and then, possibly, a reliquary). Hiller speaks of these works as 'containers that measure and contain what can't be contained'.[28] In her choice of laboratory containers, Hiller points to the empirical validation of knowledge espoused by conventional science, but she also suggests limits to the validity of an empirical approach when she submits the paintings to an irreversible process of combustion. What is left is not the sort of new knowledge that science would hope to produce but the sort of reflexive understanding that the German philosopher Kant ushered in when he spoke of our transcendental ability to conceive of not being able to conceive as a form of self-knowledge.[29] While on one level, then, the traditional divide between empirical and transcendental knowledge is tested by the rebus of *Collected Works*, the piece also represents the turn to self-reflexive practices which dwell on the meaning of art, found in the work of Conceptual artists at the time (for instance, Joseph Kosuth's *Titled (Art as Idea as Idea)* (1967) which questions the material aesthetics of the art object or Lawrence Weiner's *Statement of Intent* (1969), which queries the role of artist and viewer in the production of a work of art').

Measure for Measure addresses similar issues concerning the limits of knowledge by a literal device of containment (the burette) but repeats the key gesture of immolation annually, so that the work has built up into a series, reminiscent of the serial works of Minimalists such as Sol LeWitt and Donald Judd. This format of containment and repetition underpins another series, *Painting Blocks* (1974–1978), in which Hiller cut her paintings up into rectangles and sewed them together to form blocks, canvas side facing out, with dimensions and date stencilled on. Hiller again obscures and breaks down their original content, the effect of which is to both mystify and demystify painting, and perhaps also to call attention to the mystification of painting by concealing the remaining content. However, further to these acts of deconstruction, who speaks, how things are spoken and what is spoken were to become recurrent themes in Hiller's work using automatic writing in the 1970s and 1980s. In these works, Hiller gives play to voices and forms of address that often go unheeded by virtue of their origin in altered states of consciousness. The automatic writing works do not transmit cohesive, rational thoughts, although the visions they present and statements they make often have a dream-like lucidity. Instead, their messages seem to appear as a result either of involuntary memory or extrasensory perception – as messages from the unconscious and, in some cases, messages that are received from other realities as well as the realities of others.

Hiller embarked on this trajectory with *Sisters of Menon* (1972–1979). The work derived from a visit to a small village in France, when she felt and followed an urge to write spontaneously and unpredictably, her hand guided by 'sisters', who, on the one hand, Hiller identifies as members of a generic sisterhood who were speaking to her as 'a kind of female sensibility or entity'.[30] On the other hand, Hiller suggests that the voices might be those of her divided self. So, while an altered state of consciousness is transmitted, it is not necessarily plucked from the ether but from her own store of unconscious knowledge or memory – the point being that this knowledge is inspired and visionary and of an order that defies sense and logic in favour of intuition and divination. Moreover, as Rosemary Betterton notes, the openness of the handwritten texts allows the viewer to 'move in and out of the work and take up other positions, even perhaps to lose her own sense of boundaries'.[31] In other words, it is not just the type of knowledge and recall that is at issue in Hiller's work but also the ways in which knowledge and recall are bounded or contained – as Hiller states, 'My "self" is a locus for thoughts, feelings, sensations, but not an impermeable, corporeal boundary. I AM NOT A CONTAINER…'[32] Just as Hiller refuses rational discourse, so she refuses the notions of regulated and contained knowledge that accompanies it.

The word 'locus' of course, returns us to Nora's notion of *lieux de mémoire* and prompts me to observe that, however esoteric the automatic writing pieces may seem, they are nevertheless a means of cognition and recognition. The writings become documents – visible records or mementos of a psychical process, offered up not only for mutually intuitive communication but also for critical reflection. In an interview with Rosika Parker in 1983, Hiller stated that her work is always dialectical and that she tries to 'define and then resolve contradictions, formal, art-historical, personal etc.', noting also that her work, 'while distrusting the whole notion of the rational and the objective, had the look of the rational'. However, the documentary status of the writing is frequently held in abeyance by the alterations that are made to the original scripts when they are enlarged and reformatted, as in *The Sisters of Menon*, or filmed or photographed, as in the photo booth works. Here Hiller created a series of self-portraits using photo booths as her medium, in which the face, parts of the face, hands and feet were presented in close-up and the surface of the image covered in automatic writing. As the series progressed, the images were scaled up to near life-size and formatted within cross-shaped frames, reminiscent of the white cross that separates and formats the four photo booth images.[33] Hiller maintains that the choice of a cruciform setting for the images was tied to her preference for non-hierarchical forms such as the grid, but has also noted that the photo booth reminds her of 'a confession booth with the camera as silent witness'. As with the autobiographical works discussed in chapter 1, the conventions of self-representation are stretched, this time rendering the sitter in terms of bodily emanations, captured in writing or through photography – a psychical as much as a physical process.

Psychical traces and extrasensory perception also underpin *Magic Lantern* (1987), in which overlapping circles of coloured light are projected onto a screen accompanied by a soundtrack that includes Hiller's own voice arranged polyphonically and recordings made by Latvian scientist Konstantin Raudive, claiming to represent the voices of the dead.[34] Here, Hiller embraces Raudive's belief that the sounds of the past are harboured in the material objects and environment in which they were produced, and the suggestion that rooms and objects are not only mises en scène of past events but embody psychical as well as physical traces of the past. But, while memory is figured through auditory traces and automatist forms of suggestion in *Magic Lantern*, conscious memory-work is additionally incorporated into *Belshazzar's Feast: The Writing on the Wall* (1983–1984) in dialectic between two types of recall and knowing. The idea for the piece had emerged from newspaper articles that Hiller had seen about people who saw ghost images on their televisions after transmission closedown. Shown in installation, whether on a single screen or a set of closely grouped TV monitors, the film is meant to function symbolically in much the same way as a traditional hearth, as a vehicle for reverie.[35] As such, the piece is made up of footage of flames originally taken on super-8 film at a bonfire, intercut periodically with shots of Rembrandt's painting *Belshazzar's Feast* (c. 1635).

Hiller therefore drew a parallel between the after-hours visions of television viewers with the biblical story of Belshazzar's feast, in which the king's meal is interrupted by the appearance of a hand which writes a warning message of impending doom – punishment for transgressing the law of God. Many of the television stories that were reported similarly contained premonitions or warnings from other worldly beings, messages which today tend to be treated suspiciously or derisively. In contrast, Hiller took the visions seriously, arguing that 'these incoherent insights at the margins of society and at the edge of consciousness stand as signs of what cannot be repressed or alienated, signs of that which is always and already destroying the kingdom of law'.[36] That eccentric ways of knowing are pitted against conformist ways of knowing is made evident in the soundtrack to the flames. This is made up of Hiller whispering the newspaper reports and singing improvisationally alongside the voice of her son, Gabriel, who has been asked to describe Rembrandt's painting and recite the biblical story from memory. A contrast is struck between the halting, rehearsed memory of the child and the flow of Hiller's ramblings and improvisations, which seems to suggest the limitations of received knowledge as opposed to the vast but more spectral knowledge that lies repressed in the unconscious.

Works such as *Magic Lantern* and *Belshazzar's Feast: The Writing on the Wall* reveal another aspect of Hiller's work that is relevant to the themes of this chapter, which is that she demonstrates the sort of archival impulse that Foster identifies by basing the content of her work on collected testimonies, documents, etc. Beyond this, however, particular connections can be made between Hiller's automatist methodologies and Jacques Derrida's understanding of the psyche as an archive, reached through a discussion of what he has called 'archive fever' in the work of Sigmund Freud. For Derrida, the archive is not just a place to which knowledge is consigned, with all the attendant problems of the institutionalisation of knowledge (who authorises, who decides on what system of classification is employed, etc.) but is also a general feature of our mental lives that can be questioned and examined through the work of Freud. Derrida uses Freud's topography of conscious to unconscious layering to demonstrate his argument that psychoanalysis is an archival practice as much as an excavation of repressed memory.[37] This topographic separation between the conscious mind and the reservoir of the unconscious is epitomised by the analogy Freud himself made to the mystic writing pad – the child's wax-covered writing pad on which thoughts are inscribed and then erased, in favour of new thoughts, while always leaving a vestige below the surface.[38] Derrida goes on to tie the notion of the unconscious as an archive to the notion of an 'archive drive', the kernel of his notion of 'archive fever' (*mal d'archive*) – that we all suffer from an 'archive sickness', a compulsion towards archiving.[39] For me, the connection between Hiller's call on the unconscious in her automatist pieces and Derrida's notion of psychoanalysis as a form of archiving comes through in Derrida's singling out of Freud's 1907 reading of Wilhelm Jensen's novel *Gradiva* as an example of 'archive desire', largely because it demonstrates Freud's incorporation of phantoms, ghosts or spectres into his explorations into the understanding of the human psyche.

While in Rome, the central character in *Gradiva*, Norbert Hanold, suffers a delusion in which he is haunted by the figure of a woman (Gradiva) that he has seen in an ancient relief in a museum of antiquities. To cut a long story short, the young woman in the relief, whose ghost Hanold believes he has actually spoken with, is a sublimation of his repressed sexual desire for his childhood friend Zoe, who shared exactly the same way of walking as Gradiva. The point that Derrida makes in relation to Freud's analysis of the story, and which applies so readily to Hiller, is that Freud recognises that 'there is a truth to delusion, a truth of insanity or hauntedness… Delusion or insanity, hauntedness is not only haunted by this or that ghost, Gradiva, for example, but by the spectre of the truth that has been thus repressed. The truth is spectral, and this is its part of truth which is irreducible by explanation.'[40] As Freud himself claims, there is a grain of truth in every delusion, which, because it is so deeply repressed, is likely to resurface in a distorted form – exactly what Hiller claims to be the case with the phantom TV stories she discovered. Hanold's delusion and the stories of other-wordly visitation that Hiller whispers become more than a matter of pitting rational against intuitive ways of knowing, voluntary memory against involuntary memory; they are representative of the complex mechanisms by which the mind copes with troublesome memories or troublesome knowledge and finds surrogate ways of expressing them.

So, while Hiller's automatist works fit neatly into this notion of the psyche as archive, she can also be seen as suffering from the more general condition of archive fever, as defined by Derrida. Hiller is a habitual collector of both artefacts and information that she uses as the basis for many of her artworks (broken pieces of Pueblo pottery, British seaside postcards, film footage and newspaper clips, to name but a few). This practice undoubtedly stems from her continued interest in anthropology and has culminated in a major work, *From the Freud Museum* (1991–1996) (figs 25 and 26) – aptly, given Derrida's Freudian understanding of the archive, a product of a residency at the Freud Museum in London. However, the result of this residency is, on the surface, a far more tangible and familiar type of archive than that just discussed and consists of personally collected items and images sorted into forty-four cardboard storage boxes (left open for the purposes of display) and arranged in two layers in a long vitrine. While on one level *From the Freud Museum* can be seen as part of a wider critique of classificatory museum practices exemplified already by Broodthaers' *Museum of Modern Art: Department of Eagles* and Dion's *Tate Thames Dig*, it is also very specific not only in the personal nature of the collection but in the personal response that Hiller makes to the context of the Freud Museum, which lent itself so appropriately to Hiller's concern with the unconscious.

As might be expected, Hiller was highly conscious of the setting in which she was working, seeing the process by which things were placed in relation to one another as similar to Freud's notion of a dream as a narrative with both hidden and manifest content.[41] Nonetheless, despite the thematic commonality of the structuring of dreams, Hiller sees Freud's collection of antiquarian artefacts as concentrated on the rare and valuable, and Freud himself as early modernist in his approach to collecting. In contrast, she perceives her own collection as postmodern, made up of 'fragments and ruins and discards, appropriations etc.'.[42] This distinction raises issues about the nature of collecting, which, in turn, has implications for the role that objects can be made to play in cultural and personal memories. For Hiller, these implications still fulfil the role of dreams, but also lead to the evocation of mortality and death: 'Just as we could say that the existence of our dream life is a continual memento mori and at the same time an approach to immortality, since dreaming seems to have nothing to do with the necessities of physical existence – so collecting may be the same kind of complex activity.'[43] Freud, as Hiller notes, kept his collection of ancient artefacts around him, so that his consulting room was 'basically a tomb, connected with a dead body or vanished

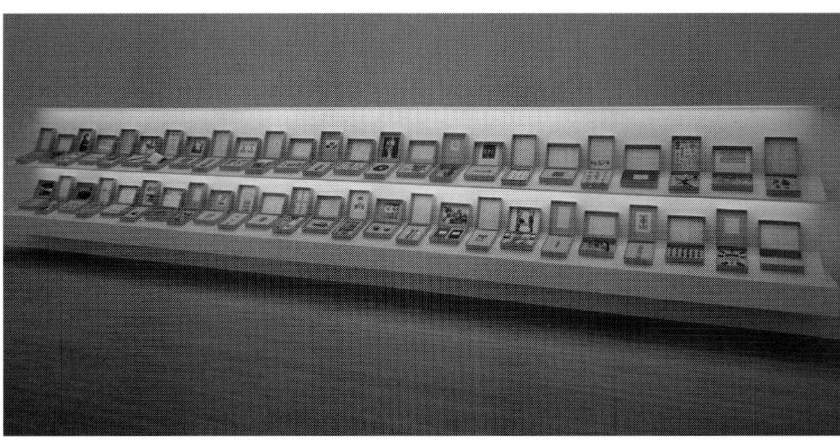

Figure 25: Susan Hiller, *From the Freud Museum*, 1991–1996. Mixed media installation, displayed: 2200 x 10000 x 600 mm. Collection Tate Modern. Purchased 1998. Copyright © Susan Hiller.

civilisation'. Hiller sees this connection with the past as a seeking of immortality and meaning through objects, and draws an analogy between the processes of collecting and Freud's view of psychoanalysis as a form of archaeology.[44]

Importantly, however, Hiller recognises that archaeology does not necessarily tell any truth but, like any narration, is a series of fictions in

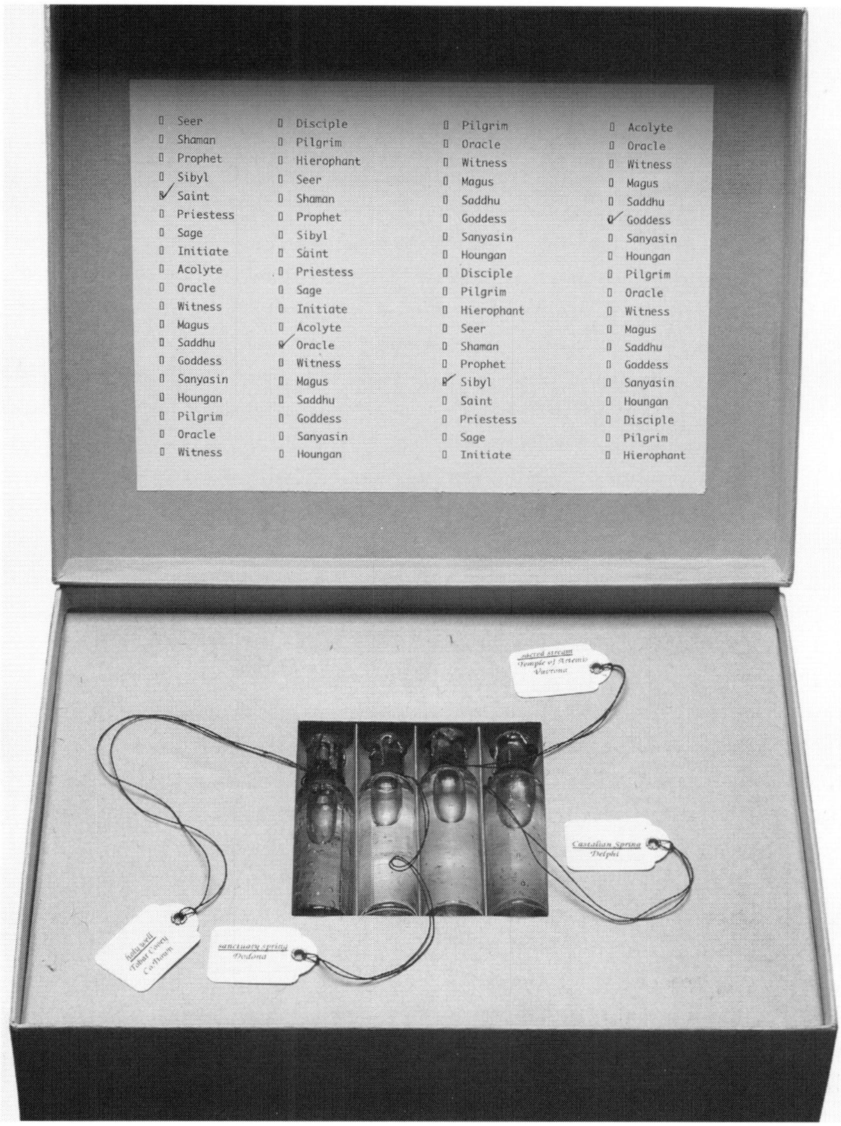

Figure 26: Susan Hiller, *From the Freud Museum*, 1991–1996. Detail, 'Sophia' Mixed media. Collection Tate Modern. Purchased 1998. Copyright © Susan Hiller.

which choices are made. In other words, she does not position herself as a neutral excavator of things but as someone who creates 'a discourse in which we could allow narratives of an archaeological nature to occur'.[45] This discourse, of course, is an intervention into the ready-made discourse of domesticity, professional practice and historicisation constituted by Freud's house functioning as a home, as a setting for his psychoanalytic practice and then as a museum. Hiller gives one of her boxes, *Cowgirl*, as an example of how such a layering of discourse is created. Here, two cow-shaped creamers are set inside the box as if on sales display while a photograph of Jenny Metcalf, a famous American outlaw, is set into the lid. Metcalf is holding a gun, which, with all its phallic connotations, was an irresistible Freudian pun for Hiller. Hiller notes that she had never heard a woman referred to derogatorily as a 'cow' before coming to England, and, for her, the box is about sexual insult and her reaction to it. The creamers also have sexual connotations, but as with so many other cultural artefacts, there is a pretended innocence which, for Hiller, is 'just a way of letting ourselves as a culture get away with quite a lot while pretending we don't know what we're saying'.[46] As Hiller also notes, putting these signifiers into the Freud Museum ('the house of the father') was a pleasing gesture for her.[47] It also chimes with Derrida's final take on Freud and the archive, which is that, ultimately, the father of psychoanalysis repeated the patriarchal logic of the archive that resides in the original and ancient sense of *arkheion*, the house of the superior magistrate in ancient Greece, the keeper of the law.[48]

In speaking of archive fever, Derrida is not only pointing to a general cultural tendency to mark or store experiences and events in a way that allows for some sort of perpetuation, he also indicates that this fever can become a pathological condition. As with fever, the word 'mal' in the original French title of the work can connote an illness or disorder as much as an intense drive, passion or obsession for collecting. For Derrida, Freud suffers from both a benign and a pathological form of archive fever, and in the latter 'he is not without his place, simultaneously, in the archive fever or disorder we are experiencing today, concerning its lightest symptoms or the great holocaust tragedies of our modern history and historiography: concerning all the detestable revisionisms as well as the most legitimate, necessary and courageous rewritings of history'.[49] While this returns directly to issues of historical approaches and methodologies already dealt with in chapters 3 and 4 of this book, it also opens up similar questions concerning the cultural politics of the archive which are, of course, always historically specific. Indeed, as Manuel Delanda notes (following Foucault), the objectification of knowledge and social regulation that archiving is now widely associated with developed in response to the rise of individualism that began in the late eighteenth century.[50] In other words, at the very time at which knowledge was being rigorously categorised by the scientists and naturalists that Dion refers us to, the archive also became a tool in the maintenance of institutional and governmental power and the control of the individual.

While this control is not total (witness the sometimes uneasy coexistence of freedom of information and data protection legislation in Western democracies), there is still a strong regulatory archival force in society (witness the ever-increasing amount of administration in our everyday lives mentioned at the start of chapter 1). However, as is already evident, this regulatory side to archiving is counterbalanced on one front at least by the artist as archivist, who, in the case of Deller, for instance, treats archiving as a way of connecting with and responding to real events and experiences. The 'archival' work done by artists is constructed outside the institution and is often at odds with the conformity of the institution. These alternative approaches to archiving can nevertheless be viewed as part of a humanist tradition in which the archive can be seen as a tool for the work of collective memory rather than mere data storage. As social scientist Arjun Appadurai suggests, the traditional humanist archive fits with the Cartesian duality of body and soul, as a corpus of knowledge or information that is animated by something less visible – usually the spirit of a people, the people or humanity in general.[51]

A distinction between a tradition of archives that are 'stiff and stable' and a tradition of 'flexible and unstable' archives that has existed in the flexible and unstable archives of oral culture has been observed by Joke Brouwer and Arjen Mulder. Brouwer and Mulder speak of more labyrinthine 'fuzzy logic' in the oral archive, to which they find a counterpart in the 'digital database'.[52] As these two authors note, hyperlinking has become so sophisticated that search engines can find a needle in a haystack, link information in unexpected ways and build patterns where there seemed to be only fragments.[53] By extension, the more elastic potentials of digital technology, such as random access, the speed of access, immersivity, interactivity and interconnectivity, have implications for the ways in which memory is produced or mediated in new-media art. For example, archiving and memory have been recurrent themes in the work of Hungarian-born new-media artist George Legrady (born 1950, now working in Santa Barbara), who has produced a number of interactive works that fit the notion of the archive as something which might be characterised as living and in a constant process of becoming rather than that which is 'stiff and stable'.

However, Legrady can be seen to have been suffering from archive fever (in its salutary form) even before he moved into interactive media. Several of his early photographic projects were predicated on the collecting of found objects and bringing a sense of order to them. For instance, Legrady gathered a number of ad hoc objects from the detritus of an empty real estate plot in

San Francisco for *Catalogue of Found Objects* (1975), photographed them and mounted the images on strips of computer printout paper, which were then placed side to side to form a grid. As Pierre Dessurault notes, the use of computer printout paper as a backdrop 'evokes electronic memory, which makes it possible to organise and process a body of information too great for the capacities of the human brain'.[54] Nonetheless, the information that Legrady gives on his website declares it to be a work of archaeological excavation that 'addresses the semiotics of objects and systems of classification'. In this approach, Legrady removes the objects from their historical specificity and juxtaposes them in ways that uncover perhaps more widely resonant subliminal meanings. For me, the 'classification' of these objects acts as a pretext (pre-text) for the suggestibility of the objects in their relationship to one another and to the paper on which they are mounted, a pretext for the sort of play of memory and imagination that electronic technology encourages and facilitates.

Legrady continued to explore ad hoc relationships between objects in other works that group objects together in grid formats, such as *Floating Objects* (1980), *Everyday Stories* (1979–1981) and *Still Lives* (1979–1983). In these, Legrady explores the narrative, even fictional, potential of objects – or, rather, of that of their photographic representation – which, for me, becomes more theatrical in its staging. For *Floating Objects*, the photographs were taken in situ (a building site) at night (evocatively) and caught in flight (Legrady has thrown them in the air). In *Still Lives*, Legrady uses both found and made objects to create disingenuously simple scenarios that rely on cultural as much as personal memory and narrative – there is, for instance, a burning of books, a game of snakes and ladders, and a dog (poodle) that is perhaps howling at the moon. But, alongside the impulse to collect, record and 'archive' images and texts that underpins these works, Legrady also demonstrates an anthropological impulse that goes back to his first major photographic project, *James Bay Cree Documentary* (1973), which records the everyday life of four Indian settlements in subarctic Canada, and is carried forward in *China Billboards Analysis* (1985), which documents the then contemporary lifestyle of Chinese citizens through the content and iconography of their billboards. This anthropological impulse also betrays an interest in socio-political relations that is manifest in Legrady's first major interactive work on memory, *An Anecdoted Archive from the Cold War* (1993) (fig. 27).

An Anecdoted Archive from the Cold War is a retrospectively built 'history' of Hungary during the Cold War. Legrady's parents had left Hungary in 1956, the year of the short-lived anti-Soviet revolution, when the artist was just six years old. So, while Legrady sees it as his 'particular hybridised history in relation to the Cold War', it is also an archive of diverse period material that has allowed him to produce memories of a time and place that he did not actually witness, as well as to recover memories of his parents' life in Hungary before they left for Canada, and, in this respect the work is another example of second-generation postmemory, as discussed in chapter 4.[55] Legrady chose to organise his virtual archive from the Cold War in a format borrowed from museums – specifically, the Worker's Movement Museum in Budapest. The 'visitor' to the archive is met with familiar orientation devices, such as an index of contents and a floor plan with thematically ordered rooms. For Legrady, this setting provides a recognisable trope that 'reminds us of the museum's cultural function, as a site of memory for the inscription of the social collective imagination and as a site of representation and power'.[56] But this is as far as the dependency on conventional museum practices goes. Legrady appropriates them only to subvert their fixity and didacticism, and, in making interactivity central to the installation, creates a space of greater play for the imagination.

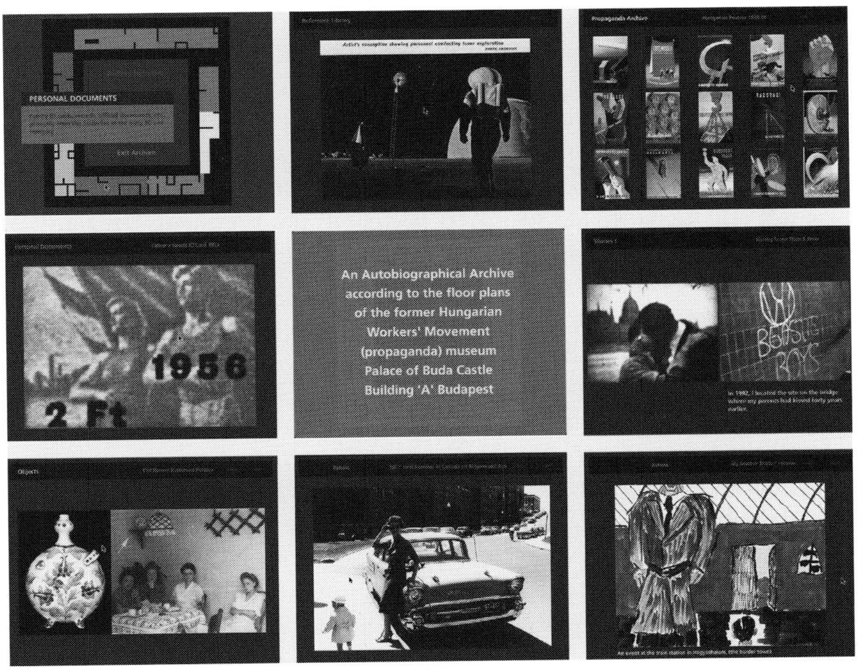

Figure 27: George Legrady, *An Anecdoted Archive from the Cold War*, 1993. An Autobiographical Archive according to the Floor Plans of the former Hungarian Worker's Movement (propaganda) Museum Palace of Buda Castle Building 'A' Budapest. Clockwise: Floorplan; Stocks Brochure Page; Hungarian Posters, 1944–1948; Kissing Scene 1948 (1992); The Border Train Station in Hegyshalom (painting by Miklo Legrady, artist's brother); Mom in Canada (First Summer in Canada, Ridgewood Ave) 1957; Old Flower Patterned Pottery and Breakfast, 1936; Father's Sports ID card, 1953. Copyright © George Legrady.

The flexibility and adaptability of digital technology is, therefore, crucial to Legrady's 'memory-work', allowing official versions of the Cold War in Hungary to be mixed freely with his own personal reminders or documents. But Legrady's archive also provides numerous aides-memoires which can be accessed randomly and connected in a non-sequential way to create variant narratives. Indeed, Legrady saw *An Anecdoted Archive from the Cold War* as an opportunity to explore the impact of non-linear media on narrative, not only raising questions about methods of storytelling but also of audience reading. The transference of authorship from the original content generator onto the interactive user has been one of the big claims concerning the paradigmatic shifts that digital technology has brought. Janet Murray has categorised this as a shift to 'procedural authorship', whereby the artist sets up a framework that encases a multiplicity of plots that can be developed in numerous and unexpected ways. So, while there is always an organising mind or author behind the project, agency is handed over to its participants and the work becomes a matter of shared authorship and, in Legrady's case, often a matter of creating what might be termed 'shared memories'.[57] In *An Anecdoted Archive from the Cold War*, this not only meant that the 'visitor' would participate in a continual structuring and restructuring of the archive, but 'walk away with a slightly different story from this Archive, situated according to their own ideological beliefs (family life, communist propaganda, pro-Western etc.)'.[58] Here, memory is not a quest for the authenticity of the past or the excavation of the past so much as a backward-looking exercise which is more about creating mutable and multiple perspectives through which the past can be experienced.

This trajectory is the opposite of that generated by the notion of *Nachträglichkeit* introduced in chapter 1, in which the unresolved past is brought to the surface to be reworked in the context of present circumstances. Legrady has no primary memory to excavate but forms a remembrance of his 'missed' heritage from the secondary sources that he gathered over a period of twenty years as an adult living in Canada and the United States, with a visiting relationship to Hungary. Moreover, the making of memory from the data that he has collected, although carried out by individual participants, is dependent upon being part of a social group with shared historical coordinates. As Maurice Halbwachs puts it, 'In order to remember, one must be capable of reasoning and comparing and of feeling in contact with a human society that can guarantee the integrity of our memory.'[59] Opened up to the unpredictable participation of others, Legrady's 'particular hybridised history' becomes shared hybridised memory which is in a continual process of becoming, or re-becoming – of integration and reintegration. Once again, it is the potential of digital technology that facilitates this process, which creates a web of multilinear and serendipitous interconnecting data. Comparing this sort of technology with that of the printed book, Florian Brody speaks of a return to a memory space akin to that of preliterate societies, in which memory existed solely in the mind – a return which he feels also signals the emergence of a new memory culture.[60]

This new memory culture might simply be called 'emergent memory', a term that Legrady has employed to describe the effect of his digital installation *Pockets Full of Memories* (2001), and, by extension, its technologically upgraded version, *Pockets Full of Memories II* (2003–2006). These works are, again, essentially exercises in archiving, this time the collection and organisation of a random selection of objects (including body parts) offered up for scanning by visitors to the installation, held initially at the Pompidou Centre in Paris. Although three thousand objects were scanned in this first installation, broad typologies and parameters were automatically established by the fact that the objects were all portable and carried within the context of the museum visit, and by the fact that the scanner would take objects only up to a certain size. In the spirit of conventional archiving, all the objects were documented by the description given by the owner on a touch-screen questionnaire, which also became the basis for their classification. As with *An Anecdoted Archive from the Cold War*, order is not relinquished but configured in a hybrid fashion, in this case by means of the Kohonen self-organising map algorithm, a program which imitates the neural networking of the brain to distinguish and map out patterns in high-density data.[61] The mapping of objects underwent continuous organisation and reorganisation until the end of the exhibition, when a final map was produced from all the objects scanned throughout the entirety of the exhibition. The resulting organisation of data was not predictable; as Legrady puts it, 'This phenomenon is called emergence as the order is not determined beforehand but emerges through the large number of local interactions on the map. This is why the system can be called "self-organising".'[62]

For me, emergent memory of this sort is a reminder of two things: firstly, that, although memory is predicated on the past, it is always constructed in the present; and, secondly, that memory is a highly and unstable changeable phenomenon. But, as has been seen throughout this book, memory is necessary to all forms of knowledge and a vital mental function for our habitual negotiations of the world, as well as negotiations of the larger societal or political arenas that we inhabit. The many works that I have discussed in this book all go to show how seriously memory and its familiars, knowledge and history, have been taken as a theme in contemporary art, and how it permeates many cultural and political contexts and practices, private and public. Even at this point, however, I have some remaining issues, in which the emphasis is not so much on how memory is formed or the many ways in which remembrance and memorisation are practised in both life and its representative, art, but on matters of memory loss, in particular the obliteration of memory. This other side to memory forms the basis of the epilogue and the concluding thoughts of this book.

EPILOGUE
OBLIVION: THE LIMITS OF MEMORY

For Freud, there was no such thing as memory loss.[1] The mind is like the wax surface of a mystic writing pad upon which that which is experienced or learnt is inscribed, leaving an imprint below the surface, which may become more and more deeply buried, but is never completely effaced.[2] Moreover, memories that the conscious mind cannot tolerate not only remain dormant but, as Freud notes, continue to be organised and reorganised, 'putting out derivatives and establishing connections, so that memory is restless and ever-expanding'.[3] Yet, as Marc Augé further observes, without the ability to forget, memory is unable to function effectively; it would become rapidly saturated if we were even to try to consciously preserve all our past experiences.[4] In order to function effectively, the mind has to find ways of limiting and selecting memory within the parameters of too much or too little memory. I began this book by noting the nightmare of severe memory loss as depicted in Christopher Nolan's film *Memento*, a counterpart to which is the story of a tragic excess of memory told in Jorge Luis Borges' 'Funes and his Memory' (sometimes translated as 'Funes the Memorius').[5] These two fictional accounts represent the limits at which memory becomes unworkable and the parameters within which all the diverse forms of memory sit.

The stretching of limits has figured as part of my analysis of the ways in which memory has been addressed in contemporary art. Some artists, for instance, have pushed at the boundaries of genre, and others have shifted the protocols of representability, but none so far have addressed the limits of memory itself. There are, however, two works that stand out for this very reason, for having probed some of the extremes of memory loss, although in ways that represent contradictory positions. These works differ from those already discussed because they summon the notion of oblivion, which is something that most of us fear, despite that fact that being able to forget is as important for mental functioning as being able to remember. United under the rubric of forgetting, the two works are different in approach, content and context and almost polar opposites in intent. One work, *Breakdown* (2001) (fig. 28), is a deliberate act of obliteration by British artist Michael Landy (born 1963), and the other, *Twelve Museums* (2002) (fig. 29), by another British artist, Becky Shaw, in collaboration with arts documentary

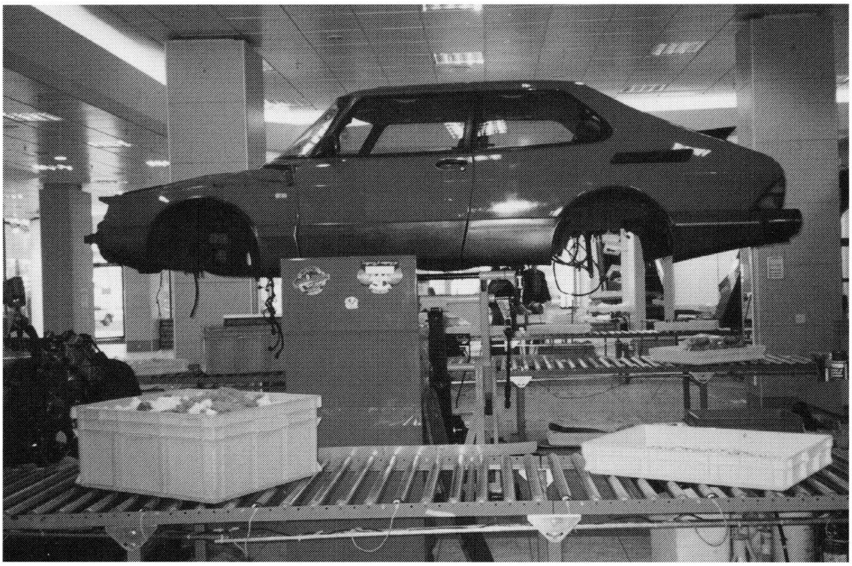

Figure 28: Michael Landy, *Breakdown*, 2001, Commissioned and Produced by Artangel. Photograph copyright © Michael Landy.

filmmaker Michael Gill, involved the capturing of the memories of an Alzheimer's sufferer before involuntary obliteration set in.

Ostensibly, Landy's *Breakdown* is not a work about memory but a way of divesting himself of his worldly goods in a grand anti-consumerist gesture. Reversing the production-line logic of the conveyer belt, Landy destroyed all his material possessions over a two-week period in February 2000 in a fully functioning mock-up of a factory. The assault on consumerism at the heart of the work was underlined by the venue chosen for the work: the vacant premises of the C&A fashion store on Oxford Street, one of central London's most famous locations for shopping. Here, a 148-metre-long conveyer belt (along with tools, tables, a shredder and a granulator) was operated by a group of volunteers who followed Landy's procedural guidelines, according to which each item had to be logged and weighed before being stripped down, reweighed and then sent to the shredder. The final stage was for the shredded parts to be ground to dust, which Landy has said he hopes will one day be buried deep beneath a shopping centre.[6] Landy's possessions totalled over five thousand in number, including photographs, his own artworks and artworks that he owned by other artists, the paraphernalia of everyday life such as receipts and vitamin pills and all his personal documents. It should be noted, at this point, that, although the possessions were effectively annihilated, a full inventory was kept, so that they persist in documentary if not in actual form and their memory is kept, albeit in an extremely reduced form.[7]

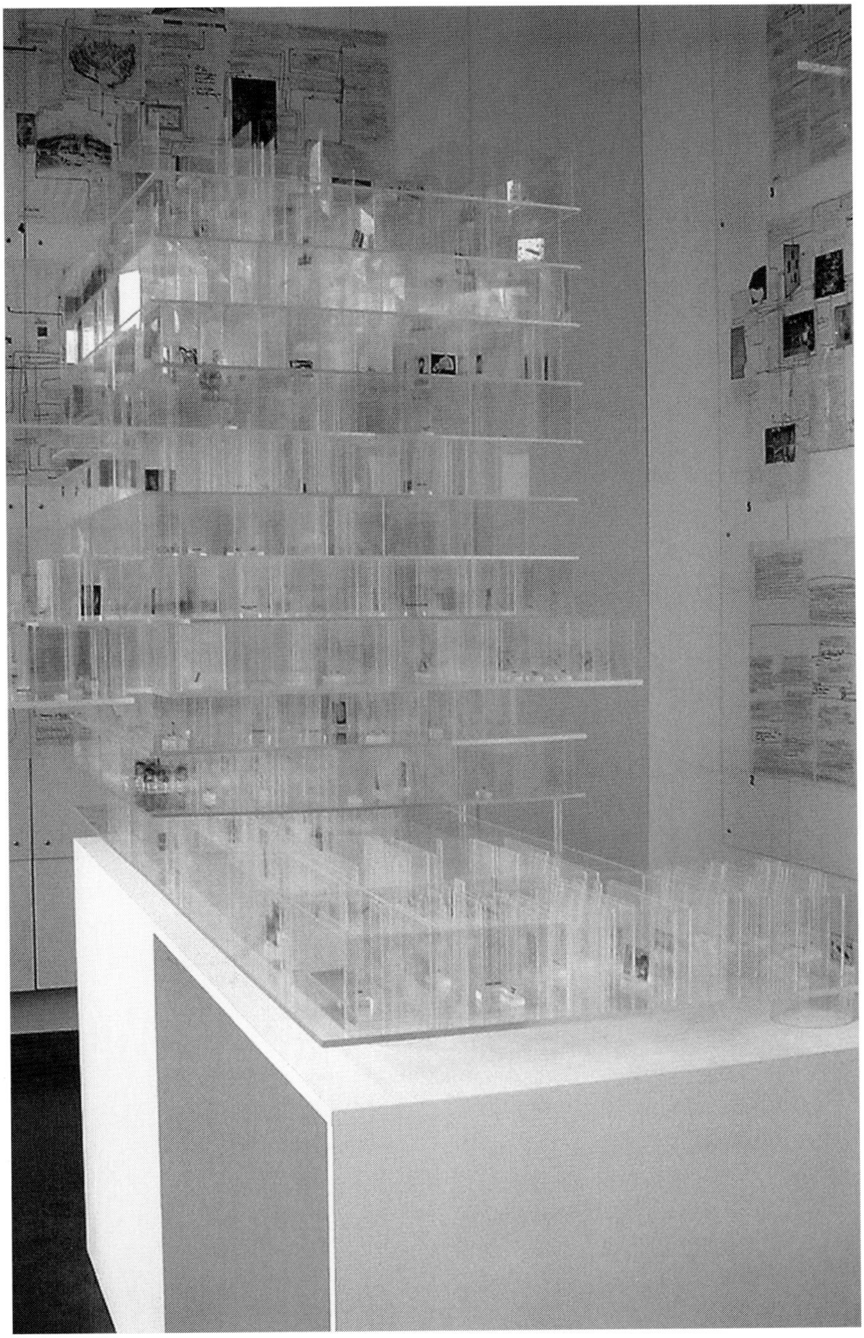

Figure 29: Becky Shaw (in collaboration with Michael Gill) *Twelve Museums*, 2002. Sackler Centre for Arts Education, Serpentine Gallery, exhibition view. Courtesy: Becky Shaw.

For me, however, this wasting of possessions raises the question of the significance of objects and documents for memory. Fittingly for Landy's *Breakdown*, the value that can be placed on objects as mementos relates to ways in which consumer objects are valued and given significance above and beyond their use value. In their research into the anthropology of consumption, for example, Mary Douglas and Baron Isherwood concluded that material possessions, including consumer goods, are used as vehicles for constructing an intelligible universe. Consumer objects are communicators that enable social meanings to be constructed and conveyed and they help establish the boundaries of social relationships.[8] Interestingly, this perspective is not so different from Halbwachs' claim that '[n]o memory is possible outside frameworks used by people living in society to determine and retrieve their recollections'. For Halbwachs, memories are constructed according to recognised conventions of representation such as language and, even when memories are experienced by those suffering from aphasia or language inhibition, for instance, the sufferers rarely forget that they are members of society, although they may forget the conventions of language that create social bonds.[9] Just as objects are part of a framework of social exchange and interaction, so are the memories that are embedded in them.

So, in an irreversible act that highlighted the materialistic values of consumerism, Landy also forfeited the symbolic value of the objects which had previously helped place him within a set of social relations. It may further be said that Landy tested the boundaries of identity by this same act of destruction. Yiannis Gabriel and Tim Lang note that while identity is inherent to the social messages that the consumer communicates through his or her possessions, the notion has achieved a privileged position in contemporary discourses of the self – even to the point of becoming a fashion.[10] Moreover, Landy was well aware of this issue when planning the work:

> I see this orgy of destruction as the ultimate consumer choice. Obviously at times I will be suffering from a certain sense of loss – probably for more sentimental possessions such as my father's sheepskin jacket which has been in our family for years, though I hardly ever wear it. I also suspect I will feel a little inadequate about the state of my belongings (my possessions aren't exactly the shiny, brand new items you usually see in window shop displays). It will be excruciatingly embarrassing at times to see my stuff being paraded in the public eye. This feeling of inadequacy is interesting in the first world country, where our success is measured in terms of how well we are doing as consumers. I will be left at the end of the 14 day period in possession of the clothes I've chosen to wear that day. Once Breakdown has finished, a more personal 'breakdown' will commence, life without my self-defining belongings.[11]

In terms of memory and material possessions, then, *Breakdown* is a highly symbolic gesture, and it can also be seen as a commemorative ritual that simultaneously removes the trappings of the past and marks a new beginning. The systematic liquidation of property is more than the loss of consumer disposables; it is an obliteration of relics or mementos that flies in the face of social convention and traditional methods of remembrance. All the primary evidence of Landy's life has been effaced, leaving a psychological gap which had previously been filled with the emotionally connective repositories of memory provided by material objects – now reduced to an inventory and the documentation of the event. Ultimately, *Breakdown* questions and highlights the need for objects as receptacles or sites of memory, and what I find most remarkable but also emotionally troubling about the work is the willingness to let go of the symbolic as well as the material value of the possessions.

While *Breakdown* tested the limits of identity and the emotional or symbolic significance of material objects for memory, *Twelve Museums* was an exploration of the realities of an identity that was slipping and becoming inchoate through a pathological loss of memory. The work resulted from a project conceived by artist David Clegg for Age Concern Kensington and Chelsea's 'Dementia Arts Project', in which artists worked collaboratively with people suffering from dementia. The aim was to explore the artistic thinking as relevant or beneficial to the needs of the person with dementia, and the emphasis was split between research into the potential of visual thinking and the production of an exhibition that acknowledged the outcome as art.[12] To make *Twelve Museums*, Shaw worked in collaboration with Alzheimer's sufferer Michael Gill, who, in the words of his son, A. A. Gill,

> was in RAF intelligence during the war and the occupation of Germany after, read philosophy at Edinburgh – the first member of his family to go to university, became a journalist on the Scotsman and then the Observer, joined the BBC. Made more than 1,000 arts documentaries, filmed Giacometti and Bacon, worked with David Sylvester, John Berger and Kenneth Clark, co-producing and directing Civilisation.[13]

As Gill's son notes, the project is not to be confused with art therapy – he considers it demeaning and humiliating to get people who have led extraordinary lives to 'end up colouring for their own good'.[14] In fact, Shaw found Michael Gill to be intellectually robust, preoccupied, for instance, not only with the conflict in Iraq but also with Iraq's long cultural history, or with the long history of the horse in art, which he saw as an emblem of warfare, community and masculinity.[15] But, while able to collaborate and put forward ideas and remaining capable of insight and revelation, Gill was unable to order and sustain his thoughts due to his illness, which led to 'repetition and sentences that lost their goal and changed direction midway'.[16] This sort of confusion is typical of senile dementia and was something that caused worry for Gill, although, in the end, it actually suggested the form that the artwork would take. Aware that Gill's memory was hampered by a lack of structure, Shaw suggested that they literally build a house or museum that replicated and externalised the architecture of his impaired thinking.

As Gill's thoughts were no longer systematically organised, it was impossible to pre-visualise the form that the building would take, and the final edifice was the result of a mapping of Shaw and Gill's conversations and of Gill's ideas and reminiscences, firstly on paper and then traced onto acetate in twelve museum floor plans. The final three-dimensional work, *Twelve Museums*, was built in transparent acrylic by a professional architectural model maker, and took over a month to build before being shown at the Sackler Centre for Arts Education at the Serpentine Gallery. The result is a translucent structure which rather poignantly makes me think of the spiritual qualities that Paul Scheerbart saw in glass architecture at the beginning of the last century – except that the utopianism that underpinned translucency for Scheerbart is obviously undercut by the reality of Gill's condition.[17] The transparency also signals the delicacy and precariousness of the illness, and the see-through layerings reflect the complexities and difficulties of thought and communication that Gill experienced as a dementia sufferer, incorporating, for instance, dead ends, false corridors, rooms that back on themselves and rooms that are too small to have anything in them.[18] Shaw made tiny versions of images and objects that held meaning for Gill, or when images were not available the word itself was used. These were inserted in the exact place that they had occurred in the diagrams of Gill's thoughts and ideas, so that, '[w]hen the museums are viewed, the same object appears many times and on many floors, internal reflections making some objects and words appear upside down and doubled-up, texts appearing in front of images that are not connected'.[19]

There is none of the bravura that characterises Landy's *Breakdown* here, but Shaw and Gill's collaboration speaks of the fortitude with which Gill responded to his dementia and the reality of oblivion. While this might make Landy's work look academic or wilful in contrast, my intention is not to compare in this way or to exact value judgements on works that were produced in different contexts for different purposes. *Breakdown*, for instance, reads differently when seen in relation to Landy's later work, *Semi-detached* (2004) which was a life-size replica of the front and back façades of his parents' home in Essex. This work shows both a respect for memory (which, for me, was only superficially absent from *Breakdown*) and acts a testimony of Landy's regard for his father (in accompanying films that show the minutiae of quotidian life in the house, including his father's bedroom shelf, for instance, and a showreel of images from DIY manuals collected by his father over decades).[20] I have brought *Breakdown* and *Twelve Museums* together not only as differing examples of works that probe the threshold at which memory tips over into oblivion but as examples of how complex and diverse memory is, even when limited to one end of the broad spectrum of remembrance and forgetting. Furthermore, there is a violence done to memory in both works, whether voluntary or involuntary, that I find particularly unsettling and affective.

From the start of this book, however, I have stressed that memory is essentially an unstable and variable phenomenon that, nevertheless, has been captured, represented, tested and contested in multiple ways in contemporary art. As the title of the book suggests, recollection and remembrance are at the heart of memory and if I am to attempt any overarching conclusion it has to be that it is these processes that underpin all the many works discussed. As Edward Casey conveniently explains, 'recollection' has two originary meanings: from the Latin, *collecta*, a 'gathering together'; and from *colligere*, which relates to the English verb 'to colligate', 'to bind together'.[21] When broken down into its stem and prefix, the word 'remembering' ('re-membering') can be seen simply as the putting back together or reassembling of parts or members. No matter how complex or obtuse the memory-work or the address to memory in contemporary art, these processes underpin it, and it is the skill and creativity sensibility with which the artist returns to the past, gathers it in, binds it and puts its parts together that bring moment and give renewed meaning to the original experience or event. The artist's ability to set the past within a social or collective framework is also vital to the success of memory, but, above and beyond this, it is the willingness to explore often difficult or sensitive subject matter and new forms that has given the works that I have discussed a cutting edge. Yet, while contemporary art with its openness and diversity has proved a rich territory for probing the significance of memory in contemporary culture, and while I have highlighted, exemplified and commented on the many guises in which memory appears in contemporary art, there is, of course, far more still to be said on this subject.

NOTES

FOREWORD

1 Arthur, C. Danto, *After the End of Art: Contemporary Art and the Pale of History* (Princeton, New Jersey: Princeton University Press, 1997) 5.
2 Hal Foster, *The Return of the Real* (Cambridge, Massachusetts: The MIT Press, 1996) xi.

INTRODUCTION

1 Frances A. Yates, *The Art of Memory*, 1966 (London: Pimlico, 1992) 45–51.
2 Ibid. 31.
3 Ibid. The memorisation of ideas or data by association with place features in many versions of the art of memory that Yates traces throughout her book, from ancient times to the late Renaissance.
4 Mary Warnock, *Memory* (London: Faber and Faber, 1987) 15–27.
5 The inverse also of the previous relationship between memory and the imagination, in which imagination had been the facilitator of memory. See Yates, 46–47, 76–77, 251–253.
6 Warnock, 78–89.
7 Ibid. 90.
8 Ibid. 94–99.
9 Ibid. 91–95.
10 The contrast between voluntary and involuntary memory is drawn in Marcel Proust, *In Search of Lost Time*, vol. 1, *Swann's Way*, 1913 (London: Vintage Classics, 2002) 50–55.
11 Edward Said, *Orientalism* (Harmondsworth: Penguin Books, 2nd edn 1995).
12 See, for example, Michel Foucault, *The Archaeology of Knowledge*, 1969 (London and New York: Routledge, 1989).
13 Andreas Huyssen, *Twilight Memories: Marking Time in a Culture of Amnesia* (London and New York: Routledge, 1995) 6.

14 The term 'memory-work' is used by Susannah Radstone in her introduction to *Memory and Methodology* (Oxford and New York: Berg, 2000) 9, 11–13. This clearly aligns with Sigmund Freud's notion of 'dream-work', which is, briefly, to digest, filter and reorganise knowledge in order to assimilate, understand or sublimate. See Sigmund Freud, *The Interpretation of Dreams*, 1901 (Harmondsworth: Penguin Books, the Penguin Freud Library, vol. 4. 1976, reprinted 1991).

15 A useful summary of this range of theories is to be found in Radstone, 2–9. The similarity between this shift and the one that is associated with Romanticism makes good sense if Romanticism is seen as seminal to current postmodern sensibilities.

16 Huyssen, 6–7.

17 Ibid. 7.

18 Ibid. 100–101.

19 Radstone, 9–11.

20 Ibid. 11–12.

21 Henri Bergson, *Matter and Memory*, 1910 (New York: Zone Books, 1991) 13.

22 That the body is as much an agent of cognition and an accumulation of memories is central to Begson's understanding of the relationship between perception and memory. Memory does not function independently in the mind but perception, cognition and recall are synaesthetic, as with Proust's *madeleine*. See Martin Jay, *Downcast Eyes: The Denigration of Vision in Twentieth-century French Thought* (Berkeley: University of California Press, 1994) 191–195.

23 Pierre Nora, 'Between Memory and History: les Lieux de Mémoire', *Representations* 26, Spring 1989, 18–20.

24 Ibid. 7–8.

25 Ibid. 15.

CHAPTER 1

1 John Pilling, ed. *Autobiography and Imagination: Studies in Self-Scrutiny* (London, Boston and Henley: Routledge and Kegan Paul, 1981) 1.

2 Sidonie Smith and Julia Watson, eds *Getting a Life: Everyday Uses of Autobiography* (Minneapolis: University of Minnesota Press, 1996) 8–12.

3 Michael Mascuch, *Origins of the Individualist Self: Autobiography and Self-identity in England, 1591–1791* (Cambridge: Polity Press, 1997) 88. As Mascuch notes, an early example of this shift is to be found in the sixteenth century in the Netherlandish scholar François du Jon's (Junius Franz, 1545–1642) autobiographical preface to his edition of *The New Testament*, c.1590.

4 Huygens was a key figure in the house of Orange, who wrote a profile of Rembrandt (along with another artist, Jan Lievens, 1607–1674) in his own autobiographical memoir, c.1629–1630, translated in Gary Schwartz, *Rembrandt: His Life, his Paintings* (London: Penguin Books, 1985) 73–77.
5 Gen Doy, *Picturing the Self: Changing Views of the Subject in Visual Culture* (London and New York: I.B. Tauris, 2005) 23–24.
6 Ibid. The first two chapters of Doy's book explore the so-called Cartesian legacy of the doubting subject (while recognising the existence of this subject type, Doy also clearly notes that it cannot be attributed to Descartes alone, but is the product of his exchanges with the available knowledge in a particular historical, social and economic context).
7 Schwartz, 363–364.
8 Sigmund Freud, 'The Ego and the Id', 1923, in *On Metapsychology*, (Harmondsworth: Penguin Books, the Penguin Freud Library, vol. 11, 1984) 367–379.
9 Simon Schama, *Rembrandt's Eyes* (London: Penguin Books, 1999) 13, 300.
10 Ibid. 616–617.
11 The need to select memories was noted by William James in *The Principles of Psychology* (New York: Henry Holt, 1890) 680, and has recently been reiterated with scientific evidence as 'creative memory' by neurobiologist James L. McGaugh in *Memory and Emotion: The Making of Lasting Memories* (New York: Columbia University Press, 2003) 115–134.
12 Oriana Baddeley, 'Reflecting on Kahlo: Mirrors, Masquerade and the Politics of Identification', in Tate Gallery, *Frida Kahlo* (London: Tate Publishing, 2005) 50.
13 Tanya Barson, 'All Art is at Once Surface and Symbol: a Frida Kahlo Glossary', ibid. 67.
14 Gannit Ankori, 'Frida Kahlo: the Fabric of Her Art', ibid. 34–35.
15 Hayden Herrera, *Frida Kahlo: The Paintings* (London: Bloomsbury, 1991) 9.
16 Ankori, 38.
17 Herrera, 9–10.
18 Cathy Caruth, *Unclaimed Experience: Trauma, Narrative and History* (Baltimore and London: Johns Hopkins University Press, 1996). Caruth refers, for instance, to Freud's example of a train accident, from which a person may escape unscathed only to suffer shock some weeks later (6, 70–71), but her interpretation of the deferred representation of trauma in the film *Hiroshima Mon Amour* (1959) is most elucidating concerning the unspeakability of trauma (25–56).
19 Nicola King, *Memory, Narrative, Identity: Remembering the Self* (Edinburgh: Edinburgh University Press, 2000) 16. See also J. Laplanche and J. B.

Pontalis, *The Language of Psychoanalysis* (London: Karnac Books, 1998) 111–114.

20 King, 11–12, 16–24. As King notes, it is a concept that has not only found purchase in the work of Sigmund Freud but in the work of later psychoanalysts such as Jacques Lacan and Jean Laplanche, as well as postmodernists such as Jean-François Lyotard and Jacques Derrida.

21 Walter Benjamin, 'Excavation and Memory', c. 1932, in Michael Jennings, Howard Eiland and Gary Smith, eds *Walter Benjamin: Selected Writings*, vol. 2, part 2, 1931–1934 (Cambridge, Massachusetts, and London: Belknap Press, 2005) 576; see also 'Berlin Chronicle', in ibid. 611.

22 Frances Morris, *Louise Bourgeois: Stitches in Time* (London: August Projects, 2003) 10. In 'Brief Account of Career', c. 1965, Bourgeois makes no reference to the personal meanings in her sculpture to date; see Louise Bourgeois, *Destruction of the Father, Reconstruction of the Father: Writings and Interviews 1923–1997* (Cambridge, Massachusetts: MIT Press, 1998) 77–79.

23 Louise Bourgeois, 'Statements 1979' and 'Statements from an Interview with Donald Kuspit', ibid. 115 and 158 respectively.

24 Ibid. 157.

25 Louise Bourgeois, 'Interview with Susi Bloch', ibid. 104.

26 Louise Bourgeois, 'Child Abuse', ibid. 133–135.

27 Louise Bourgeois, 'Self Expression is Sacred and Fatal', ibid. 225.

28 Louise Bourgeois, 'On Twosome', ibid. 209.

29 Yates, 18–24.

30 Louise Bourgeois, 'On Cells', in Bourgeois, 205.

31 Robert Storr, 'A Sketch for a Portrait: Louise Bourgeois', in Robert Storr, Paulo Herkenhoff and Allan Schwartzman, eds *Louise Bourgeois* (London: Phaidon Press, 2003).

32 Andrew Bennett and Nicholas Royle, *Literature, Criticism and Theory* (Harlow: Pearson Longman, 3rd edn 2004) 34.

33 Mandy Merck and Chris Townsend, eds *The Art of Tracey Emin* (London: Thames and Hudson, 2002).

34 Janice Peck, 'The Mediated Talking Cure: Therapeutic Framing of Autobiography in TV Talk Shows', in Smith and Watson, 134–155.

35 For instance, Tracey Emin, *Strangeland* (London: Hodder and Stoughton, 2005).

36 See www.jeanettewinterson.com/pages/content/index.asp?PageID=357.

37 Renée Vada, 'Another Dimension: Tracey Emin's Interest in Mysticism', in Merck and Townsend, 184.

38 For the relationship between Emin's art and feminist aesthetics, see Rosemary Betterton, 'Why is my Art not as Good as Me?', in Merck and Townsend, 22–39.

39 Joan Gibbons, *Art and Advertising* (London and New York: I. B. Tauris, 2005) 21.

40 Lorna Healy, 'We Love You Tracey', in Merck and Townsend, 160–164.
41 Sidonie Smith and Julia Watson, 'The Rumpled Bed of Autobiography: Extravagant Lives, Extravagant Questions', *Biography* 24, 1, Autumn 2001.
42 Here Smith and Watson refer to Philippe Lejeune's influential work 'The Autobiographical Pact', in Paul John Eakin, ed. *On Autobiography* (Minneapolis: University of Minnesota Press, 1989).
43 Ibid. 3–30. (This version of 'The Autobiographical Pact' was published in *Poetique* 14, 1973.)
44 Leigh Gilmore, *The Limits of Autobiography: Trauma and Testimony* (Ithaca, New York and London: Cornell University Press, 2001) 14.
45 Philippe Lejeune, 'The Autobiographical Pact', in Eakin, *On Autobiography* 125–126. This is a revised version of the essay written for the same 1989 anthology.
46 Paul John Eakin, *How our Lives Become Stories* (Ithaca, New York and London: Cornell University Press, 1999); see chapter 2, 'Relational Selves, Relational Lives: Autobiography and the Myth of Autonomy', 43–98.
47 Dipankar Gupta, *Learning to Forget: The Anti-memoirs of Modernity* (Oxford and New York: Oxford University Press, 2005) 61–62.
48 Gilmore, 14–15. For Gilmore, limit cases also raise many issues concerning the roles and functions of autobiography. She addresses this through reference to a number of literary case studies, the theoretical outcomes of which are summed up in the concluding chapter, 143–148.
49 See Nancy Spector, *Felix Gonzalez-Torres* (New York: Guggenheim Museum, 1995) 22, for examples of political irony in such works. Andrea Rosen notes *'Untitled' (Loverboy)* (1990) and *'Untitled' (Ross in LA)* (1991) as part of a group of works that focused on Gonzalez-Torres' relationship with his partner, Ross, produced in the early 1990s; see "'Untitled: the neverending portrait', in Dietmar Elgar, ed. *Felix Gonzalez-Torres: Text* (catalogue raisonné) (Stuttgart: Cantz Verlag, 1997) 56.
50 Richard Serra's corner pieces of the mid-1960s to early 1970s provide an obvious example. It is also worth noting that Gonzalez-Torres was included in *Primary Matters: The Minimalist Sensibility from 1959 to the Present*, held at the San Francisco Museum of Modern Art, November 2003 to January 2004.
51 Pasi Falk has written on the symbolic value given to communal eating in *The Consuming Body* (London, Thousand Oaks, California, and New Delhi: Sage Publications, 1994), in which he notes a correlation between eating practices and the social body; 11–14, 20–22.
52 See Roland Waspe, 'Private and Public', in Elgar, 18. Waspe refers to a statement made by Gonzalez-Torres in an interview with Hans-Ulrich Obrist in *Der Standard*, 10 January 1996. I discuss the billboard in a chapter on the abject and the sublime entitled 'Reality Bites' in *Art and Advertising* 92–96.

53 Jean-François Lyotard, 'The Sublime and the Avant-Garde', *Artforum*, April 1984, 36–43.
54 Spector, 25. See also Gibbons, 93–94.
55 It may be worth noting that the case had figured earlier in a billboard produced by Gonzalez-Torres in 1989, which carried a number of references to gay politics and history in a band of text at the bottom of a largely blank black background.
56 Felix Gonzalez-Torres, 'Practices: the Problem of Divisions of Cultural Labour', *Art and Design* 9, January–February 1994, 91.
57 Spector, 154.
58 Ibid. 154–156.
59 Gonzalez-Torres, 73.
60 Rosen, 56–57.
61 Ibid. 57.

CHAPTER 2

1 Susan Sontag, *On Photography* (Harmondsworth: Penguin Books, 1977) 154.
2 These definitions recur throughout Peirce's writings but have conveniently been collated in *The Commens Dictionary of Peirce's Terms*, which gives precise reference to the original writings. See www.helsinki.fi/science/commens/dictionaryfront.html.
3 The 'having been thereness' of the indexical sign is something that Roland Barthes speaks of in several works on the theory of photography, firstly in 'The Photographic Message', 1961, in *Image, Music, Text* (London: Fontana, 1977), but later and more notably as a theme in the more widely read *Camera Lucida*, 1980 (London: Vintage, 2000) 76–77, 85–89.
4 Charles Sanders Peirce, 'A Syllabus of Certain Topics of Logic', 1903, in Nathan Houser and Christian Koesel, eds *The Essential Peirce: Selected Writings*, vol. 2 (Bloomington and Indianapolis: Indiana University Press, 1998) 273, and Rosalind Krauss, 'Notes on the Index: Part 1', 1977, in *The Originality of the Avant-garde and Other Modernist Myths* (Cambridge, Massachusetts: MIT Press, 1994) 198.
5 Neville Wakefield, 'Separation Anxiety and the Art of Release', *Parkett* 42, 1994, 77–78.
6 Ibid. 78–79.
7 Susan Lawson, 'Sensitive Skin: *infra mince* and *difference* in the work of Rachel Whiteread', in Chris Townsend, ed. *The Art of Rachel Whiteread* (London: Thames and Hudson, 2004) 78.
8 Ibid. 69–84. Lawson goes into the role of deferral in Whiteread's work in some detail in relation to Derrida in particular. It is best to read the whole essay for a comprehensive view of her insights.

9 See interview with Craig Houser; ibid. 52.
10 Patrick Elliot, 'Sculpting Nothing: an Introduction to the Work of Rachael Whiteread', in Scottish National Gallery of Modern Art and Serpentine Galley, *Rachel Whiteread* (exhibition catalogue) (Edinburgh: Trustees of the National Gallery, Scotland, 2001) 10–11.
11 Interview with Houser; Townsend, 54.
12 Simon Watney, 'About the House', *Parkett* 42, 1994, 105.
13 Molly Nesbit explains the stages involved in the casting processes and notes the implications of Whiteread's stopping at stage one in 'Casting Out', in Deutsche Guggenheim Berlin, *Transient Spaces* (exhibition catalogue) (New York: Guggenheim Museum Publications, 2001) 113. See also Sally Hornstein, 'Matters Immaterial: on the Meaning of Houses and the Things Inside Them', in Townsend, 56–58.
14 Barthes, *Camera Lucida* 76.
15 John Berger, 'Appearances', in John Berger and Jean Mohr, eds *Another Way of Telling* (Cambridge: Granta, 1987) 120–121.
16 See Watney, 105.
17 See Geoffrey Batchen, *Forget Me Not: Photography and Remembrance* (New York: Princeton Architectural Press, 2004) 75. See also Charles S. Peirce, 'Logic as Semiotic: The Theory of Signs', c.1897–1910, in Robert Innis, ed. *Semiotics: An Introductory Anthology* (Bloomington: Indiana University Press, 1985) 8, 13. Even if not always so precisely named, indexicality has since been discussed in the work of key photographic theorists: Barthes, 'The Photographic Message', in *Image, Music, Text* 17, Sontag, 154; Victor Burgin, 'Photographic Practice and Art Theory', in Victor Burgin, ed. *Thinking Photography* (Basingstoke and London: Macmillan, 1982) 61; and Berger and Mohr, 95.
18 Victor Burgin, 'Photography, Phantasy, Function', in Burgin, 198. See also Barthes, *Camera Lucida* 4.
19 Burgin, 'Photographic Practice and Art Theory' 47.
20 Allan Sekula, 'The Traffic in Photographs', *Art Journal*, Spring 1981, 15–16.
21 Allan Sekula, 'On the Invention of Photographic Meaning', in Burgin, 94.
22 Barthes, *Camera Lucida* 82–85.
23 Quoted in Don Slater, 'Photography and Modern Vision: the Spectacle of "Natural Magic"', in Chris Jenks, ed. *Visual Culture* (London and New York: Routledge, 1995) 222.
24 Barthes, *Camera Lucida* 67–71.
25 Ibid. 64.
26 Kasahara Michiko, 'Ishiuchi Miyako: Traces of Time', in Ishiuchi Miyako, *Mother's 2000–2005: Traces of the Future* (Tokyo: The Japan Foundation, 2005) 125–126.

27 Barthes, *Camera Lucida* 109.
28 Michiko, 124.
29 Barthes, *Camera Lucida* 25–27.
30 Sekula in Burgin, 94.
31 Rosalind Krauss, 'The Photographic Conditions of Surrealism', in Krauss, 111–114.
32 Ibid. 112. The poet and leading figure in the movement, André Breton, speaks of the marvellous as part of a 'great revelation' in the first Manifesto of Surrealism and notes that it has different manifestations at different points in history. André Breton, 'Manifesto of Surrealism', 1924, in *Manifestoes of Surrealism*, 1955 (Ann Arbor: University of Michigan Press, 1972).
33 Guido Costa, *Nan Goldin* (London and New York: Phaidon, 2001) introduction unpaginated.
34 Nan Goldin, *The Ballad of Sexual Dependency* (New York: Aperture Foundation Books, 1986) 6, 9.
35 Ibid. 6.
36 Ibid.
37 Ibid.
38 Annette Kuhn, *Family Secrets: Acts of Memory and Imagination* (London and New York: Verso, 1995).
39 Ibid. See chapters 4 and 6, in particular 47–69, 6–123.
40 The titles of the works quoted are: *Cookie with Max at my Birthday Party* (1976); *Cookie and Millie in the Girls' Room at the Mudd Club* (1979); *Cookie and Vittorio's Wedding: The Ring* (1986); and *Cookie in her Casket* (1989).
41 Nan Goldin, 'Cookie Mueller: March 2, 1949 – November 10, 1989', in Nan Goldin, *I'll Be Your Mirror* (New York: Whitney Museum of American Art, 1996) 256.
42 Ibid.
43 See www.digitaljournalist.org/issue0106/voices_goldin.htm.
44 It is worth noting that the Salpêtrière was the scene of pioneering French psychologist Jean-Martin Charcot's public treatment of so-called 'hysterical' women by hypnosis in the 1880s, which were also documented through the medium of photography. For a critical account of Charcot's practices and their representation, see Georges Didi-Huberman, *Invention of Hysteria, Charcot and the Photographic, Iconography of the Salpêtrière* (Cambridge, Massachusetts: MIT Press, 2003).
45 These are the words of the dedication on the last page of the publication that accompanied the exhibition: Nan Goldin, *Soeurs, Saints et Sibylles* (Paris: Editions du Regard, 2004) unpaginated.
46 In the publication that accompanied the exhibition, Goldin adds: 'My parents started to treat me like Barbara. At 13, I wanted to grow up to be a junkie.' Ibid.

47 Walter Benjamin, 'The Work of Art in the Age of its Technological Reproducibility: Second Version', in Howard Eilard and Michael Jennings, eds, *Walter Benjamin: Selected Writings*, vol. 3, *1935-1938* (Cambridge, Massachusetts, and London: Belknap Press, 2006) 103.
48 'On Acceptance: a Conversation, Nan Goldin Talking with David Armstrong and Walter Keller', in Goldin, *I'll Be Your Mirror* 449–450.
49 'In Conversation: Bill Fontana and Ben Borthwick', in Joan Gibbons and Kaye Winwood, eds, *The Hothaus Papers: Perspectives and Paradigms in Media Arts* (Birmingham: Article Press, in association with VIVID, 2006) 136.
50 Ibid. 137.
51 Conversation between Bill Fontana and composer Anthony Moore, www.resoundings.org/Pages/Interview2.htm.
52 Gibbons and Winwood, 141.
53 Ibid.
54 See www.resoundings.org/Pages/Interview2.htm.

CHAPTER 3

1 Keith Jenkins, *Re-thinking History* (London and New York: Routledge, 1991, republished as a Routledge Classic in 2003) 6–24.
2 Classic examples include Michel Foucault, *The Birth of the Clinic: An Archaeology of Medical Perception*, 1963 (London: Tavistock, 1970), and *Discipline and Punish: The Birth of the Prison*, 1975 (New York: Vintage Books, 1995).
3 What might be termed the 'naturalisation' of discourse permeates much of Foucault's writing, but a summative account can be found in *The Archaeology of Knowledge* 21–39.
4 Anita Brookner, *Jacques Louis David* (London: Thames and Hudson, 1987).
5 Dominick LaCapra, *History and Memory after Auschwitz* (Ithaca, New York and London: Cornell University Press, 1998) 17.
6 Ibid. 21–23.
7 Barbara A. Misztal, *Theories of Social Remembering* (Maidenhead and Philadelphia: Open University Press, 2003) 12–14.
8 Judy Chicago, *The Dinner Party* (Harmondsworth: Penguin Books, 1996) 3.
9 For concise discussion of these issues and others, see Norma Broude and Mary Garrard, *The Power of Feminist Art* (London: Thames and Hudson, 1996) 21–29.
10 Chicago, 6–7.
11 It also received adverse criticism from male art critics such as Hilton Kramer, who, rather than analysing its content, saw it as vulgar and kitsch:

Amelia Jones, 'The Sexual Politics of *The Dinner Party*: a Critical Context', in Amelia Jones, ed. *Sexual Politics: Judy Chicago's Dinner Party in Feminist Art History* (Berkeley, Los Angeles and London: University of California Press, 1996).

12 The Ethel Smythe plate is another exception, depicting a bird's-eye view of a grand piano.

13 See Nancy Ring, 'Identifying with Judy Chicago', in Jones, 131–132.

14 Anette Kubitza, 'Rereading the Readings of *The Dinner Party* in Europe', in Jones, 155–162.

15 Ibid. 165–166.

16 Jean-François Lyotard, *The Postmodern Condition: A Report on Knowledge*, 1979 (Manchester: Manchester University Press, 1984).

17 See Chicago's own account of the various receptions of *The Dinner Party*, in which she attempts to counter the criticisms made against it and demonstrate its symbolic value: Chicago, 213–224.

18 These alternative venues include a black box theatre space at the University of Houston, a disused temple in Cleveland, a converted cyclorama in Boston, an old commercial building in Chicago, an old theatre in Atlanta, an alternative space in the 1984 Edinburgh Festival and a warehouse in London. Ibid.

19 Misztal, 21.

20 Writing in 1986, for instance, Tamar Garb was highly critical of what she saw as Chicago's wish to enshrine *The Dinner Party* in the context of the museum, although this may not be representative of a long-term position, as by 1996 Griselda Pollock and Rozsika Parker, other leading feminist critics in the United Kingdom, were putting forward arguments for the advantages of working within the 'system'. Tamar Garb, 'Engaging Embroidery', *Art History* 9, 1986, 132. Rozsika Parker and Griselda Pollock, eds, *Framing Feminism: Art and the Women's Movement, 1975–1985* (London: Pandora, 1987).

21 Misztal, 15–16.

22 See www.brooklynmuseum.org/collections/eascfa.php.

23 'Carlos Basualdi in Conversation with Doris Salcedo', in Carlos Basualdi, Andreas Huyssen and Nancy Princethal, eds, *Doris Salcedo* (London: Phaidon Press, 2000) 16, and 'Interview with Charles Merewether', ibid. 137.

24 Nancy Princenthal, 'Survey', ibid. 55.

25 Ibid. 51–54.

26 Taken from the definition of 'atrabilious' in *The Shorter Oxford English Dictionary* (Oxford: Clarendon Press, 1993).

27 Sigmund Freud, 'Mourning and Melancholia', 1917, in *On Metapsychology* (Harmondsworth: Penguin Books, the Penguin Freud Library, vol. 11, 1984) 251–268.

28 'Interview with Charles Merewether', 140.
29 Don Cameron, cited in Jill Bennett, *Empathic Vision: Affect, Trauma, and Contemporary Art* (Stanford, California: Stanford University Press, 2005) 60.
30 Andreas Huyssen, 'Doris Salcedo's Memory Sculpture: *Unland: The Orphan's Tunic*', in *Present Pasts: Urban Palimpsests and the Politics of Memory* (Stanford, California: Stanford University Press, 2003) 113.
31 Princenthal, 63.
32 Salcedo's interest in theatre is noted in her interview with Carlos Basualdo: Basualdi, Huyssen and Princenthal, 8.
33 Bennett, 7–8.
34 Bennett has located this making strange in relation to the strategy of estrangement (or defamiliarisation) developed by the Russian Formalists in the early twentieth century (the idea that by making the work strange, the writer (or artist) would be able to alter the mental and political perspectives of the viewer): Bennett, 67. Princenthal has noted that this sense of strangeness also derives from other historical sources, for example, or the anarchic ready-mades of Duchamp and the way that Beuys integrated political awareness with sculpture: Princenthal, 40. See also 'Carlos Basualdi in Conversation with Doris Salcedo'.
35 'The absurd' was a principal term used by existentialist philosopher Jean Paul Sartre to characterise the human condition in the lead-up to and during and after World War II, a world that he and associates such as Albert Camus saw as outside reason. The concept is discussed in Sartre's *Being and Nothingness*, 1943, and appears in many of his literary works, e.g. *Nausea*, 1938, or *The Wall*, 1939.
36 'Interview with Charles Merewether', in Basualdi, Huyssen and Princenthal, 137.
37 Bennett, 67.
38 Misztal, 61–63.
39 Edlie Wong, 'Situating Memory in the Art of Doris Salcedo', *Critical Sense*, Winter 2001, 74–79.
40 Ibid. 71–72.
41 Ibid. 69–70.
42 Ibid. 70, 71.
43 A summary of the varying applications and connotations of 'black' is to be found in the introduction to Gen Doy's *Black Visual Culture: Modernity and Postmodernity* (London and New York: I.B. Tauris, 2000), including a useful distinction between the generic use of the term (with a lower-case 'b') and its more specific usage in relation to particular identities (with an upper case 'B'), as in 'Black history', 'Black liberation', etc. Without denying the complexity of the term, for the purposes of this chapter I use the term

'black art' in its lower-case form to refer simply to art by postcolonial artists of both African and Near Eastern origin that addresses issues of racially constructed identity and history. 'Postcolonial' is also a term which requires some qualification. Peter Childs and Patrick Williams summarise a number of positions concerning the where, when, who and what of postcolonialism, demonstrating how impossible it is to construct an hegemonic account in the face of the wide chronological and geographical, political and economic contexts of colonialism: Childs and Williams, *An Introduction to Postcolonial Theory* (London, New York, Toronto, Sydney, Tokyo, Singapore, Madrid, Mexico City, Munich and Paris: Prentice Hall/Harvester Wheatsheaf, 1997) 1–25. They also note that the idea that colonial legacies have actually reached a point at which they can be regarded as 'post' rather than 'neo' has been strongly contested on the grounds that many previously colonised societies have replicated colonial rule in their governmental structures and infrastructures, as well as on the evidence of its covert survival in the economic imperialism of the West. For some, the prefix 'post' in itself is problematic implying a finality to colonialism that does not exist – not to mention the related issue of the hyphen, which, when employed, is said to signal a historical stage rather than the ideological orientation of the unhyphenated 'postcolonialism'. As Gen Doy notes (in *Black Visual Culture* 205), despite the diversity of approaches within it, postcolonial theory (without the hyphen) does carry a set of main characteristics (aiming to overturn the Eurocentric emphasis of colonial history and the crude binary classifications that came with it), and it is in this very broad, unhyphenated sense that I use the term.

44 Kobena Mercer, 'Black Art and the Burden of Representation', *Third Text* 10, Spring 1990, 61–77; see 61–62 and 65–66 in particular. *The Other Story* was held wanting by several black artist critics for not being fully representative of the 'totality' of black art, especially through the neglect of black women artists: see Steve Edwards, ed. *Art and its Histories: A Reader* (New Haven, Connecticut, and London: Yale University Press, in association with the Open University, 1999) 263–276, for a postscript from Araeen and critical responses from Homi Bhaba and Rita Keegan (as well as those of white conservative critics Brian Sewell and Peter Fuller).

45 Ibid.

46 David A. Bailey, 'Keith Piper: Some Thoughts on a Portrait of an Artist', in *A Ship Called Jesus* (Birmingham: Ikon Gallery, exhibition catalogue, 1991) unpaginated.

47 Rasheed Araeen, 'The Success and Failure of Black Art', *Third Text* 18, March 2004, 143–147.

48 Mercer, 74–77 in particular.

49 Keith Piper, 'A Ship Called Jesus', in Bailey.

50 As Piper notes, slavery was often justified on the grounds that it brought the 'gift of Christianity' in compensation for the forced removal from the homeland: Keith Piper, 'The Ghosts of Christendom', in Bailey. He also notes that allegiance with the Church was facilitated because it provided a space in which African ritual traditions are known to have survived and because parallels were easily drawn between the exile and sufferings of the Hebrews and those of black people: Piper, 'The Rites of Passage', in Bailey.

51 Angela McRobbie, 'The African Dandy', in Jaap Guldemond, Gabriele Mackert and Barbera van Kooij, eds, *Yinka Shonibare: Double Dutch* (Rotterdam: NAi Publishers, 2004) 65.

52 It is interesting to note here that *Diary of a Victorian Dandy* entered the realm of the popular in October 1998 when, with the support of inIVA (International Institute of Visual Arts), it was produced as a large-scale poster for the London underground.

53 McRobbie, 65.

54 For a detailed essay, see John Picton, 'Laughing at Ourselves', in Guldemond, Mackert and van Kooij, 46–58.

55 John Berger, *Ways of Seeing* (Harmondsworth: Pelican Books, in conjunction with the BBC, 1972) 83–109, 106–108 in particular.

56 Max Ernst, 'What is the Mechanism of Collage?', 1936, in Herschel B. Chipp, ed. *Theories of Modern Art* (Berkeley, Los Angeles and London: University of California Press, 1968) 427.

57 Divya Tolia-Kelly and Andy Morris have made a similar claim in 'Disruptive Aesthetics? Revisiting the Burden of Representation in the Art of Chris Ofili and Yinka Shonibare', *Third Text* 18, 2, 2004, 155–156.

58 Araeen, 147–148.

59 Yinka Shonibare, 'Poetic Licence', in David Burrows, ed. *Who's Afraid of Red, White and Blue?* (Birmingham: Article Press, 1998) 73.

60 See Brian O'Doherty, *Inside the White Cube: The Ideology of the Gallery Space*, 1986 (Berkeley and Los Angeles: University of California Press, 1999) 87–10.

61 Tolia-Kelly and Morris, 154–155, 159.

62 Nora, 7–9.

63 Ibid. 19.

64 Gibbons and Winwood, eds 170.

CHAPTER 4

1 Marianne Hirsch, *Family Frames: Photography, Narrative and Postmemory* (Cambridge, Massachusetts, and London: Harvard University Press, 1997) 243.

2 Lawrence L. Langer, *Holocaust Memories: The Ruins of Memory* (New Haven, Connecticut, and London: Yale University Press, 1991).

3 Following Langer, I will refer to 'former victims' rather than 'survivors' as the term 'survivor' has the potential to signal a leaving behind of trauma, which does not do justice to former victims having to 'live' with the Holocaust for the rest of their lives. I will use the term 'survivor' only in relation to my discussion of Art Spiegelman's *Maus*, in deference to the fact that it is the term that he employs.
4 Caruth, 1–4.
5 Julia Kristeva, *Powers of Horror: An Essay on Abjection* (New York and Guildford: Columbia University Press, 1982). See also Charles Penwarden, 'Of World and Flesh: an Interview with Julia Kristeva', in Stuart Morgan, ed. *Rites of Passage: Art for the End of the Century* (London: Tate Gallery Publications, 1995) 21–27.
6 LaCapra, 20–21.
7 Imre Kertész, 'Who Owns Auschwitz?', *Yale Journal of Criticism* 14, 1, 2001, 267–272.
8 Ernst Van Alphen, *Caught by History: Holocaust Effects in Contemporary Art, Literature and Theory* (Stanford, California: Stanford University Press, 1997). 17–20.
9 Ibid. 28–29.
10 Ibid. 37.
11 Hirsch, 245.
12 Ibid. 256–264.
13 Lynn Gumpert quotes from Boltanski in Gumpert, *Christian Boltanski* (Paris: Flammarion, 1994) 33–34.
14 Hirsch, 257.
15 'Tamar Garb in Conversation with Christian Boltanski', in Didier Semin, Tamar Garb, Donald Kuspit and Georges Perec, *Christian Boltanski* (London: Phaidon Press, 1997) 19.
16 Langer, 62–63.
17 'Tamar Garb in Conversation with Christian Boltanski'.
18 *Reserves: The Purim Holiday* commemorates the escape of Jewish peoples from massacre in ancient Persia, told in the Biblical book of Esther.
19 See Gumpert, 102–110.
20 'Tamar Garb in Conversation with Christian Boltanski', 27.
21 Some Western historians became involved in the debate itself. British historians Richard J. Evans and Ian Kershaw, for instance, reacted against the right-wing attempt to redeem Germany, while US historian Gordon A. Craig took a more middle-of-the-road perspective.
22 Andreas Huyssen, 'Anselm Kiefer: the Terror of History, the Temptation of Myth', in *Twilight Memories* 214–215.
23 Ibid. 215.
24 Mark Rosenthal, *Anselm Kiefer* (Chicago and Philadelphia: the Art Institute of Chicago and the Philadelphia Museum of Art, 1988) 17.

25 Huyssen, *Twilight Memories* 216–217.
26 Ibid. 218–219.
27 Lisa Saltzman, *Anselm Kiefer and Art after Auschwitz* (Cambridge, New York and Melbourne: Cambridge University Press, 1999) 82.
28 Saltzman gives a lengthy account of Kiefer's reception at home and abroad in ibid. 97–123.
29 Death is expressed principally through the image of 'black milk'. The drinking of 'black milk' is a repetitive motif that takes the reader through a day-long narrative of Jewish labour (grave digging) and Aryan control (hounds and 'shot made of lead'). Moreover, as the first three lines imply, this is an ongoing and relentless daily narrative. The fugue is written in the first person plural (a collective Jewish 'we') and addresses Margarete and Sulamith in their second person singular forms, through the repetition of 'Your golden hair, Margarete' and 'Your ashen hair, Sulamith', The man (camp guard) is referred to in the third person and acts as a further figure of death. A parallel narrative of the blue-eyed guard writing to his lover, Margarete, is woven into the poem, describing him as playing with vipers while he tyrannises his victims before he shoots them with 'shot made of lead shots'.
30 Saltzman, 28.
31 Richard Walter Darré, Reichsminister for food and agriculture 1933–1942 and a leading influence in the Race and Resettlement programme, was a key figure in emphasising the importance of blood and soil in Nazi Germany. Chapter XIII of *The Hitler Youth Handbook* (1937) is dedicated to the topic of German soil.
32 Rosenthal, 96.
33 Saltzman, 29.
34 Huyssen, *Twilight Memories* 225–227.
35 Ibid. 222–223.
36 Saltzman, 31.
37 Ibid. 65–66.
38 Ibid. 67–70.
39 Ibid. 82–92.
40 Georgia Marsh, 'The White and the Black: an Interview with Christian Boltanski', *Parkett* 22, 1989, 37.
41 Andreas Huyssen, 'Of Mice and Mimesis: Reading Spiegelman with Adorno', in *Present Pasts*, 122.
42 The two parts have been editioned together, firstly in the United States in 1996, and then in the United Kingdom as Art Spiegelman, *The Complete Maus* (Harmondsworth: Penguin Books, 2003). Page references given later are to *The Complete Maus*.
43 See Gary G. Groth 'Grown-UP Comics: Breakout from the Underground', *Print*, November/December 1988, 98–111. *An Argument at Work* was part

of a larger series, *American Splendor*, begun in 1976 and made into a feature film in 2003.

44 Art Spiegelman, 'Commix: an Idiosyncratic Historical and Aesthetic Overview', *Print*, November/December 1988, 61.

45 Spiegelman makes these points in an interview with Gary G. Groth, 'Art Spiegelman and Françoise Mouly', in Gary G. Groth and Robert Fiore, *The New Comics* (New York: Berkley Books, 1988) 190–191.

46 Joshua Brown, 'Of Mice and Memory', *Oral History Review*, Spring 1988, 91. Although grateful for the recognition, Spiegelman took the *New York Times Book Review* to task when he was listed among their fiction rather than non-fiction best-sellers: *New York Times Book Review*, 29 December 1991.

47 War comics of the 1950s and 1960s (as in EC comics, for instance) were invariably couched in the genre of the adventure story. *Maus* does, however, align with the literary genre of the new non-fiction (or creative non-fiction), pioneered by writers such as Truman Capote (*In Cold Blood*, 1965) and Norman Mailer (*Armies of the Night*, 1968).

48 LaCapra, 142.

49 *Prisoner on the Hell Planet: A Case History* first appeared in *Short Order Commix #1*, 1973. For the insert, see Spiegelman, *The Complete Maus* 102–105.

50 Hirsch, 31–32.

51 Spiegelman, *The Complete Maus* 5–6.

52 Ibid. 160–161.

53 Hirsch, 35.

54 Spiegelman, *The Complete Maus* 111.

55 Ibid. 175.

56 Ibid. 238, 249–250.

57 Ibid. 294.

58 Hirsch, 38–39.

59 Holocaust monuments have received extensive attention in two publications by James E. Young: *The Texture of Memory: Holocaust Memorials and Meaning* (New Haven, Connecticut, and London: Yale University Press, 1993) and *At Memory's Edge: After Images of the Holocaust in Contemporary Art* (New Haven, Connecticut, and London: Yale University Press, 2000).

60 Spiegelman, *The Complete Maus* 84.

61 Young, *At Memory's Edge* 128.

62 Ibid. 130.

63 Ibid. 131.

64 Ibid. 138–139.

CHAPTER 5

1 Arlene Raven, *Art in the Public Interest* (Cambridge: Da Capo Press, 1993) 1–2.
2 Suzi Gablik, *The Reenchantment of Art* (London: Thames and Hudson, 1991) 106; see also 162–163.
3 Lacy gives brief profiles of eighty-six such artists in the introduction to section 5 of Suzanne Lacy ed. *Mapping the Terrain: New Genre Public Art* (Seattle and Washington: Bay Press, 1995) 191–285. The range of practices she cites include outdoor installation work (Victor Acconti and Christo, for instance), performance (Ant Farm and herself, for instance), community-based projects (Group Material and Tim Rollins and KOS, for instance) and environmentally conscious art (Mel Chin and Merle Ukeles Laderman, for instance).
4 Nicolas Bourriaud, *Relational Aesthetics*, 1998 (Dijon: Les Presses du Réel, 2002) 13.
5 Ibid. See essay participation and transitivity, 25–40.
6 Ibid. 30–31.
7 Ibid. 15.
8 For more on memory and place, see Edward Casey, *Remembering: A Phenomenological Study*, 1987 (Bloomington: Indiana University Press, 2nd edn 2000) 181–189.
9 Endel Tulving and Wayne Donaldson, 'Episodic and Semantic Memory', in E. Tulving and W. Donaldson, eds *Organisation of Memory* (New York: New Academic Press, 1972) 381–403.
10 Casey, 182.
11 Simon Sadler, *The Situationist City* (Cambridge, Massachusetts: MIT Press, 1999) 17–19, 108–110.
12 See www.socialfiction.org. An applet is a program written in the Java[™] programming language that can be included in an HTML page.
13 See www.proboscis.org.uk.
14 Ibid.
15 Loaded with *Urban Tapestries* software and connected to the Orange GPRS network, or General Packet Radio Service (high-speed non-verbal transmission of info-supplements SMS).
16 Gabe Sawhney in Abigail Pugh, 'Flaneur by Phone: the [murmur] Project Brings Cellular Psychogeography to the Annex', *eye weekly*, 19 August 2004; www.eye.net.
17 Ibid.
18 Ibid.
19 See www.oneblockradius.org.
20 Walter Benjamin speaks of producing this kind of alternative map of the city in 'Berlin Chronicle', 596.

21 See www.rhizome.org.
22 Huyssen, *Twilight Memories* 6–7, and Nora, 18–20.
23 Benjamin, 'Excavation and Memory', 576; see also 'Berlin Chronicle', 611.
24 Michel de Certeau, 'Walking in the City', c. 1984, in *The Practice of Everyday Life* (Berkeley and London: University of California Press, 1988) 91–110.
25 Giles Lane, *Proboscis Cultural Snapshots Number Nine: July 2004, Social Tapestries*, ISSN 145–8474; see www.proboscis.org.uk.
26 A look at the list of Cardiff's walks between 1991 and 2007 quickly demonstrates the substantial support and funding that she has received internationally from respected art institutions and organisations. See Mirjam Schaub, *Janet Cardiff: The Walk Book* (Vienna: Thyssen-Bornemisa Art Contemporary, in collaboration with the Public Art Fund, New York, 2005) 342–343.
27 Ibid. 25.
28 Ibid. 15.
29 Carolyn Christov-Bakargiev, *Janet Cardiff: A Survey of Works Including Collaborations with George Bures Miller* (New York: P.S.1 Contemporary Arts Center, 2002) 23.
30 Casey, 216–217.
31 Janet Cardiff, 'Anatomy of a Walk', in ibid. 34.
32 Ibid. See also working notes for script, 52–55.
33 From CDRom recorded excerpts of selected walks, issued with ibid.
34 In Christov-Bakargiev, 80.
35 Schaub, 260.
36 From script of *Münster Walk*, in Christov-Bakargiev, 87.
37 Alex Ohlin, 'Something to be Desired: Janet Cardiff and the Pull of Film Noir', *Art Papers* 28, 1, January/February 2004, 34–39.
38 Script for *Münster Walk*, in Christov-Bakargiev, 87.
39 Script for *The Missing Voice (Case Study B)*, in ibid. 116.
40 Ibid. 118.
41 The first double-page spread of this feature is reproduced in the Pompidou Centre's, *Pierre Huyghe: The Third Memory* (New York, Paris and Chicago: the Pompidou Centre, the Renaissance Society at the University of Chicago and the Bohen Foundation, 2000) 68–69.
42 Pierre Huyghe, 'Pierre Huyghe', (part of round-table discussion), *October* 100, Spring 2002, 34.
43 Roland Barthes, 'The Third Meaning: Research Notes on some Eisentein Stills, 1970', in *Image, Music, Text* 60, 62. See also Ernst 'What is the Mechanism of Collage?', in Chipp, 427.
44 Huyghe. Huyghe paraphrases Barthes closely when talking of a fold of information; see Barthes, *Image, Music, Text* 62. Robert Hobbs also makes

the connection between Huyghe and Barthes, in 'Pierre Huyghe's Ellipses', *Parkett* 66, 2002, 160.

45 Guy Debord, *Society of the Spectacle*, 1967 (London: Rebel Press, 1992), and Theodor Adorno and Max Horkheimer, *The Dialectic of Enlightenment*, 1947 (London and New York: Verso, 1997).

46 Jean Baudrillard, 'Simulacra and Simulations', in Mark Poster, ed. *Jean Baudrillard: Selected Writings* (Oxford: Polity Press, in association with Basil Blackwell, 1988).

47 Jean-Charles Masséra, 'The Lesson of Stains', in *Pierre Huyghe: The Third Memory* 95.

48 Fourier's communities were nevertheless hierarchical in the distribution of wealth, on the understanding that some of the less pleasant work could be compensated by more pay. For more on Fourier, see Jonathan Beecher, *Charles Fourier: The Visionary and his World*, (Berkeley, Los Angeles and London: University of California Press, 1986). Huyghe links the *Streamside Day* project to Fourier in George Baker, 'An Interview with Pierre Huyghe', *October* 110, Fall 2004, 81.

49 Ibid. 85–86.

50 Ibid. 85.

51 Paul Connerton, *How Societies Remember* (Cambridge and New York: Cambridge University Press, 1989) 6.

52 Ibid. 21–24. Connerton names these three types of memory as 'personal memory', 'cognitive memory' and 'habit memory'. See also Maurice Halbwachs, *On Collective Memory*, 1925 (Chicago and London: University of Chicago Press, 1992).

53 Baker, 83.

54 See Laurence Bossé, Emma Dexter, Julia Garimorth, Vincent Honoré Hans Ulrich Obrist, 'Introduction', and Hans Ulich Obrist, 'Conversation with Pierre Huyghe', in Tate Gallery, *Pierre Huyghe: Celebration Park* (London: Tate Gallery, Exhibition Catalogue, 2006) 110 and 120 respectively.

55 Details of the journey, its rationale and the musical are to be found in the archive section of the Public Art Fund's extensive website: www.publicartfund.org.

56 See note 51, above.

57 See www.publicartfund.org.

58 See Nicholas Serota's retrospective account 'A New Direction: New Labour Sparked a Cultural Revolution – but Now it's Time for a New Arts Manifesto', *The Guardian*, 5 June 2006.

59 Michael Morris, 'Jeremy Deller: the Battle of Orgreave', in *Off Limits: 40 Artangel Projects* (London: Merrell Publishers, 2002) 91.

60 Ibid.

61 Jeremy Deller, *The English Civil War Part II: Personal Accounts of the 1984–1985 Miners' Strike* (London: Artangel Publishing, 2001) 7.

62 Ibid. 12–13.
63 Ibid. 23.
64 John Slyce, 'Jeremy Deller: Fables of the Reconstruction', *Flash Art*, February 2003, 75–76.
65 Ibid. 76.
66 Ibid.
67 Jenny Thomas, *War Games: Inside the World of 20th Century War Reenactors* (Washington: Smithsonian Books, 2004) 286.
68 Ibid. 284–285.

CHAPTER 6

1 Hal Foster, 'An Archival Impulse', *October* 110, Fall 2004, 3–4. Foster names Thomas Hirschhorn, Tacita Dean, Sam Durant, Douglas Gordon, Pierre Huyghe, Mark Dion and Renée Green, among others.
2 Ibid. 5.
3 Nato Thompson, 'Jeremey Deller: for the Love of the People', *Parkett* 74, 2005, 153.
4 Jeremy Deller and Alan Kane, *Folk Archive: Contemporary Popular Art from the UK* (London: Bookworks, 2005) 2.
5 Waldemar Januszczak, 'Folk Archive: under Jeremy Deller's Guidance, Folk Art Kicks off its Clogs for Ever', *The Times*, 15 May 2005.
6 Ibid.
7 See Brian O'Doherty, *Inside the White Cube: The Ideology of the Gallery Space*, 1986 (Berkeley and Los Angeles: University of California Press, 1999) 87–90.
8 Barr organised the Museum of Modern Art in New York according to a chronology that was represented in a diagram, *The Development of Abstract Art*, published in 1936. This charted the 'isms' of modern art, descending from Synthesism and Neo-Impressionism in 1890 to non-geometric abstract art and geometric abstract art in 1935, mentioning all the usual suspects, such as Fauvism, Cubism and Surrealism, along the way. In contrast to this and in line with criticism concerning the linearity of the chronological approach, the collection at Tate Modern is organised according to four themes, 'Material Gestures', 'Poetry and Dream', 'Idea and Object' and 'States of Flux', which allows for a more contextual and conceptual reading of the works. In its recent refurbishment MoMA has kept to the notion of a historical overview, but this is broader and not dependent on Barr's diagram. It also has a rotating or sampling system of display for its contemporary collection, which moves far from the historical overview of the earlier part of the collection.

9 See Brigit Pelzer, 'Les Indices de l'Exchange', in *Marcel Broodthaers* (Paris: Galerie National du Jeu de Paume, exhibition catalogue, 1992) 24.
10 These are listed in Rainer Borgemeister, 'The Eagle from the Oligocene to the Present', in Benjamin Buchloh, ed. *Broodthaers: Writings, Interviews, Photographs* (Cambridge, Massachusetts, and London: MIT Press, 1988) 137.
11 Douglas Crimp, 'This is Not a Museum of Art', in *On the Museums Ruins* (Cambridge Massachusetts, and London: MIT Press, 1993) 205.
12 Pelzer, 28.
13 Crimp, 212.
14 Borgemeister, 137–138.
15 Ibid. 139 for a more detailed list of contents.
16 Ibid. 142.
17 Pelzer, 221.
18 Dion speaks of the natural history museum in this way in 'Field Work and the Natural History Museum: Mark Dion Interview', in Alex Coles, ed. *The Optic of Walter Benjamin* (London: Black Dog Publishing, 1999) 43. Coles tries unsuccessfully to draw Dion out on the subject of Broodthaers in this interview.
19 Carolyn Christov-Bakargiev, 'Ursus Maritimus', in *Natural History and Other Fictions: An Exhibition by Mark Dion* (Ikon Gallery, Birmingham, De Appel, Amsterdam, and Kunstverein, Hamburg, 1997) 45.
20 Ibid. 45–48.
21 Jackie McAllister, 'The Desks of Mickey Cuvier', in ibid. 24.
22 Ibid. 25.
23 Helen Molesworth, *The Delirium of Alfred Russel Wallace*, in ibid. 32.
24 Ibid.
25 These are Fribourg, Switzerland (1995), Umbertide, Italy (1996), Venice (1997–1998) and London (1999).
26 While showing appreciation of the art in Dion's work, archaeologist Colin Renfrew has reservations about the extent to which Dion's amateur archaeology can be considered genuine, as it is essentially a critical art practice and does not, for instance, use traditional stratigraphic methodologies. See Colin Renfrew, 'It May Be Art, but Is It Archaeology? Science as Art and Art as Science', in Mark Dion and Alex Coles, eds *Mark Dion: Archaeology* (London: Black Dog Publishing, 1999) 13–22.
27 Ibid. 22
28 'Beyond Control: an Interview with Stuart Morgan', in Barbara Einzig, ed. *Thinking about Art: Conversations with Susan Hiller* (Manchester and New York: Manchester University Press, 1996) 244.
29 Immanuel Kant, *The Critique of Judgement*, 1790 (Oxford, Toronto and New York: Oxford University Press, 1952); see the discussion of the sublime, for instance, 119.

30 'Beyond Control' 247.
31 Rosemary Betterton, 'Susan Hiller's Painted Works', in James Lingwood, ed. *Susan Hiller: Recall, Selected Works, 1964–2004* (Gateshead: Baltic, 2004) 19.
32 Ibid.
33 'Portrait of the Artist as a Photomat', talk given to the Patrons of New Art from the Tate Gallery, 1983, in Einzig, 60–61.
34 Raudive spend almost ten years scientifically researching 'electronic voice phenomena', publishing his findings in *Breakthrough* (London: Colin Smythe, 1971).
35 Tate Liverpool, *Susan Hiller* (London: Tate Publishing, 1996) 72.
36 Ibid. See also Susan Hiller, 'Belshazzar's Feast: the Writing on the Wall', an interview with Catherine Kinley, in Einzig, 90–91.
37 For the archive as a place of consignment, see Jacques Derrida, *Archive Fever: A Freudian Impression* (Chicago: University of Chicago Press, 1995) 3–5. For the start of his claim to Freud as representative of the 'question of the archive', see ibid. 7–23. It may be worth noting that much of this book does not speak directly to these issues but is taken up with a rather lengthy discussion of whether psychoanalysis is a Jewish science and the Oedipal implications of this (through an engagement with Yosef Hayim Yerushelmi's *Freud's Moses: Judaism Terminable and Interminable* (New Haven, Connecticut: Yale University Press, 1991) 3–81. The more pointed discussion occurs either side of this.
38 Derrida, 13–20.
39 Ibid. 19, 90–91.
40 Ibid. 87.
41 Einzig, 227.
42 Ibid. 228.
43 Ibid.
44 Ibid. 229.
45 Ibid. 230.
46 Ibid. 231.
47 Ibid.
48 Derrida, 2, 95.
49 Ibid. 90.
50 Manuel Delanda, 'The Archive: before and after Foucault', in Joke Brouwer and Arjen Mulder, eds, *Information Is Alive* (Rotterdam: V2_Publishing and NAi publishers, 2003) 8–13.
51 Arjun Appadurai, 'Archive and Inspiration', in ibid. 14–15.
52 Brouwer and Mulder, 4.
53 Ibid. 5.
54 See www.georgelegrady.com.
55 Ibid.
56 Ibid.

57 Janet Murray, *Hamlet on the Holodeck: The Future of Narrative in Cyberspace* (Cambridge, Massachusetts: MIT Press, 1997) 188–194, 153.
58 See www.georgelegrady.com.
59 Halbwachs, 41. *An Anecdoted Archive from the Cold War* contains movie extracts, video footage of Eastern European places and events, objects, books, family documents, socialist propaganda, money, sound recordings, news reports, identity cards, Western media reports, etc. See www.georgelegrady.com.
60 Florian Brody, 'The Medium Is the Memory', in Peter Lunenfeld, ed. *The Digital Dialectic: New Essays on New Media* (Cambridge, Massachusetts: MIT Press, 1999) 135–148.
61 Teuvo Kohonen, *Self Organising Maps* (Berlin Heidelberg, New York: Springer, 3rd edn 2001).
62 See www.georgelegrady.com.

EPILOGUE

1 Sigmund Freud, 'Civilisation and its Discontents', 1930 in *Civilization, Society and Religion* (Harmondsworth: Penguin Books, the Penguin Freud Library, vol. 12, 1991) 256.
2 Sigmund Freud, 'A Note on the Mystic Writing Pad', 1925, in *On Metapsychology* (Harmondsworth: Penguin Books, the Penguin Freud Library, vol. 11, 1984) 429–434.
3 Sigmund Freud, 'Repression', 1915, in *On Metapsychology* (Harmondsworth: Penguin Books, the Penguin Freud Library, vol. 11, 1984) 148.
4 Marc Augé, *Oblivion* (Minneapolis: University of Minnesota Press, 2004) 20.
5 Jorge Luis Borges, 'Funes and his Memory', in *Fictions* (Harmondsworth: Penguin Classics, 1999) 91–99. In this short story, the son of a Uruguayan ironing woman, Ireneo Funes, develops a seemingly limitless capacity to remember after a riding accident, the penalty for which is to be so drowned in specificities that he becomes incapable of platonic abstractions and ends up without the powers of discrimination that the opportunity to think and reflect that being able to selectively forget brings. There are, of course, real-life versions of profound amnesia and over-saturated memory. The tragic consequences of memory saturation are demonstrated by the case of the Russian mnemonist Solomon Shereshevskii (1886–1958), who, unable to place his memories into a context and distinguish something that happened minutes before from things that had happened years before, ended up in an asylum: see Alexander R. Luria, *The Mind of a Mnemonist: A Little Book about a Vast Memory*, 1968 (Cambridge, Massachusetts: Harvard University Press, 1987). The tragedy of severely limited recall is witnessed in the case

of Clive Wearing, who was the subject of an ITV documentary, *The Man with the 7 Second Memory*, 2005.

6 Michael Landy, 'The Breakdown in Oxford Street', *Creative Review* 21, 2, 2001.

7 Michael Landy, *Breakdown* (London: Artangel Publishing, 2001)

8 Mary Douglas and Baron Isherwood, *The World of Goods: An Anthropology of Consumption*, 1979 (London and New York: Routledge, 1996) 38–39, 43–45.

9 Halbwachs, 43.

10 Yiannis Gabriel and Tim Lang, *The Unmanageable Consumer* (London, Thousand Oaks, California, and New Delhi: Sage Publications, 2nd edn 2006) 55, 95.

11 Landy, 'The Breakdown in Oxford Street'.

12 Becky Shaw, 'Twelve Museums', in Claire Doherty, *Contemporary Art: From Studio to Situation* (London: Black Dog Publishing, 2004) 170.

13 A. A. Gill, 'Mind Games', *Sunday Times Magazine*, 2 March 2003.

14 Ibid.

15 Shaw, 173.

16 Ibid. 170–171.

17 Paul Scheerbart, *Glass Architecture*, 1914 (London: November Books, 1972).

18 Shaw, 172.

19 Ibid.

20 See Tate Gallery, *Michael Landy: Semi Detached* (London: Tate Publishing, 2004), with essays by Judith Nesbitt and John Slyce.

21 Casey, 293.

BIBLIOGRAPHY

Adorno, Theodor, and Horkheimer, Max, *The Dialectic of Enlightenment*, 1947 (London and New York: Verso, 1997)

Ankori, Gannit, 'Frida Kahlo: the Fabric of Her Art', in Tate Gallery, *Frida Kahlo* (London: Tate Publishing, 2005)

Araeen, Rasheed, 'The Success and Failure of Black Art', *Third Text* 18, March 2004

Augé, Marc, *Oblivion* (Minneapolis: University of Minnesota Press, 2004)

Baddeley, Oriana, 'Reflecting on Kahlo: Mirrors, Masquerade and the Politics of Identification', in Tate Gallery, *Frida Kahlo* (London: Tate Publishing, 2005)

Bailey, David A., *A Ship Called Jesus* (Birmingham: Ikon Gallery, exhibition catalogue, 1991)

Baker, George, 'An Interview with Pierre Huyghe', *October* 110, Fall 2004

Barson, Tanya, 'All Art is at Once Surface and Symbol: a Frida Kahlo Glossary', in Tate Gallery, *Frida Kahlo* (London: Tate Publishing, 2005)

Barthes, Roland, *Image, Music, Text* (London: Fontana, 1977)

— *Camera Lucida*, 1980 (London: Vintage, 2000)

Basualdi, Carlos, Huyssen, Andreas, and Princenthal, Nancy, eds, *Doris Salcedo* (London: Phaidon Press, 2000)

Batchen, Geoffrey, *Forget Me Not: Photography and Remembrance* (New York: Princeton Architectural Press, 2004)

Beecher, Jonathan, *Charles Fourier: The Visionary and his World*, (Berkeley, Los Angeles and London: University of California Press, 1986)

Benjamin, Walter, 'Excavation and Memory', c. 1932, in Michael Jennings, Howard Eiland and Gary Smith, eds, *Walter Benjamin: Selected Writings*, vol. 2, part 2, 1931–1934 (Cambridge, Massachusetts: MIT Press, 1998)

Bennett, Andrew, and Royle, Nicholas, *Literature, Criticism and Theory* (Harlow: Pearson Longman, 3rd edn 2004)

Bennett, Jill, *Empathic Vision: Affect, Trauma, and Contemporary Art* (Stanford, California: Stanford University Press, 2005)

Berger, John, *Ways of Seeing* (Harmondsworth: Pelican Books, in conjunction with the BBC, 1972)

Berger, John, and Mohr, Jean, eds *Another Way of Telling* (Cambridge: Granta, 1987)

Bergson, Henri, *Matter and Memory*, 1910 (New York: Zone Books, 1991)

Borges, Jorge Luis, 'Funes and his Memory', in *Fictions* (Harmondsworth: Penguin Classics, 1999)

Bourgeois, Louise, *Destruction of the Father, Reconstruction of the Father: Writings and Interviews 1923–1997* (Cambridge, Massachusetts: MIT Press, 1998)

Bourriaud, Nicolas, *Relational Aesthetics*, 1998 (Dijon: Les Presses du Réel, 2002)

Breton, André, *Manifestoes of Surrealism*, 1955 (Ann Arbor: University of Michigan Press, 1972)

Brody, Florian, 'The Medium Is the Memory', in Peter Lunenfeld, ed. *The Digital Dialectic: New Essays on New Media* (Cambridge, Massachusetts: MIT Press, 1999)

Brookner, Anita, *Jacques Louis David* (London: Thames and Hudson, 1987)

Broude, Norma, and Garrard, Mary, *The Power of Feminist Art* (London: Thames and Hudson, 1996)

Brouwer, Joke, and Mulder, Arjen, eds *Information Is Alive* (Rotterdam: V2_Publishing and NAi publishers, 2003)

Brown, Joshua, 'Of Mice and Memory', *Oral History Review*, Spring 1988

Buchloh, Benjamin, ed. *Broodthaers: Writings, Interviews, Photographs* (Cambridge, Massachusetts, and London: MIT Press, 1988)

Burgin, Victor, ed. *Thinking Photography* (Basingstoke and London: Macmillan, 1982)

Burrows, David, ed. *Who's Afraid of Red, White and Blue?* (Birmingham: Article Press, 1998)

Caruth, Cathy, *Unclaimed Experience: Trauma, Narrative and History* (Baltimore and London: Johns Hopkins University Press, 1996)

Casey, Edward, *Remembering: A Phenomenological Study*, 1987 (Bloomington: Indiana University Press, 2nd edn 2000)

Chicago, Judy, *The Dinner Party* (Harmondsworth: Penguin Books, 1996)

Childs, Peter, and Williams, Patrick, *An Introduction to Postcolonial Theory* (London, New York, Toronto, Sydney, Tokyo, Singapore, Madrid, Mexico City, Munich and Paris: Prentice Hall/Harvester Wheatsheaf, 1997)

Chipp, Herschel B., ed. *Theories of Modern Art* (Berkeley, Los Angeles and London: University of California Press, 1968)

Christov-Bakargiev, Carolyn, 'Ursus Maritimus', in *Natural History and Other Fictions: An Exhibition by Mark Dion* (Ikon Gallery, Birmingham, De Appel, Amsterdam, and Kunstverein, Hamburg, 1997)

— *Janet Cardiff: A Survey of Works Including Collaborations with George Bures Miller* (New York: P.S.1 Contemporary Arts Center, 2002)

Coles, Alex, ed. *The Optic of Walter Benjamin* (London: Black Dog Publishing, 1999)

Connerton, Paul, *How Societies Remember* (Cambridge and New York: Cambridge University Press, 1989)
Costa, Guido, *Nan Goldin* (London and New York: Phaidon Press, 2001)
Crimp, Douglas, *On the Museums Ruins* (Cambridge, Massachusetts, and London: MIT Press, 1993)
Danto, Arthur C., *After the End of Art: Contemporary Art and the Pale of History* (Princeton, New Jersey: Princeton University Press, 1997)
De Certeau, Michel, *The Practice of Everyday Life* (Berkeley and London: University of California Press, 1988)
Debord, Guy, *Society of the Spectacle*, 1967 (London: Rebel Press, 1992)
Deller, Jeremy, *The English Civil War Part II: Personal Accounts of the 1984–1985 Miners' Strike* (London: Artangel Publishing, 2001)
Deller, Jeremy, and Kane, Alan, *Folk Archive: Contemporary Popular Art from the UK* (London: Bookworks, 2005)
Derrida, Jacques, *Archive Fever: A Freudian Impression* (Chicago: University of Chicago Press, 1995)
Didi-Huberman, Georges, *Invention of Hysteria, Charcot and the Photographic Iconography of the Salpêtrière* (Cambridge, Massachusetts: MIT Press, 2003)
Dion, Mark, and Coles, Alex, eds *Mark Dion: Archaeology* (London: Black Dog Publishing, 1999)
Douglas, Mary, and Isherwood, Baron, *The World of Goods: An Anthropology of Consumption*, 1979 (London and New York: Routledge, 1996)
Doy, Gen, *Black Visual Culture: Modernity and Postmodernity* (London and New York: I.B. Tauris, 2000)
— *Picturing the Self: Changing Views of the Subject in Visual Culture* (London and New York: I.B. Tauris, 2005)
Eakin, Paul John, ed. *On Autobiography* (Minneapolis: University of Minnesota Press, 1989)
— *How our Lives Become Stories* (Ithaca, New York, and London: Cornell University Press, 1999)
Edwards, Steve, ed. *Art and its Histories: A Reader* (New Haven, Connecticut, and London: Yale University Press, in association with the Open University, 1999)
Eiland, Howard, and Jennings, Michael, eds, *Walter Benjamin: Selected Writings*, vol. 3, *1935–1938* (Cambridge, Massachusetts, and London: Belknap Press, 2006)
Einzig, Barbara, ed. *Thinking about Art: Conversations with Susan Hiller* (Manchester and New York: Manchester University Press, 1996)
Elgar, Dietmar, ed. *Felix Gonzalez-Torres: Text* (catalogue raisonné) (Stuttgart: Cantz Verlag, 1997)
Elliot, Patrick, 'Sculpting Nothing: an Introduction to the Work of Rachel Whiteread', in Scottish National Gallery of Modern Art and Serpentine

Galley, *Rachel Whiteread* (exhibition catalogue) (Edinburgh: Trustees of the National Gallery, Scotland, 2001)
Emin, Tracey, *Strangeland* (London: Hodder and Stoughton, 2005)
Falk, Pasi, *The Consuming Body* (London, Thousand Oaks, California, and New Delhi: Sage Publications, 1994)
Foster, Hal, 'An Archival Impulse', *October* 110, Fall 2004
Foucault, Michel, *The Birth of the Clinic: An Archaeology of Medical Perception*, 1963 (London: Tavistock, 1970)
— *The Archaeology of Knowledge*, 1969 (London and New York: Routledge, 1989)
— *Discipline and Punish: The Birth of the Prison*, 1975 (New York: Vintage Books, 1995)
Freud, Sigmund, *The Interpretation of Dreams*, 1901 (Harmondsworth: Penguin Books, the Penguin Freud Library, vol. 4, 1976, reprinted 1991)
— 'Repression', 1915, in *On Metapsychology* (Harmondsworth: Penguin Books, the Penguin Freud Library, vol. 11, 1984)
— 'Mourning and Melancholia', 1917, in *On Metapsychology* (Harmondsworth: Penguin Books, the Penguin Freud Library, vol. 11, 1984)
— 'The Ego and the Id', 1923, in *On Metapsychology*, (Harmondsworth: Penguin Books, the Penguin Freud Library, vol. 11, 1984)
— 'A Note on the Mystic Writing Pad', 1925, in *On Metapsychology* (Harmondsworth: Penguin Books, the Penguin Freud Library, vol. 11, 1984)
— 'Civilisation and its Discontents', 1930, in *Civilization, Society and Religion* (Harmondsworth: Penguin Books, the Penguin Freud Library, vol. 12, 1991)
Gablik, Suzi, *The Reenchantment of Art* (London: Thames and Hudson, 1991)
Gabriel, Yiannis, and Lang, Tim, *The Unmanageable Consumer* (London, Thousand Oaks, California, and New Delhi: Sage Publications, 2nd edn 2006)
Garb, Tamar, 'Engaging Embroidery', *Art History* 9, 1986
Gibbons, Joan, *Art and Advertising* (London and New York: I.B. Tauris, 2005)
Gibbons, Joan, and Winwood, Kaye, eds, *The Hothaus Papers: Perspectives and Paradigms in Media Arts* (Birmingham: Article Press, in association with VIVID, 2006)
Gill, A. A., 'Mind Games', *Sunday Times Magazine*, 2 March 2003
Gilmore, Leigh, *The Limits of Autobiography: Trauma and Testimony* (Ithaca, New York, and London: Cornell University Press, 2001)
Goldin, Nan, *The Ballad of Sexual Dependency* (New York: Aperture Foundation Books, 1986)

— *I'll Be Your Mirror* (New York: Whitney Museum of American Art, 1996)
— *Soeurs, Saints et Sibylles* (Paris: Editions du Regard, 2004)
Gonzalez-Torres, Felix, 'Practices: the Problem of Divisions of Cultural Labour', *Art and Design* 9, January–February 1994
Groth, Gary G., 'Grown-UP Comics: Breakout from the Underground', *Print*, November/December 1988
Groth, Gary G., and Fiore, Robert, *The New Comics* (New York: Berkley Books, 1988)
Guldemond, Jaap, Mackert, Gabrielle, and van Kooij, Barbera, eds *Yinka Shonibare: Double Dutch* (Rotterdam: NAi Publishers, 2004)
Gumpert, Lynn, *Christian Boltanski* (Paris: Flammarion, 1994)
Gupta, Dipankar, *Learning to Forget: The Anti-memoirs of Modernity* (Oxford and New York: Oxford University Press, 2005)
Halbwachs, Maurice, *On Collective Memory*, 1925 (Chicago and London: University of Chicago Press, 1992)
Herrera, Hayden, *Frida Kahlo: The Paintings*, (London: Bloomsbury, 1991)
Hirsch, Marianne, *Family Frames: Photography, Narrative and Postmemory* (Cambridge, Massachusetts, and London: Harvard University Press, 1997)
Hobbs, Robert, 'Pierre Huyghe's Ellipses', *Parkett* 66, 2002
Houser, Nathan, and Koesel, Christian, eds, *The Essential Peirce: Selected Writings*, vol. 2 (Bloomington and Indianapolis: Indiana University Press, 1998)
Huyghe, Pierre, 'Pierre Huyghe', *October* 100, Spring 2002
Huyssen, Andreas, *Twilight Memories: Marking Time in a Culture of Amnesia* (London and New York: Routledge, 1995)
— *Present Pasts: Urban Palimpsests and the Politics of Memory* (Stanford, California: Stanford University Press, 2003)
Innis, Robert, ed. *Semiotics: An Introductory Anthology* (Bloomington: Indiana University Press, 1985)
Ishiuchi, Miyako, *Mother's 2000–2005: Traces of the Future* (Tokyo: Japan Foundation, 2005)
James, William, *The Principles of Psychology* (New York: Henry Holt, 1890)
Januszczak, Waldemar, 'Folk Archive: under Jeremy Deller's Guidance, Folk Art Kicks off its Clogs for Ever', *The Times*, 15 May 2005
Jay, Martin, *Downcast Eyes: The Denigration of Vision in Twentieth-century French Thought* (Berkeley: University of California Press, 1994)
Jenkins, Keith, *Re-thinking History* (London and New York: Routledge, 1991, republished as a Routledge Classic in 2003)
Jenks, Chris, ed. *Visual Culture* (London and New York: Routledge, 1995)

Jennings, Michael, Eiland, Howard, and Smith, Gary, eds, *Walter Benjamin: Selected Writings*, vol. 2, part 2, *1931–1934* (Cambridge, Massachusetts, and London: Belknap Press, 2005)

Jones, Amelia, ed. *Sexual Politics: Judy Chicago's Dinner Party in Feminist Art History* (Berkeley, Los Angeles and London: University of California Press, 1996)

Kant, Immanuel, *The Critique of Judgement*, 1790 (Oxford, Toronto and New York: Oxford University Press, 1952)

Kertész, Imre, 'Who Owns Auschwitz?', *Yale Journal of Criticism* 14, 1, 2001

King, Nicola, *Memory, Narrative, Identity: Remembering the Self* (Edinburgh: Edinburgh University Press, 2000)

Kohonen, Teuvo, *Self Organising Maps* (Berlin Heidelberg, New York: Springer, 3rd edn 2001)

Krauss, Rosalind, *The Originality of the Avant-garde and Other Modernist Myths* (Cambridge, Massachusetts: MIT Press, 1994)

Kristeva, Julia, *Powers of Horror: An Essay on Abjection* (New York and Guildford: Columbia University Press, 1982)

Kuhn, Annette, *Family Secrets: Acts of Memory and Imagination* (London and New York: Verso, 1995)

LaCapra, Dominick, *History and Memory after Auschwitz* (Ithaca, New York, and London: Cornell University Press, 1998)

Lacy, Suzanne, ed. *Mapping the Terrain: New Genre Public Art* (Seattle and Washington: Bay Press, 1995)

Landy, Michael, *Breakdown* (London: Artangel Publishing, 2001)

— 'The Breakdown in Oxford Street', *Creative Review* 21, 2, 2001

Langer, Lawrence L., *Holocaust Memories: The Ruins of Memory* (New Haven, Connecticut, and London: Yale University Press, 1991)

Laplanche, J., and Pontalis, J. B., *The Language of Psychoanalysis* (London: Karnac Books, 1998)

Lejeune, Philippe, 'The Autobiographical Pact', in John Paul Eakin, ed. *On Autobiography* (Minneapolis: University of Minnesota Press, 1989)

Lingwood, James, ed. *Susan Hiller: Recall, Selected Works, 1964–2004* (Gateshead: Baltic, 2004)

Lunenfeld, Peter, ed. *The Digital Dialectic: New Essays on New Media* (Cambridge, Massachusetts: MIT Press, 1999)

Luria, Alexander R., *The Mind of a Mnemonist: A Little Book about a Vast Memory*, 1968 (Cambridge, Massachusetts: Harvard University Press, 1987)

Lyotard, Jean-François, *The Postmodern Condition: A Report on Knowledge*, 1979 (Manchester: Manchester University Press, 1984)

— 'The Sublime and the Avant-Garde', *Artforum*, April 1984

Marsh, Georgia, 'The White and the Black: an Interview with Christian Boltanski', *Parkett* 22, 1989

Mascuch, Michael, *Origins of the Individualist Self: Autobiography and Self-identity in England, 1591–1791* (Cambridge: Polity Press, 1997)

McAllister, Jackie, 'The Desks of Mickey Cuvier', in *Natural History and Other Fictions: An Exhibition by Mark Dion* (Ikon Gallery, Birmingham, De Appel, Amsterdam, and Kunstverein, Hamburg, 1997)

McGaugh, James L., *Memory and Emotion: The Making of Lasting Memories* (New York: Columbia University Press, 2003)

Mercer, Kobena, 'Black Art and the Burden of Representation', *Third Text* 10, Spring 1990

Merck, Mandy, and Townsend, Chris, eds *The Art of Tracey Emin* (London: Thames and Hudson, 2002)

Misztal, Barbara A., *Theories of Social Remembering* (Maidenhead and Phiadelphia: Open University Press, 2003)

Morgan, Stuart, ed. *Rites of Passage: Art for the End of the Century* (London: Tate Gallery Publications, 1995)

Morris, Frances, *Louise Bourgeois: Stitches in Time* (London: August Projects, 2003)

Morris, Michael, 'Jeremy Deller: the Battle of Orgreave', in *Off Limits: 40 Artangel Projects* (London: Merrell Publishers, 2002)

Murray, Janet, *Hamlet on the Holodeck: The Future of Narrative in Cyberspace* (Cambridge, Massachusetts: MIT Press, 1997)

Nesbit, Molly, 'Casting Out', in Deutsche Guggenheim Berlin, *Transient Spaces* (exhibition catalogue) (New York: Guggenheim Museum Publications, 2001)

New York Times Book Review, 29 December 1991

Nora, Pierre, 'Between Memory and History: les Lieux de Mémoire', *Representations* 26, Spring 1989

O'Doherty, Brian, *Inside the White Cube: The Ideology of the Gallery Space*, 1986 (Berkeley and Los Angeles: University of California Press, 1999)

Ohlin, Alex, 'Something to be Desired: Janet Cardiff and the Pull of Film Noir', *Art Papers* 28, 1, January/February 2004

Parker, Rozsika, and Pollock, Griselda, eds *Framing Feminism: Art and the Women's Movement, 1975–1985* (London: Pandora, 1987)

Pelzer, Brigit, 'Les Indices de l'Exchange', in *Marcel Broodthaers* (Paris: Galerie National du Jeu de Paume, exhibition catalogue, 1992)

Pilling, John, ed. *Autobiography and Imagination: Studies in Self-Scrutiny* (London, Boston and Henley: Routledge and Kegan Paul, 1981)

Pompidou Centre, *Pierre Huyghe: The Third Memory* (New York, Paris and Chicago: the Pompidou Centre, the Renaissance Society at the University of Chicago and the Bohen Foundation, 2000)

Poster, Mark, ed. *Jean Baudrillard: Selected Writings* (Oxford: Polity Press, in association with Basil Blackwell, 1988)

Proust, Marcel, *In Search of Lost Time*, vol. 1, *Swann's Way*, 1913 (London: Vintage Classics, 2002)
Pugh, Abigail, 'Flaneur by Phone: the [murmur] Project Brings Cellular Psychogeography to the Annex', *eye weekly*, 19 August 2004
Radstone, Susannah, ed. *Memory and Methodology* (Oxford and New York: Berg, 2000)
Raudive, Konstantin, *Breakthrough* (London: Colin Smythe, 1971)
Raven, Arlene, *Art in the Public Interest* (Cambridge: Da Capo Press, 1993)
Rosenthal, Mark, *Anselm Kiefer* (Chicago and Philadelphia: the Art Institute of Chicago and the Philadelphia Museum of Art, 1988)
Sadler, Simon, *The Situationist City* (Cambridge, Massachusetts: MIT Press, 1999)
Said, Edward, *Orientalism* (Harmondsworth: Penguin Books, 2nd edn 1995)
Saltzman, Lisa, *Anselm Kiefer and Art after Auschwitz* (Cambridge, New York and Melbourne: Cambridge University Press, 1999)
Schama, Simon, *Rembrandt's Eyes* (London: Penguin Books, 1999)
Schaub, Mirjam, *Janet Cardiff: The Walk Book* (Vienna: Thyssen-Bornemisa Art Contemporary, in collaboration with the Public Art Fund, New York, 2005)
Scheerbost, Paul, *Glass Architecture*, 1914 (London: November Books, 1972)
Schwartz, Gary, *Rembrandt: His Life, his Paintings* (London: Penguin Books, 1985)
Sekula, Allan, 'The Traffic in Photographs', *Art Journal*, Spring 1981
Semin, Didier, Garb, Tamar, Kuspir, Donald, and Perec, Georges, *Christian Boltanski* (London: Phaidon Press, 1997)
Shaw, Becky, 'Twelve Museums', in Claire Doherty, *Contemporary Art: From Studio to Situation* (London: Black Dog Publishing, 2004)
Slyce, John, 'Jeremy Deller: Fables of the Reconstruction', *Flash Art*, February 2003
Smith, Sidonie, and Watson, Julia, eds *Getting a Life: Everyday Uses of Autobiography* (Minneapolis: University of Minnesota Press, 1996)
— 'The Rumpled Bed of Autobiography: Extravagant Lives, Extravagant Questions' *Biography* 24, 1, Autumn 2001
Sontag, Susan, *On Photography* (Harmondsworth: Penguin Books, 1977)
Spector, Nancy, *Felix Gonzalez-Torres* (New York: Guggenheim Museum, 1995)
Spiegelman, Art, 'Commix: an Idiosyncratic Historical and Aesthetic Overview', *Print*, November/December 1988
— *The Complete Maus* (Harmondsworth: Penguin Books, 2003)
Storr, Robert, Herkenhoff, Paulo, and Schwartzman, Allan, eds *Louise Bourgeois* (London: Phaidon Press, 2003)

Tate Gallery, *Michael Landy: Semi Detached* (London: Tate Publishing, 2004)
— *Frida Kahlo* (London: Tate Publishing, 2005)
— *Pierre Huyghe: Celebration Park* (London: Tate Gallery, exhibition catalogue, 2006)
Tate Liverpool, *Susan Hiller* (London: Tate Publishing, 1996)
Thomas, Jenny, *War Games: Inside the World of 20th Century War Reenactors* (Washington: Smithsonian Books, 2004)
Thompson, Nato, 'Jeremey Deller: for the Love of the People', *Parkett* 74, 2005
Tolia-Kelly, Divya, and Morris, Andy, 'Disruptive Aesthetics? Revisiting the Burden of Representation in the Art of Chris Ofili and Yinka Shonibare', *Third Text* 18, 2, 2004
Townsend, Chris, ed. *The Art of Rachel Whiteread* (London: Thames and Hudson, 2004)
Tulving, Endel, and Donaldson, Wayne, eds *Organisation of Memory* (New York: New Academic Press, 1972)
Van Alphen, Ernst, *Caught by History: Holocaust Effects in Contemporary Art, Literature and Theory* (Stanford, California: Stanford University Press, 1997)
Wakefield, Neville, 'Separation Anxiety and the Art of Release', *Parkett* 42, 1994
Warnock, Mary, *Memory* (London: Faber and Faber, 1987)
Waspe, Roland, 'Private and Public', in Dietmar Elgar, ed. *Felix Gonzalez-Torres: Text* (catalogue raisonné) (Stuttgart: Cantz Verlag, 1997)
Watney, Simon, 'About the House', *Parkett* 42, 1994
Yates, Frances A., *The Art of Memory*, 1966 (London: Pimlico, 1992)
Young, James E., *The Texture of Memory: Holocaust Memorials and Meaning* (New Haven, Connecticut, and London: Yale University Press, 1993)
— *At Memory's Edge: After Images of the Holocaust in Contemporary Art* (New Haven, Connecticut, and London: Yale University Press, 2000)
Wong, Edlie, 'Situating Memory in the Art of Doris Salcedo', *Critical Sense*, Winter 2001

WEBSITES

www.brooklynmuseum.org/collections/eascfa.php
www.digitaljournalist.org/issue0106/voices_goldin.htm
www.georgelegrady.com
www.helsinki.fi/science/commens/dictionaryfront.html
www.publicartfund.org

www.resoundings.org/Pages/Interview2.htm
www.jeanettewinterson.com/pages/content/index.asp?PageID=357
www.oneblockradius.org
www.socialfiction.org
www.proboscis.org.uk
www.eye.net
www.rhizome.org

INDEX

Adorno, Theodor 75, 87, 109
Age Concern 145
AIDS 24, 25, 42, 44
Alamo 119
amnesia 1
Amnesty International 114
Angus, Alice 98
Anhalter Bahnhof 50
Ankori, Gannit 14, 15
Antarctic 112
anthropology 131, 136
Appadurai, Arjun 135
Araeen, Rasheed 64–65, 71
Aragon, Louis 98
Arc de Triomphe 49
archaeology 125–126, 133–134
archival practices 76–77, 119, 120, 134, 135 (in George Legrady 136–138)
archives 4, 8, 118 (virtual, 135–136)
    archive as psyche 131
    archive fever 130, 131
    archival impulse (drive) 119, 130
Aristotle 1
art of memory (ancient) 17
Artangel 114
artificial memory 2
Artpace (Texas) 119
audio walks 103–107
Augé, Marc 141
Auschwitz 78, 89
autobiography 8, 9–28, 30, 129
automatic writing 40, 128–129

Bailey, David A. 65
Bambi 112
Barr, Alfred 121
Barthes, Roland 32, 38–39, 108
Baudelaire, Charles 53
Baudrillard, Jean 109
Benjamin, Walter 5, 15–16, 48, 102
Bennett, Jill 60, 63
Berger, John 32, 70
Bergson, Henri 5, 6
Betterton, Rosemary 128
biomorphic surrealism 16
black art 64–71
black identity 65
Bloch, Susi 17
blood and soil 84, 86
Boiffard, Jacques-André 41
Bold, Alf 45, 46
Boltanski, Christian 76–80, 87, 88, 92, 94
Borgemeister, Rainer 123
Borges, Jorge-Luis 141
Bourgeois, Louise 16–19, 22, 23, 28, 34
Bourriaud, Nicolas 96–97
Bowers v. Hardwick 26
Brancusi, Constantin 16
Breton, André 40, 98
Brody, Florian 139

Broodthaers, Marcel 120–123, 124, 126, 127, 132
Brouwer, Jake 135
Brown, Joshua 89
Brucker-Cohen, Jonah 102
Buchenwald 82
Buren Daniel 120
Burgin, Victor 37
Bush, President George B. 119

Campbell, Ian 114
Cardiff, Janet 103–107
Caruth, Cathy 15, 74–75
Casey, Edward 98, 147
Cash, Johnny 47
Cave, Nick 47
Celan, Paul 75, 83
Celebration (Florida) 110
Celebration Park 111
Central Park (NY) 104–105, 112
Certeau, Michel de 102, 103
Chambers, Eddie 65
chat show 9, 19
Checkpoint Charlie 50
Chicago, Judy 55–58, 67
Christo 120
Christov-Bakargiev, Carolyn 124
cinema verité 44
Cladders, Johannes 123
Cody, Joshua 113
Cohen, Leonard 47
Cold War 137, 138
Coleridge, Samuel Taylor 3
colonialism 4, 66, 68, 70, 71
Columbus, Christopher 112
comics 88
commemoration 33, 41, 46, 49, 92, 104, 111, 114, 145
Connerton, Paul 111, 112
convulsive beauty 40, 41
Cook, Captain James 112
counter-history 67, 71, 73
counter-memory 51, 54, 58, 63, 64, 71, 73
Courbet, Gustave 54
Crawford (Texas) 19
Crimp, Douglas 123
Crumb, Robert 88
Cuvier, Baron Georges 124

Dada 18, 21
daguerreotype 37, 40
Danto Arthur C. xiii
data/databases 4, 118, 135
data protection 135
David, Jacques-Louis 53
Dean, Tacita 120
Debord, Guy 109
Delacroix, Eugene 13
Delanda, Manuel 134
Deleuze, Gilles 63
Deller, Jeremy 107, 113–117, 119–120, 126, 135
dementia 145
derive 98
Derrida, Jacques 31, 59, 130–131, 134
Descartes, René 1
Dessurault, Pierre 136
détournement 98
Dimitrijevic, Braco 97
Dion, Mark 124–126, 127
Douglas, Mary 144
Doy, Gen 10
Duchamp, Marcel 31
Durand-Dessert, Michel 77

Eakin, Paul John 22
Elizabeth A. Sackler Centre for Feminist Art 58
Elliot, Patrick 32
Emin, Tracey 19–23, 31, 34
enactment 8, 97
Ernst, Max 70, 108
Eubank, Chris 68
Expressionism 83
Extrasensory perception 128

false memory syndrome 4
family photography 30, 34

Félibien, André 53
fetish 37, 41
Fibonacci numerical system 98
Figgis, Mike 114
film noir 105–106
Fontana, Bill 29, 30, 48–51
forgetting 8, 140, 141, 147
Fortunoff Video Archive for Holocaust Testimonies 74
Foster, Hal xiii, 119
Foucault, Michel 4, 53, 134
Fourier, Charles 110
Fragonard, Honoré 68
French Academy 53
French Revolution 53–54
Freud Museum 132, 134
Freud, Sigmund 5, 11, 15, 102, 130, 131, 132–133, 134, 141
Friedrich, Casper David 82

Gablik, Susi 92
Gabriel, Yiannis 144
Gainsborough, Thomas 68–69
Gauguin, Paul 3
Gerz, Jochen 92, 94–95
Gill, A. A. 145
Gill, Michael 141, 145–146
Gilmore, Leigh 22, 23
Gitlin, Todd 88
Glowlab 100
Goldin, Barbara Holly 43, 46–48
Goldin, Nan 28, 29, 42–48, 51
Goldwater, Robert 17
Gonzalez-Torres, Felix 24–28, 52
Graham, Dan 110
Guattari, Felix 97
Gupta, Dipankar 22

Halbwachs, Maurice 111, 138, 144
Hanning, Jens 97
Healy, Lorna 21
Heimatfilm (Homeland film) 82
Heizer, Michael 49
High Modernism/High Modernist Abstraction xiii
Hill, Reginald 106
Hiller, Gabriel 130
Hiller, Susan 127–134
Hirsch, Marianne 8, 73, 76, 77, 89, 90
Historians Debate (Historikerstreit) 80
History
- and archaeology 125–126, 133–134
- and black art 64–71
- and fiction 6, 52
- and historicism 67, 70
- and ideology 4
- and institutions 54
- and memory 5, 7, 51, 52–55, 76
- colonial 68
- repressed 58

History Painting 53, 55
Hitchens, Christopher 116
Hitler, Adolf 90
HIV 24
Hogarth, William 68
Holocaust (Nazi) 8, 73–94
Horkheimer, Max 109
Huygens, Constantijn 10
Huyghe, Pierre 105–113, 124, 126
Huyssen, Andreas 5–6, 7, 60, 81, 82, 85, 87

Icarus 86
imperialism 70
indexicality 8, 29–51, 77–78
Isherwood, Baron 144

Januszczak, Waldemar 120
Jenkins, Keith 52

Jensen, Wilhelm 131
Judd, Donald 128

Kahlo, Frida 13–15, 16, 22, 23, 28, 34
Kane, Alan 119–120
Kant, Immanuel 25, 127
Kertész, Imre 75
Kiefer, Anselm 80–87, 88, 92
Kirk, Simon 114
Klein, Yves 120
knowledge
- and archaeology 125–126
- and discourse 53
- and power 53
- eccentric 130
- empirical 127
- experiential v. conceptual 97
- institutionalisation of 53, 72
- rational v. intuitive 131
- reflexive 97
- transcendental 127

Kohonen, Teuvo 139
Kosuth, Joseph 127
Krauss, Rosalind 30, 40
Kreis, Wilhelm 85
Kristeva, Julia 74
Kubitza, Anette 57
Kuhn, Annette 44
Kurtzman, Harvey 88

La Llorona 14
La Reunion (Dallas) 110
LaCapra, Dominick 54, 75, 89
Landy, Michael 141, 142–145, 146–147
Lane, Giles 98
Lang, Tim 144
Langer, Lawrence L. 73, 74
Lawson, Susan 31
Legrady, George 135–139
Lejeune, Philippe 21, 22
Levi, Primo 75
LeWitt, Sol 128
liberal arts 2
lieux de mémoire 7, 71–72, 98, 118, 128
Locke, John 2
Lumet, Sidney 108
Lyotard, Jean-François 25–26, 57

Magritte, René 123
Malthus, Thomas 125
Mandl, David 100
Manet, Edouard 53
Manic Street Preachers 114
marvellous, the 37, 40, 41
Mascuch, Michael 10
Maus 88–92, 94
McGregor, Ian 115
McRobbie, Angela 68
melancholy 59
memento-mori 40, 80, 126, 132
memoir 9, 22
memorials 92
memory
- ancient art of 2, 17
- and autobiography 8, 9–28, 117
- and death 29–30, 32, 59–60, 63, 78
- and clothes 18, 38–39, 41, 59, 62–63, 77
- and confession 9, 19
- and emotion 4, 17–18, 19
- and furniture 18, 60–63
- and grief 59, 60
- and history 5, 51, 52–55, 76
- and indexicality 8, 29–51
- and imagination 2–3, 70–71, 108

and knowledge 1–3, 5, 52–53, 118
and liminality 6, 31
and mourning 59
and museums 4, 8, 71, 120–123
and recognition (re-cognition) 1, 6, 60
and revisionism 8, 52–72, 134
and sound 48–51
and self 3, 5
and testimony 118–140
and trauma 14, 15, 19–20, 23, 24, 60, 73, 74, 85, 87
artificial 2
as diaristic practice 12, 42–43
as psychotherapy 34
cognitive 112, 124
collective 28, 73–74, 111, 137
emergent 139
episodic 97, 117
experiential 94
habit 117
hegemonic 63
institutionalised 63, 92
involuntary 2, 4, 128
'large' 78
natural 2
popular 32–33, 63
semantic 117
'small' 78
somatic 31
subjective 5, 7
veracity of 2–3
voluntary 2

Mercer, Kobena 65, 66
Merewether, Charles 63
Metcalf, Jenny 134
Micallef, Shawn 99
Minimalism 24, 25, 75, 128
Misztal, Barbara 55, 58
Molesworth, Helen 125
monuments 33, 92, 94–95
Morris, Frances 16
Mouly, Françoise 89, 92
Mueller, Cookie 44–45
Mulder, Arjen 135
Murray, Janet 138
[murmur] 98, 99–100, 102, 107

Nachgeborenen (the ones born afterwards) 80, 87
nachträglichkeit 15, 16, 17, 21, 34, 138
National Coal Board 115
National Union of Mineworkers 114
Nazism 81–83, 85
neocolonialism 64
Nelson, Willie 119
new genre public art 96
Nolan, Christopher 1, 141
Nora, Pierre 7, 71–72, 98, 118, 128
North American Phalanx 110

oblivion 8, 141
Odyssey, The 2
Ofili, Chris 65
One Block Radius 98, 100–102, 107
Orozco, Gabriel 96

Pacino, Al 108
Peirce, Charles Sanders 30, 34
Pekar, Harvey 88
personal/political 14, 25
Piper, Keith 65–67, 70
Plato 1, 3
postcolonialism 14, 64, 65, 68, 69, 158
postmemory 8, 73–95, 137
Princenthal, Nancy 59

private/public 8, 22–23, 24–25, 26, 32
Proboscis 98, 99
Proust, Marcel 2, 3, 5, 6, 7
Psychogeographic walks 98–102 (in Janet Cardiff, 103–107)
Psychogeography 97
public art 96
Pugh, Abigail 100

Radstone, Susannah 6
Raudive, Konstantin 129
Raven, Arlene 96
Ray, Christina 100
Realism 54
re-enactment 8, 97, 113, 114–117
relational aesthetics 96–97
Rembrandt, van Rijn 9–13, 130
remembrance 41, 42, 46, 117, 140, 145, 147
Renfrew, Colin 126
Rhizome 102
Ridley, Nicholas 115
Rivera, Diego 13–14
Romantic poets 3
Romanticism 11, 54, 82
Rosen, Andrea 27
Rosenthal, Mark 82, 85
Roussel, James 99, 100
Royal Photographic Society 37
Rude, Françoise 49

Saint Augustine 10
Saint Barbara 46–47
Said, Edward 4
Salcedo, Doris 51, 58–64, 67, 73, 78
Saltzman, Lisa 84, 85, 87
Sawhney, Gabe 99
Scargill, Arthur 114
Schama, Simon 12
Scheerbart, Paul 146
Schmitt-Rottluff, Karl 90
Schwartz, Gary 10
Scott, Robert Falcon 112
Sekula, Allan 37, 40
Shalev-Gerz, Esther 92, 94–95
Shaw, Becky 141, 145–146
Shoah Foundation 74
Shonibare, Yinka, MBE 52, 64, 67–71
Situationist International/ Situationists 97, 98
Smith, Sidonie 21–22
Smithson, Robert 49
Social Fiction 98
Speer, Albert 82
spectacle/simulation 109, 113
Spector, Nancy 26
Spiegelman, Anja 89, 90, 92
Spiegelman, Art 87–92
Spiegelman, Mala 92
Spiegelman, Nadja 89
Spiegelman, Richieu 89, 90–91
Spiegelman, Vladek 89–92, 94
Spielberg, Steven 75
Storr, Robert 18, 19
Streamside Knolls (Fishkill, NY), 110
sublime, the 25–26
Surrealist Map of the World (1929) 97
Surrealists/Surrealism 18, 40–41, 98, 108, 121
Symbolism/Symbolists 3, 18

Talbot, William Henry Fox 37
testimony 74, 119, 130
Thatcher, Margaret 115
Third Reich 82
Thomas, Jenny 116–117
Thompson, Nato 119
trauma 14, 15, 19–20, 23, 60, 73, 74, 85, 87, 116
Truth, Sojourner 57
Turner Prize 65, 11

Urban Tapestries 98, 99, 100, 102, 107
Uylenburgh, Saskia 10

Van Alphen, Ernst 75–76
Van Gogh, Vincent 3, 12–13
vanitas 80, 83
Vara, René 20

Waco (Texas) 119
Wakefield, Neville 30
Walker, Alice 57
Wallace, Alfred Russel 125
Warnock, Mary 3
Watney, Simon 31
Watson, Julia 21–22
Whiteread, Rachel 29, 30–34, 51, 52, 94
Wilder, Billy 106
witness 75, 76, 79
Wojtowicz, John 108
Wong, Edlie 63–64
Wordsworth, William 3

Yates, Frances 2
yBas (young British artists) 20
Young, James E. 95
Younghusband, Jan 114